# BOOK OF BOUTIQUE CRAFTS

© Joan Moloney 1974

ISBN 0 7063 1816 1

First published in Great Britain in 1974
by Ward Lock Limited, 116 Baker Street,
London, W1M 2BB

All Rights Reserved. No part of this
publication may be reproduced, stored in a
retrieval system, or transmitted, in any form
or by any means, electronic, mechanical,
photocopying, recording, or otherwise,
without the prior permission of the
Copyright owner.

Designed by Andrew Vargo

Text set in Century Schoolbook
by Nickeloid & Co. Ltd. London

Made and printed in Great Britain by
Butler & Tanner Ltd., Frome and London

# CONTENTS

**Boutique Crafts**
| | |
|---|---|
| Sewing Notions | 2–1 |
| Sewing Basket | 3–1 |
| Elephant Egg Cosies | 4–1 |
| Elephant Mirror | 5–1 |
| Lavender Bags | 6–1 |
| Handkerchief or Pencil Case | 7–1 |
| Record Cover | 8–1 |
| Portfolio | 9–1 |
| Shoe Bag and Box Board | 10–1 |
| Mirror and Comb Case | 11–1 |
| Purse Belt | 12–1 |
| Stitched Bedding | 13–1 |
| Gift Boxes | 14–1 |
| With What You've Got: Socks | 16–1 |
| With What You've Got: Jeans | 17–1 |
| Gloves – New from Old | 18–1 |
| Hats | 19–1 |
| Sponge Bag and Hat | 23–1 |
| Slippers and Sandals | 24–1 |
| Make Some Clothes | 25–1 |
| Beach Top | 26–1 |
| Make a Blouse | 27–1 |
| Gathered Skirt | 28–1 |
| A Simple Dress | 29–1 |
| Bath Robe | 30–1 |
| Making Flowers | 31–1 |
| Pom-poms and French Knitting | 32–1 |
| How to Knit | 33–1 |
| Knitted Squares | 34–1 |
| Knitted Doll | 35–1 |
| Shawl | 37–1 |
| Hood | 38–1 |
| How to Crochet | 39–1 |
| (a) Belt | 40–1 |
| (b) Waistcoat | 41–1 |
| Crochet Circles | 43–1 |
| Metrication | 46–1 |

**Making Jewellery**
| | |
|---|---|
| What You Will Need | 2–2 |
| Jewellery from Oddments | 4–2 |
| Paper Beads | 6–2 |
| Straws, Labels and Beads | 7–2 |
| Paper Jewellery | 8–2 |
| Use of Acetate | 10–2 |
| Fabric and Wire | 11–2 |
| Make Your Own Beads | 12–2 |
| Cook Your Own Beads | 14–2 |
| Strung Beads | 16–2 |
| Looped Beads | 20–2 |
| Indian Beadwork | 22–2 |
| Bead Weaving | 24–2 |
| Chains | 28–2 |
| Copperwire Jewellery | 30–2 |
| Simple Enamelling | 32–2 |
| Simple Enamelling – Wire and Loops | 34–2 |
| Simple Enamelling – Rings and Things | 35–2 |
| Making Links and Chains | 36–2 |
| Silver Jewellery | 38–2 |
| Jewellery Boxes | 46–2 |

**Patchwork and Applique**

| | |
|---|---|
| Templates for Patchwork | 2–3 |
| Assembling Patches | 4–3 |
| Techniques of Applique | 6–3 |
| Some Small Patchwork Hems | 8–3 |
| Some Small Patchwork Hems: Toys from Patches | 9–3 |
| Diamond Fish | 10–3 |
| Square Duck | 11–3 |
| Triangle Bird | 12–3 |
| Triangle Fish and Doll | 13–3 |
| Square Patch Dog and Lion | 14–3 |
| Hexagon Spider | 16–3 |
| Hexagon Turtle | 17–3 |
| Pentagon Dolls | 18–3 |
| Pentagon Ball Toys | 20–3 |
| "Spotty Doll" | 22–3 |
| Square Patch Basket | 23–3 |
| Free Patchwork Doll | 24–3 |
| Patchwork Pot Holders | 26–3 |
| Hot Water Bottle Cover | 27–3 |
| Square Patch Bag | 28–3 |
| More Patchwork Ideas | 29–3 |
| Cushions | 30–3 |
| Applique Motifs | 32–3 |
| Quilts and Bedspreads | 33–3 |
| Applique Gifts | 38–3 |
| Applique Box | 39–3 |
| Making and Covering a Box | 40–3 |
| Covering a Book | 41–3 |
| Little Applique | 42–3 |
| Applique on Clothes | 43–3 |
| Applique Pictures | 44–3 |
| Mounting Pictures | 46–3 |
| Applique Pictures | 47–3 |
| Box Tote | 48–3 |

**Leather and Fur Crafts**

| | |
|---|---|
| Skins and Things | 2–4 |
| Fur and Fake | 3–4 |
| Sewing and Lacing | 4–4 |
| Skiving and Decorating | 5–4 |
| Some Small Items | 6–4 |
| Jewellery in Leather and Suede | 8–4 |
| Chamois Sewing Doll | 10–4 |
| Doll in Leather and Fur | 11–4 |
| Fur Bird | 12–4 |
| Fur Mouse | 13–4 |
| Fake Snake | 14–4 |
| Doll in Chamois and Fur | 16–4 |
| Painted Leather Frog | 20–4 |
| Purses | 22–4 |
| Bag and Purse | 24–4 |
| Drawstring Bag and Beaded Bag | 26–4 |
| Knitting Bag | 27–4 |
| Fur Mittens | 28–4 |
| Slippers | 30–4 |
| Slippers Slipper | 31–4 |
| Moccasin Slippers | 32–4 |
| Leather Gloves | 33–4 |
| Some Bright Ideas | 34–4 |
| For the Real Thing – Leather | 36–4 |
| Ten Belts | 38–4 |
| Fur Hat | 40–4 |
| Sewing Leather and Fur for Clothes | 42–4 |
| Full B/W Waistcoat | 44–4 |
| Clothes in Fur and Leather | 45–4 |
| Fakers – Fur, Leather and Suede | 46–4 |
| Tough Guy | 47–4 |
| Cleaning Up | 48–4 |

# BOOK OF BOUTIQUE CRAFTS

# BOUTIQUE CRAFTS

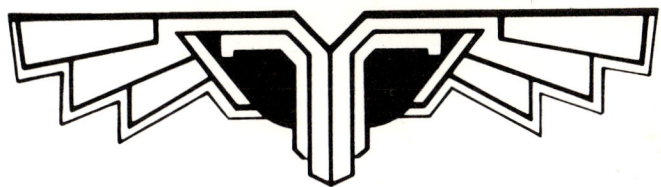

Open the door of any Boutique and you are confronted by a dazzling variety of clothes, toys, gifts, colours, textures and crafts. The kind of things, in fact, that you will find in this book—your very own boutique—and you can make them yourself.

You can learn to knit and crochet. To make not just pretty sensible things, like the shawl, but also jolly things, like the knitted doll. Or perhaps you like the crochet flowers, or fancy yourself in a bright crochet waistcoat.

If you have never even attempted dressmaking, the dress, blouse and skirt, even the bathrobe, are incredibly easy to make.

As well as pretty gift boxes, there are many gifts. A neat little mirror and comb case, lavender bags, record cover, portfolio, and many more.

There are suggestions on what you can make out of outgrown jeans, an odd sock, a pair of gloves. Stitched beading will surely appeal to you when you see the pretty designs and simple instructions...

Treat this book as a Boutique.

# Sewing Notions

1. The needle case. Cut two pieces of material 5½ x 7 in (14 x 18 cm)—half-inch (13 mm) turnings have been allowed. Cut a firm piece of card 4½ x 3 in (11·4 x 7·6 cm) and score down the centre to fold. Sew the material pieces together on the wrong side, leaving one end open. Turn through and insert the card. Sew opening. Sew felt or flannel pieces inside to hold needles.

2. Pincushion. My daughter Pania made this lemon pin cushion for me. You can see it in the photograph of gift boxes. It is simply two yellow felt lemon shapes sewn together and filled with cotton wool. Two flat felt leaves are sewn to the top.

3. Transparent Bag. Cut out two hanger shapes from firm card. Paint and then glue or sew them to each side of a strong polythene bag. This useful, see-through bag, can contain silks and cottons, or socks, stockings, handkerchiefs and so on.

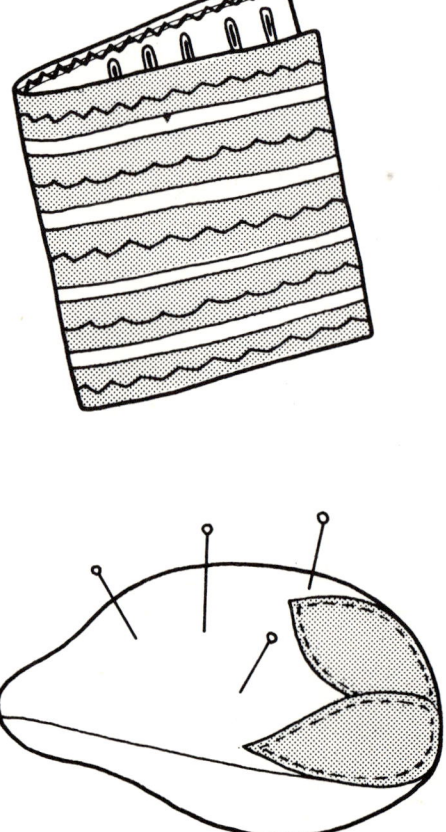

# Sewing Basket

Line a small basket by measuring it across as shown. Use this measurement for the diameter. Cut and bind the edge of the circle with bias binding or ribbon. Lay the material in the basket, and from the fullness, form cone-shaped pockets. Pin and space them evenly. Now remove lining and sew the pockets. Sew the lining into the basket so that the stitches do not show.

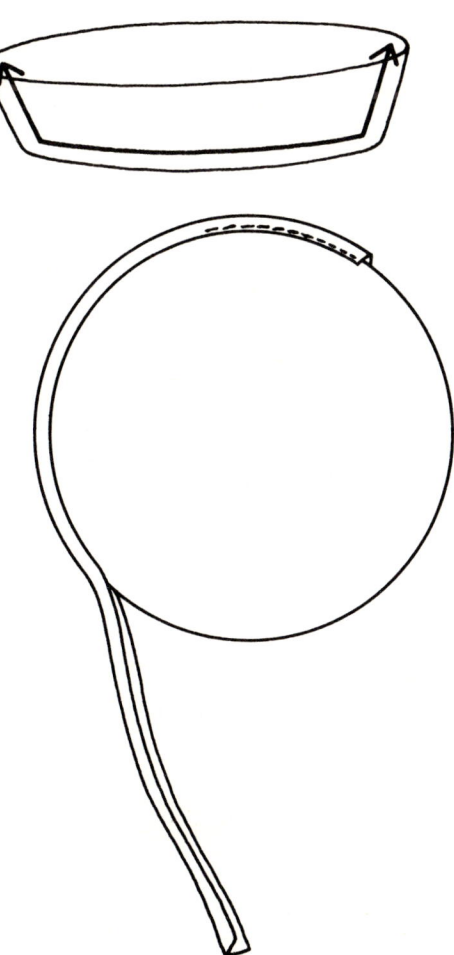

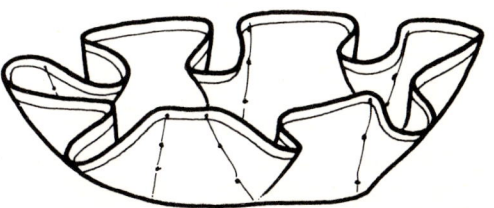

3–1

# Elephant Egg Cosies

Brighten up the breakfast table with these elephant egg cosies. Use the pattern below. The main body part is mauve, the trunk is pink, the tusks white, ears mauve, eyes black. For the first elephant stitch trunk and tusks to front before sewing to back. Insert ears into sides at this stage.

The second is in profile and his trunk and ear are stitched to the front before sewing round edge. Number three is made as for the first, but his trunk is turned up. Embroider white cotton 'water' coming out of it.

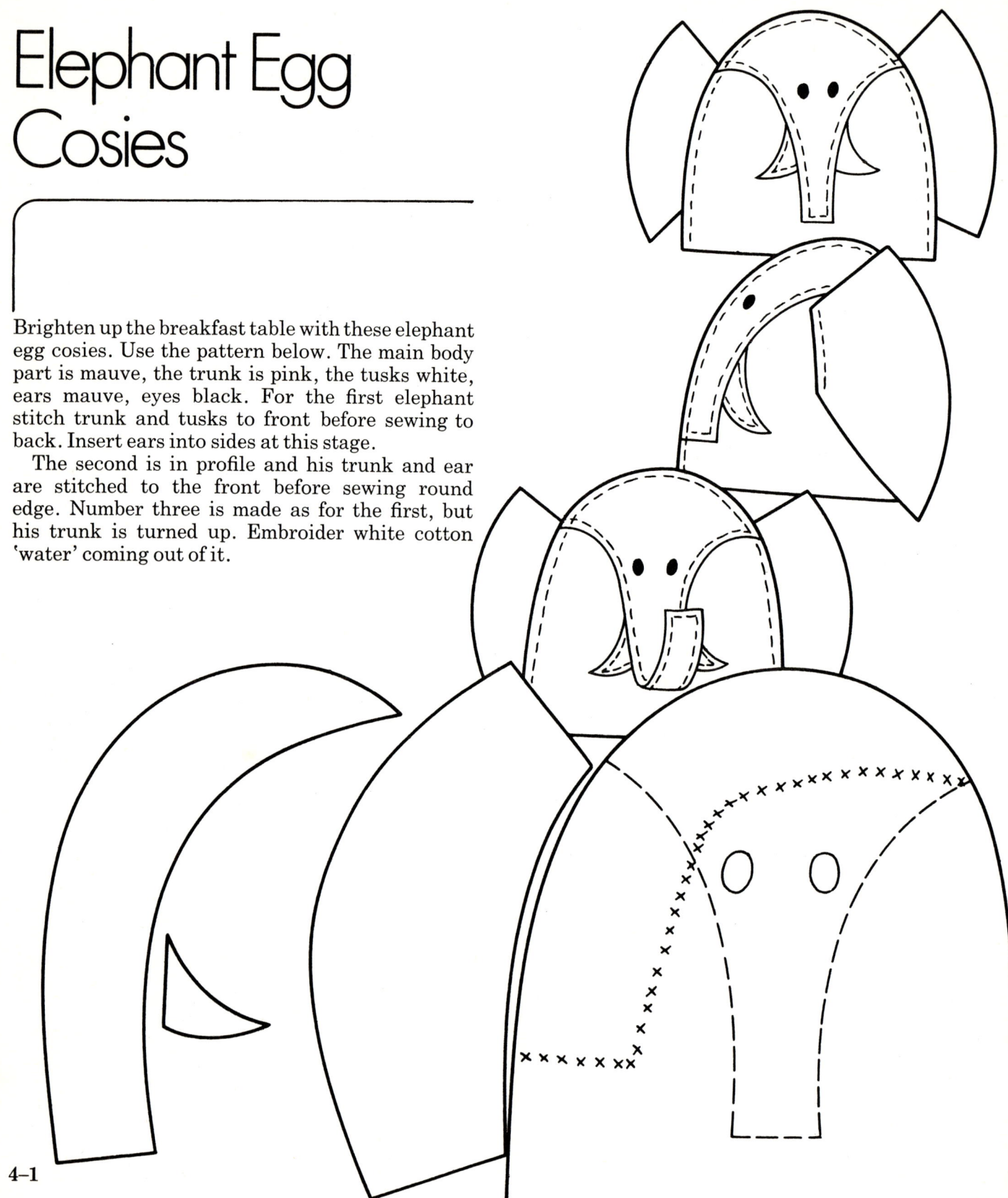

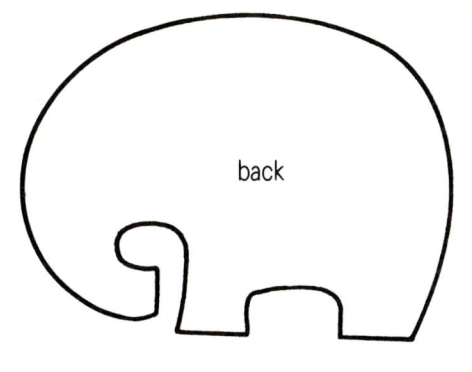

back

# Elephant Mirror

This elephant is also made of felt and he has a mirror for an ear. Trace off the shape below, cut two in felt, and one, fractionally smaller, in card. Glue a small mirror to the card where the ear is positioned. Cut out the ear shape from the front only. Blanket stitch around this ear edge. Sew or glue eye. Now make a sandwich of the back felt, card, and front felt and blanket stitch all round.

card with mirror

front

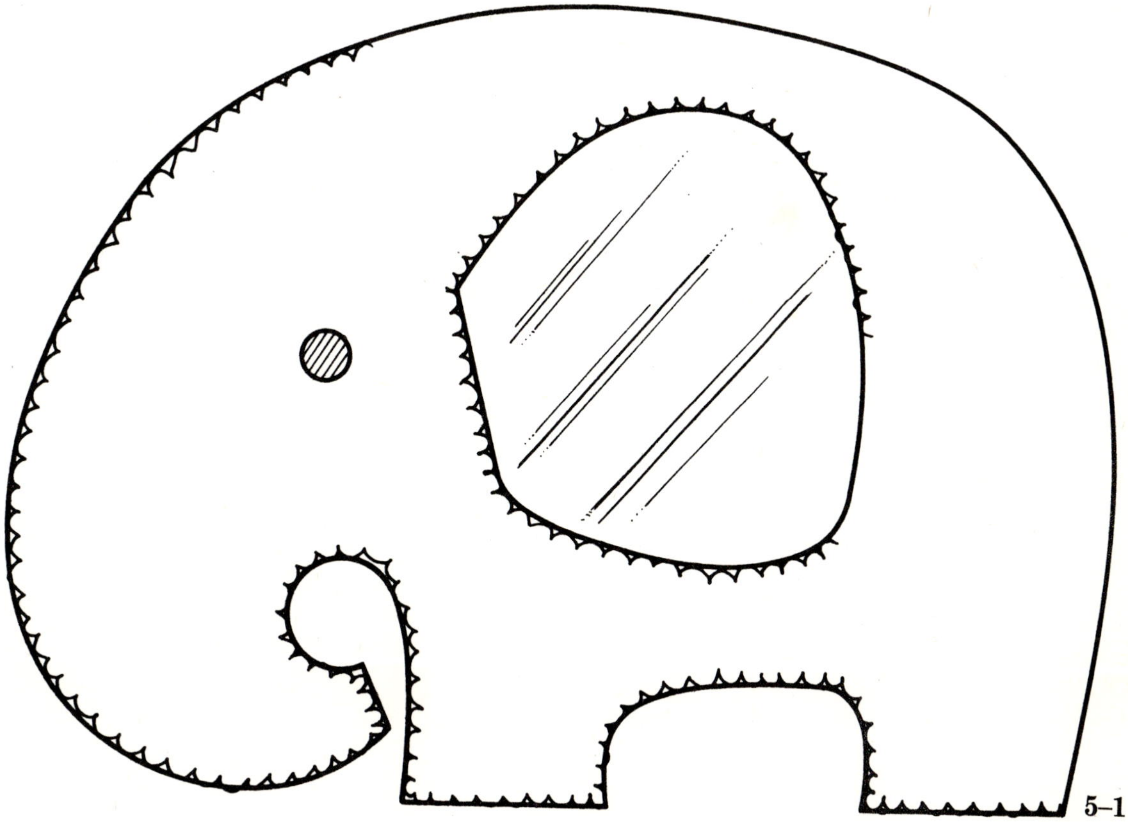

5–1

# Lavender Bags

1. This pretty flower shaped lavender bag is cut from flower-print lawn and the underside is plain cotton material. Sew them together, right sides facing, clip curved seams, turn through and fill with lavender. Sew opening and sew a tiny bow in the centre.

2. This one is a tiny doll shape cut from double white cotton material. Allow small turnings when you trace the pattern. Using soft coloured pencils or textile crayons, draw face, hair and dress. Make as for the first one, clipping curved seams before turning through. Sew bow to head.

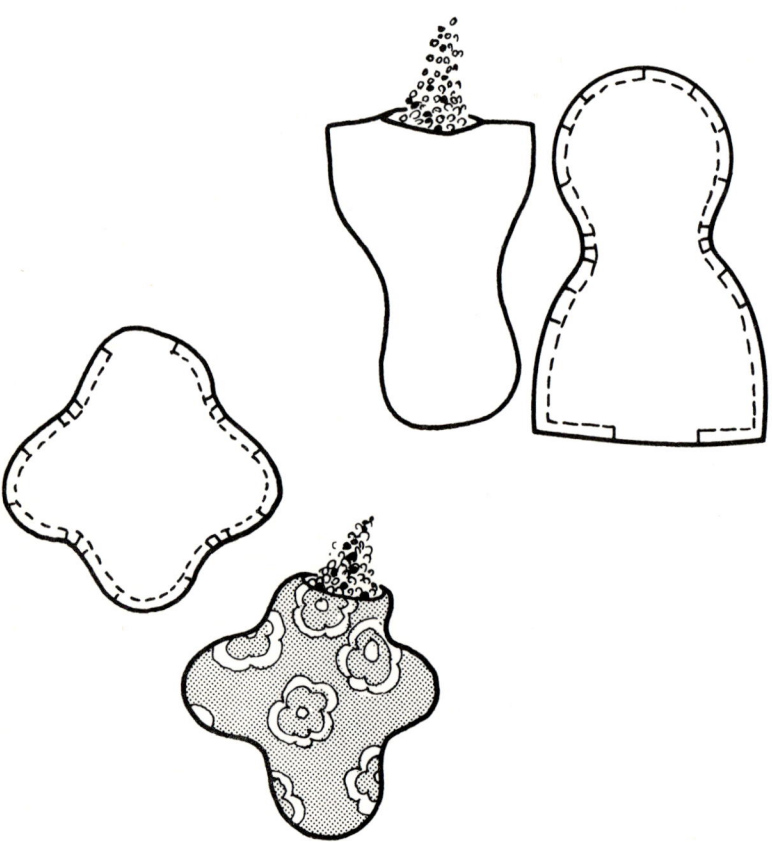

# Handkerchief or Pencil Case

Cut out two pieces of material 8½ x 4½ in (22·6 x 11·4 cm)—half-inch (13 mm) turnings have been allowed. Tack turnings on two long edges as shown. Lay edges on zip, right side up, tack and machine or back stitch. Open zip and turn through. Sew down both sides and along bottom. Turn case through and close zip.

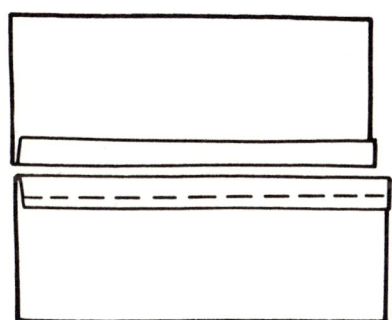

Fig 1

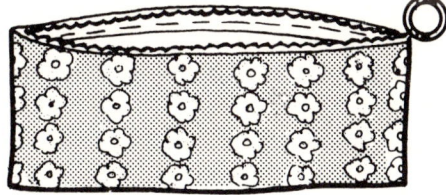

Fig 4

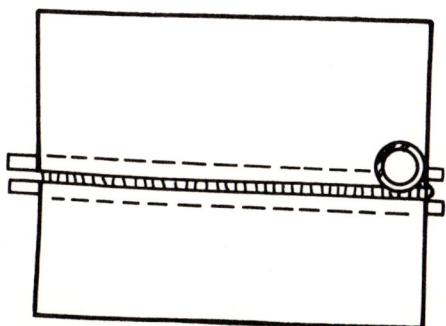

Fig 2

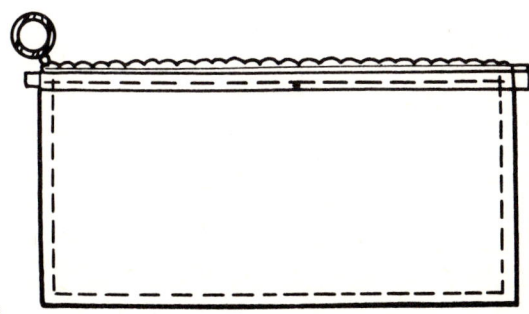

Fig 3

7–1

# Record Cover

To make a pattern for the record case, lay a record, in its sleeve, on a piece of card. Allow a margin all round it, with a scored ¾ in spine. Cut a second piece of card like the first. Cover the card both sides with material, turning in edges and sewing all round. Make fabric pockets wider at sides, pleat and sew to inside of cover. A tab and popper would hold the cover together, and if the material is plain, you can sew or appliqué a design or name on it.

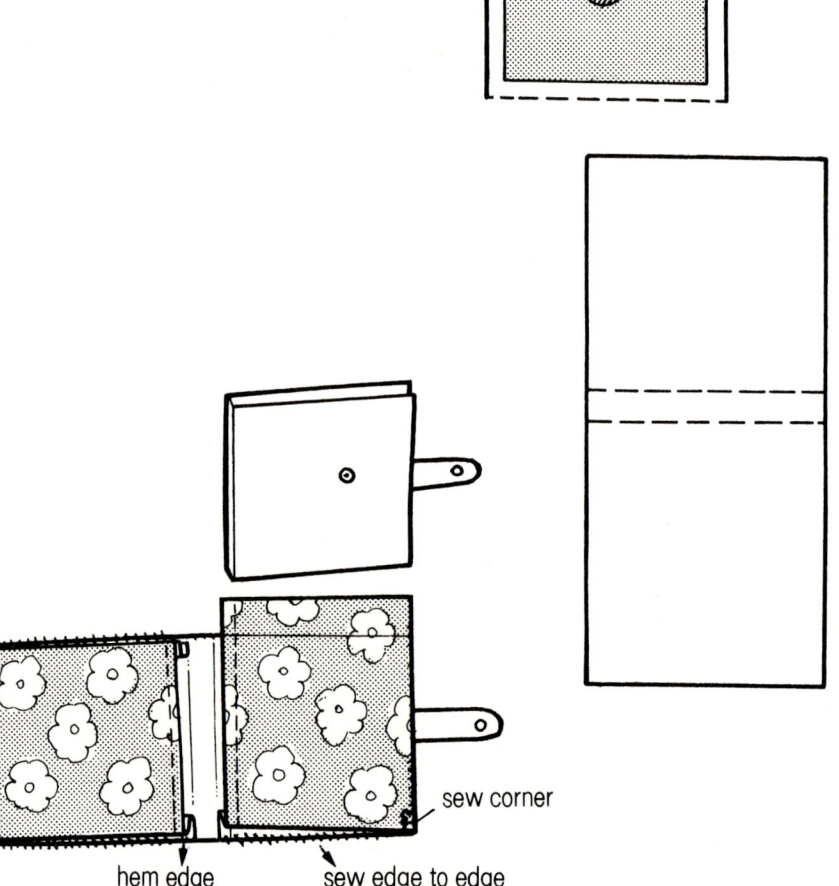

hem edge    sew edge to edge    sew corner

8–1

# Portfolio

This portfolio measures 20 x 12 in (50·8 x 30·4 cm), but you can, if you wish, make it larger by increasing the measurements given. It is made in firm card and has felt appliqué and pencil pockets glued to it. Cut two pieces of card 20 x 12 in (50·8 x 30·4 cm) and join them, with a 1 in (2·5 cm) space between, with a strip of 2 in (5 cm) wide tape, glued to each edge, overlapping $\frac{1}{2}$ in (13 mm). Cut four pieces of thin card 12 x 7 in (30·4 x 17·8 cm) cut to shape as shown. Cut two pieces of thin card 20 x 7 in (50·8 x 17·8 cm) also shaped. Fold along the score lines and glue the edge to the pieces of card, inserting tapes, with glue, in these 'seams'.

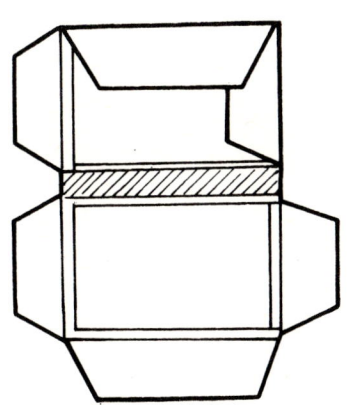
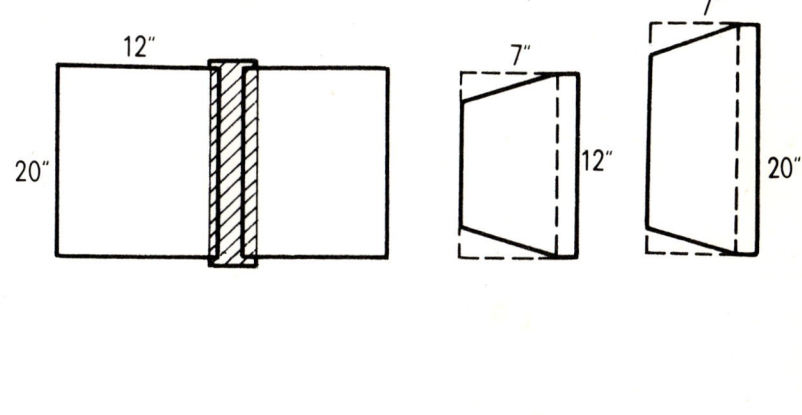

# Shoe Bag and Box Board

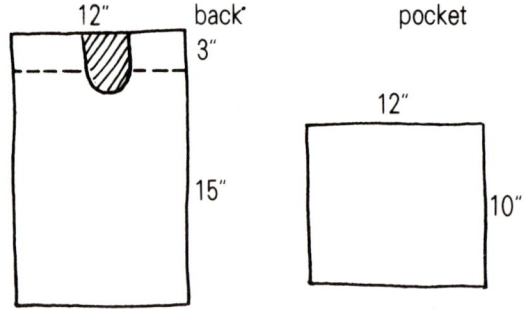

The shoe bag is made in clear plastic, and you will need a straight hanger for it. Cut a piece 15 in (36 cm) deep, + 3 in (7·6 cm) turn over at top, x 12 in (30·4 cm) wide. Cut away shaded area. Cut a pocket 12 in (30·4 cm) wide by 10 in (25·4 cm) deep. Edge top of pocket with bias tape. Lay pocket on back and edge with tape all round. Lay tape down centre of pocket and stitch straight down. Fold turnovers over hanger and sew across.

The box board is useful also, and as easy to make. Collect boxes in different sizes—toothpaste boxes, a small size cereal box, large match boxes etc. Cut away lids. Cover a large square of very firm card with bright print paper. Paint the boxes and glue them to the board. Add a cord, through punched holes, knotted at the back.

# Mirror and Comb Case

Cut a piece of felt lining 6 x 4 in (15·2 x 10·2 cm) and a piece of print material 7 x 5 in (17·8 x 12·7 cm)—(half-inch (13 mm) turnings have been allowed for this). Cut one piece of felt 4 x 1½ in (10·2 x 3·8 cm) and one piece 4 x 2 in (10·2 x 5 cm) and shape both as shown. Fold in the turning on the print material, lay the felt piece onto it and then the pockets on top. Oversew all round. A tiny comb goes into one narrow pocket and a tiny mirror into the other.

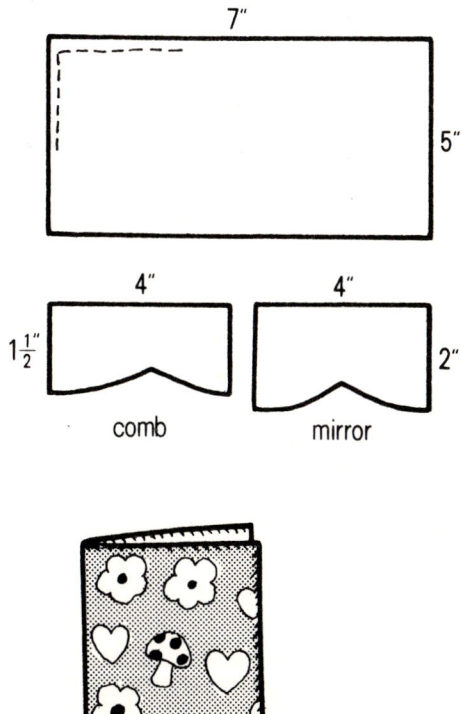

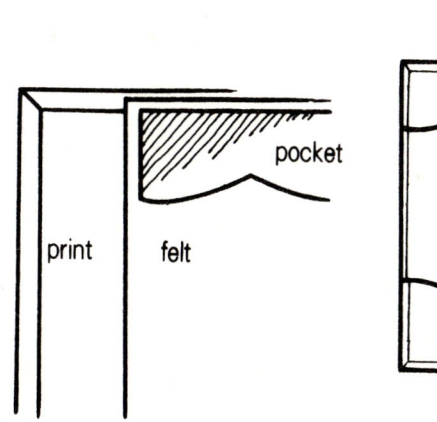

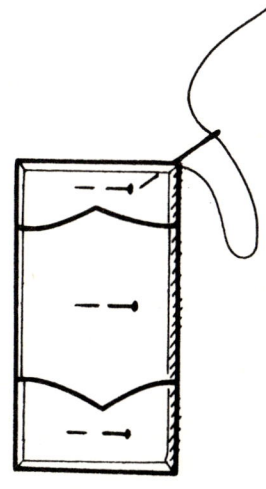

# Purse Belt

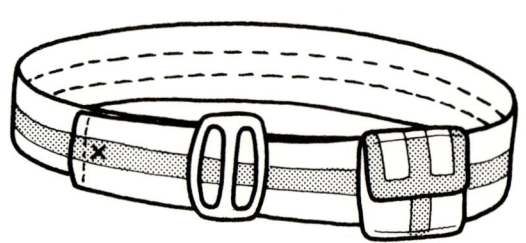

## Belt

You will need a length of 3 in (7·6 cm) carpet braid the measurement of your waist plus 5 in (12·7 cm) overlap, and a decorative ribbon the same length and width. Stitch the ribbon to the braid all round. Slot one end through a buckle and stitch the turning down. Sew a popper to the overlap and belt to hold.

## Purse

Cut a piece of 3 in (7·6 cm) carpet braid 8 in (20·3 cm) long. Stitch a band of ribbon down the centre, and then bind upper and lower ends up 3 in (7·6 cm) and sew each side. Sew a popper to flap and purse. Sew purse to belt at the back.

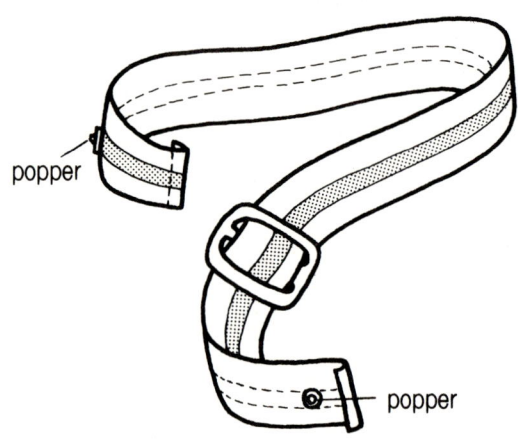

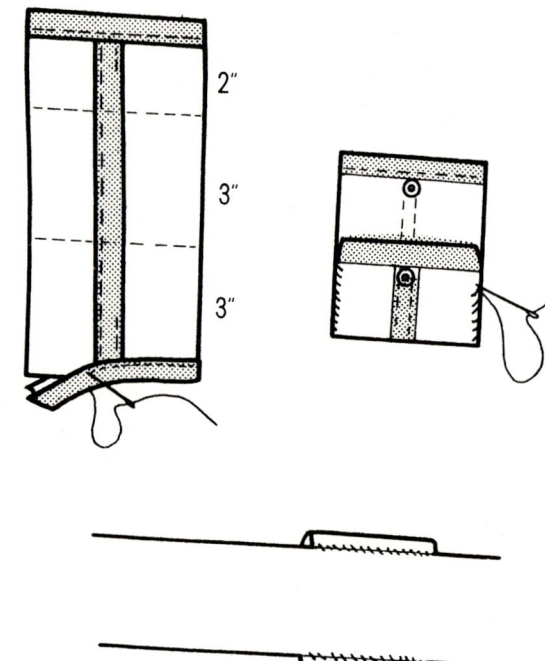

sew back of purse to belt.

# Stitched Beading

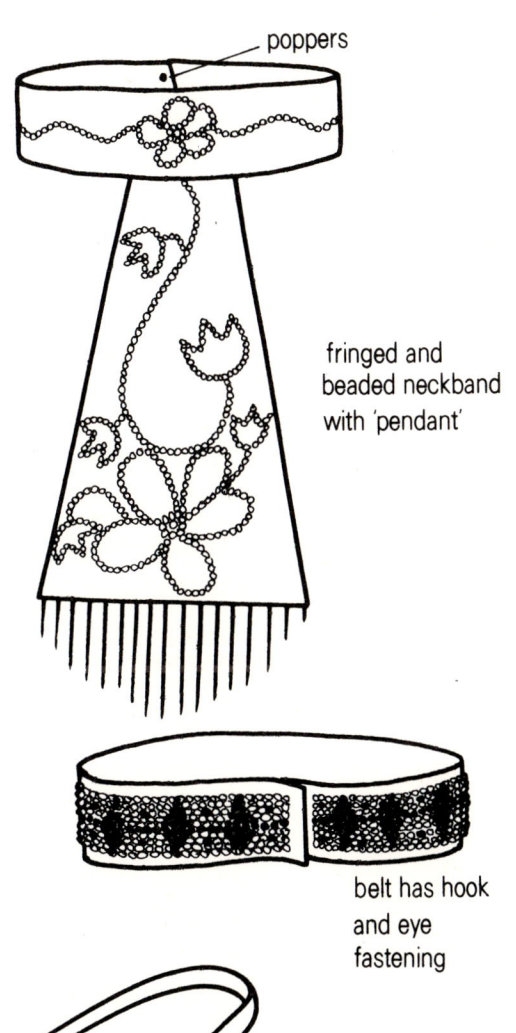

fringed and beaded neckband with 'pendant'

poppers

belt has hook and eye fastening

bag has beaded square sewn onto it.

Stitched beading is a simple and attractive form of decoration which can be applied to a variety of objects. You will need tiny beads and a fine beading needle. To apply the beads to the background material, you bring the threaded needle up through cloth, then thread six beads, make a stitch as close as possible to the last bead, then thread six more beads. You continue in this way until you have covered the line of your design. If you are filling an area, you make rows of beads, one below another, until you have filled it. Contrast coloured beads can be added for design, but the process is the same. To save dragging, the work should be lined and a light canvas interlining inserted between material and lining. You can, of course, sew down fewer than six beads if the pattern requires this. Here are three beaded items to start you off. A neckband with a pendant, a belt and a bag.

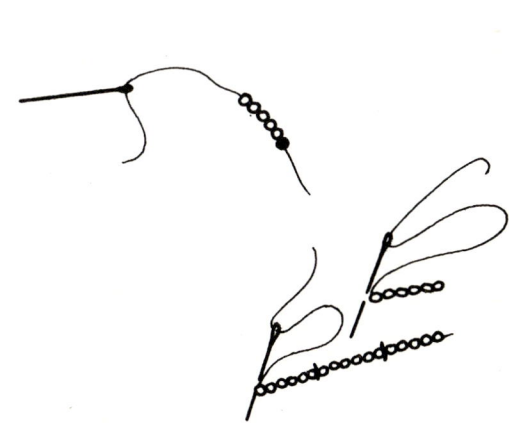

# Gift Boxes

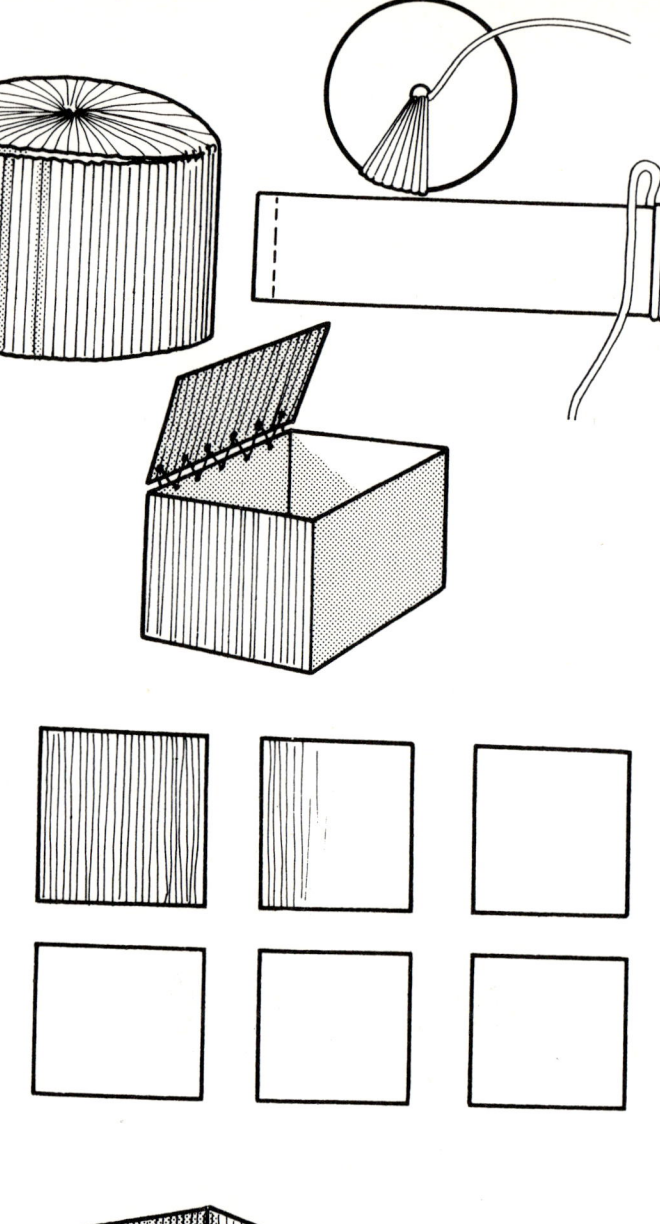

Attractive boxes can easily be made by winding raffia over card shapes. The round box is made using two circles of card, the same size, with holes in the centre, and a straight piece of card long enough to go round the circle with ½ in (13 mm) overlap. Using a long needle thread the raffia through the hole in one circle and keep winding until the card is covered. Repeat for the second circle, which makes the lid. Overlap and glue the long strip of card, then wind the raffia over it until the ring is covered. Using raffia sew the ring to one circle neatly and securely. Catch the lid to the box with a few loose stitches as shown.

The square box is made of six equal sized squares of card wrapped with raffia. Sew four sides together and then sew to the base. Sew the lid to the box with loose stitches along one side. These boxes would be even nicer lined, and you can add decorative stitching to them with contrast coloured raffia.

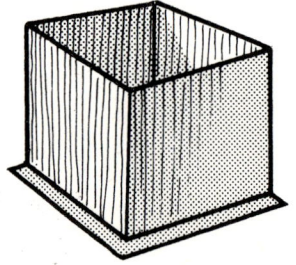

14–1

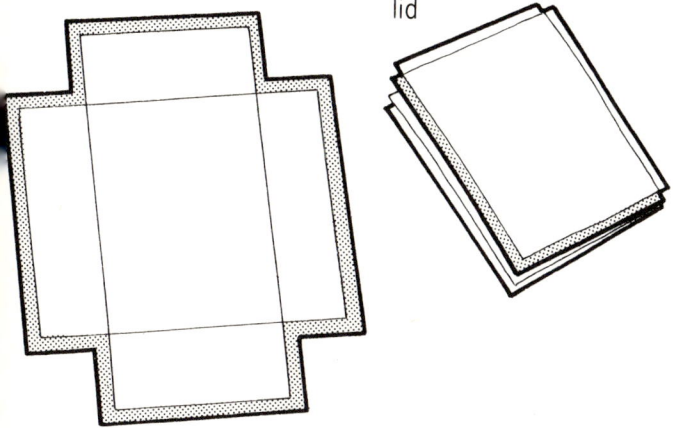

Here are two very pretty gift boxes. One is for sewing and the smaller is for jewellery. The box is simple to make. Cut a pattern to the size required. Cut print material ½ in (13 mm) larger than pattern all round and cut a lining the same size. Score and fold the dotted lines and tape corners. Sew the corners of the print with the turnings inside. Sew the lining with the turnings outside. Lay the box in the print material and the lining in the box. Turn the hems of both in, and neatly oversew together. The lid is made slightly larger than the box and has a piece of quilt wadding for padding. Cut the card, lining, wadding and print. Lay wadding on the card with the lining underneath and the print on top. Turn under hems and neatly sew all round. A wide piece of tape or matching material is placed between the long edge of the box and the lid to make a hinge.

# With what you've got

## Old or Odd Socks

Don't throw away odd or outgrown socks. Make them into something else—a soft wool doll, for example. Cut the socks as shown in the diagram. Sew round the dotted line at D to form legs, then fill the legs and body with foam clips, other odd socks, cotton wool or kapok. Gather in the neck at C with a running thread, then stuff the head B. Gather and sew the top, then stitch the hat A over it. Sew and stuff the arms and stitch these to the body. If you have used patterned socks, you will not need to make clothes. If the socks are plain you can make simple felt clothes which will contrast well with the wool.

Or you can make a funny sock glove puppet. Take an odd sock and put your hand into it—your fingers in the toe and your thumb in the heel. Open and close your fingers and thumb and already your puppet is trying to talk . . . So give it a mouth, red felt lips cut out and glued to the sole of the sock. Now cut out felt eyes and glue these to the top of the foot where your knuckles are. If you happen to have some false eyelashes, glue them to white felt 'eyelids' and fix these over the eyes. You can use strips of black felt cut to form eyelashes instead of false ones. Now bunch and plait lengths of wool as shown and stitch the 'hair' in place.

You can make all kinds of characters in this way, even animals, adding simple bold trimmings and features to suit the character.

# Jeans

Look at what you can do with jeans or trousers that don't fit you any more. Are they too short? Then cut them shorter to make bloomers. Cut bands from the spare parts, fold them and turn in edges. Gather ends of trousers slightly and stitch them to the bands. Make pockets out of any left-over pieces.

Or make a drawstring bag cut from the base of a trouser leg. Sew the bottom edge on the wrong side. Make a hemmed edge through which you insert a tape or cord to draw in the top.

Or cut straight across the seat part of the jeans as shown. Stitch the lower edge inside, and make a strap cut from one trouser leg. Sew this to each side of the opening. Sew in a zip, or poppers, to close the bag.

You can make a doll in the same way as the sock doll, but without the hat. The head is A, neck is B, body and legs C, and the arms, cut from the other leg, are D. Add wool hair and embroidered features. Dress her in your outgrown dresses.

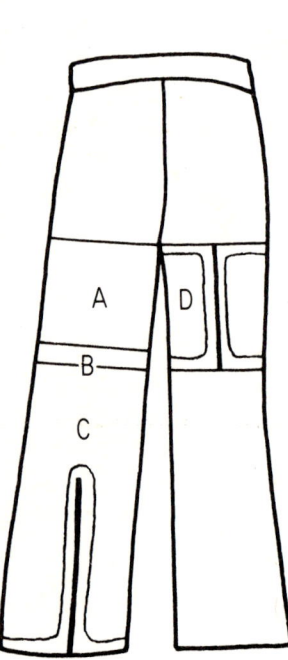

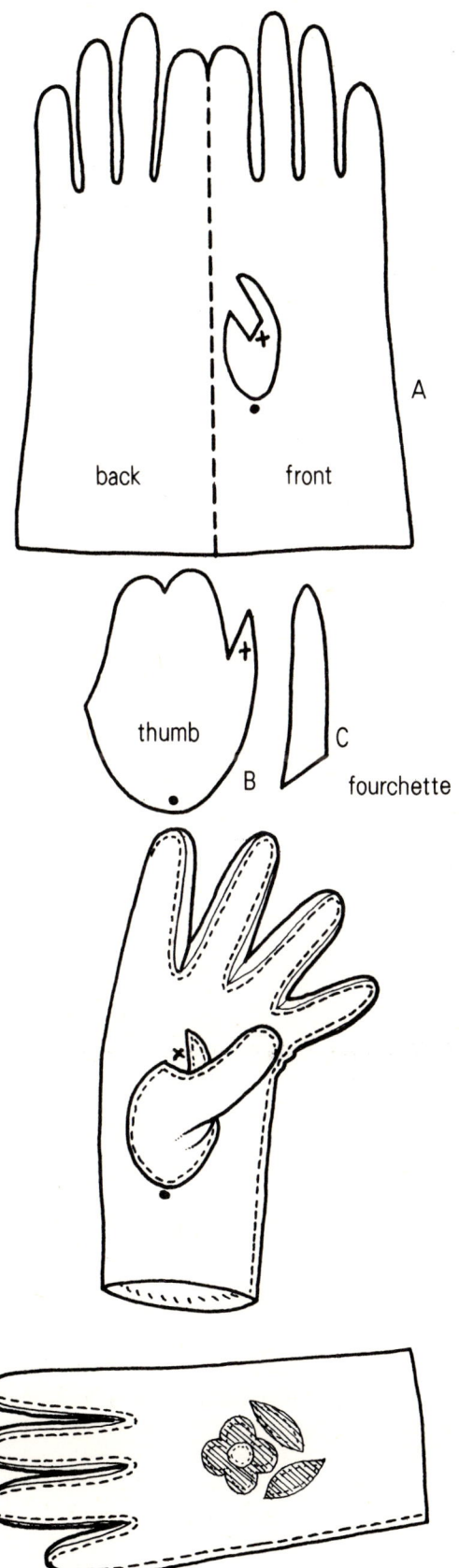

# New Gloves from Old

Don't be alarmed by the strange-shaped patterns here. They represent the parts of a glove which has been carefully cut along the seam lines and taken apart. Cut one glove for the pattern but leave one made up so that you can refer to it. Fabric and leather gloves are almost always made in this way. A seam runs up the side of the glove to the tip of the little finger, and is folded beside the thumb up to the point of the first finger-dotted line. The fourchettes, c, are the strips which are inserted between the fingers and are joined together in pairs. You will have six for each glove. When you have taken your glove apart, make very accurate paper patterns for each part, making sure they all fit together. If you make the gloves in leather you can sew them on the right side with flat stitch. If you are making stretch fabric gloves, allow small turnings. Cut out one set of all pieces for one hand, then turn the patterns over to cut out the reverse, other hand. The side seam is sewn last.

Begin by sewing the thumbs. Place thumb edge marked with a cross against X on glove and begin sewing together to point marked with a dot. Fold thumb and sew rest of seam. Sew fourchettes together in pairs, insert between fingers and sew the backs and then front fingers. Finally sew the side seam. If you are making fabric gloves, hem wrist edge.

# Hats

These hats would look great in any boutique, and you can make one very easily. If you have difficulty choosing which one, make a set of them to go with different outfits in different materials. A neat denim hat with rick-rack trim, a pretty flower print with cool green brim lining, a dressy hat with ribbon and artificial flowers, or felt hats with appliqué stars or flowers. A hat to suit your mood —any female understands that!

On the next two pages you will find the patterns and diagrams for making the hat. There are just two pattern pieces, the crown and the brim. Since there is not enough space to draw the whole of the brim pattern, trace off the quarter section and make a pattern as shown. Fold a piece of paper and lay the broken line edge of the brim pattern against the fold. Draw round the pattern and cut it out. Open out the new brim pattern and cut away the turning allowance to make a new fold line. This is placed on the fold of the material and cut out twice. Cut out four crown pieces. Sew the four crown pieces together (A) and try this 'cap' shape on so that if it does not quite fit, you can adjust it. Place the two brim pieces together, right sides facing, and sew round the outer edge (B). Turn the brim through and stitch up the back seam. Top stitch the edge for a neat finish (C). Place the brim and crown together and stitch them together (D). Stitch a band of petersham round this edge (E), then turn the edge in and catch it down (F).

This hat could be made in a bright towelling material to go with a towelling version of the simple dress shown later.

Another version could be trimmed with crochet flowers, which you can learn how to make in the crochet section. It is as versatile as your imagination.

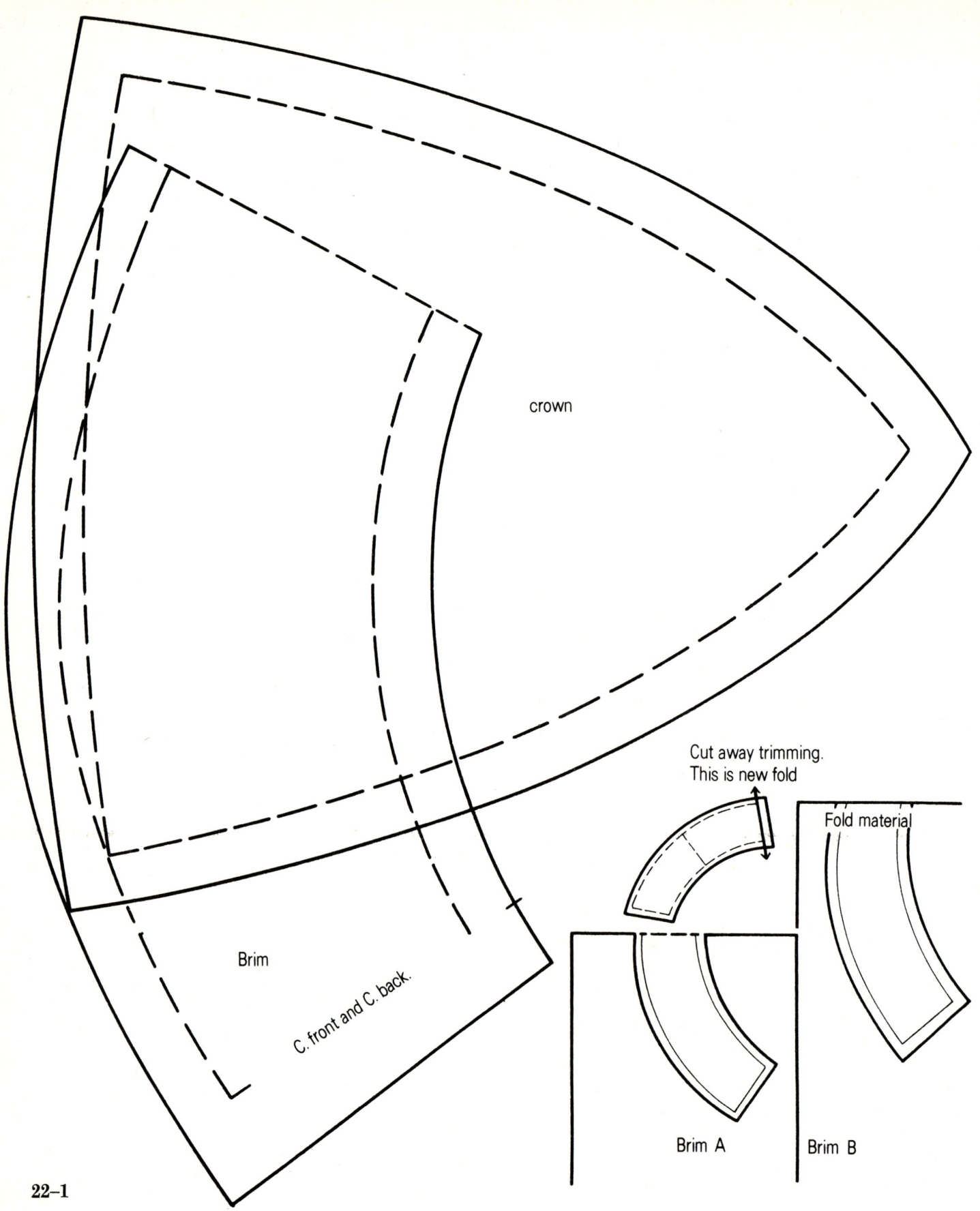

22–1

23–1

# Sponge Bag and Hat

Cut a 22 in (56 cm) diameter circle in print cotton and one in clear plastic material. Neatly hem the two together all round. Stitch a band of bias tape 1½ in (3·8 cm) from the edge, and insert a strip of elastic into this channel to fit your head. Oversew the ends and sew channel opening.

Cut a piece of print cotton and one of the clear plastic material 21 x 11½ in (53·3 x 31·8 cm). Stitch a tape channel 2½ in (6·3 cm) from edge. Sew down side seam and along the bottom. Make 1 in (2·5 cm) hem at top edge. Insert tape or cord for drawstring.

# Slippers and Sandals

The slippers have plaited raffia soles, with towelling strip uppers. Stand with one foot on a piece of paper and draw round it to make a pattern. Make long raffia plaits and coil and stitch them to fit your foot pattern. Cut a strip of towelling 7 in (17·8 cm) and the length needed to go over your foot and overlap $\frac{1}{2}$ in (13 mm) on to sole each side. Stitch edges together $\frac{1}{2}$ in (13 mm) and turn through. Flatten the piece with the seam underneath and stitch each end to the sole. Glue or sew bought inner soles, or felt shapes to the sole under the upper.

The soles of the sandals are made in the same way as the slippers. Instead of towelling, plait and stitch raffia to the same shape and line with felt or hemmed material, to make the upper and finish the sandal in the same way as the slippers.

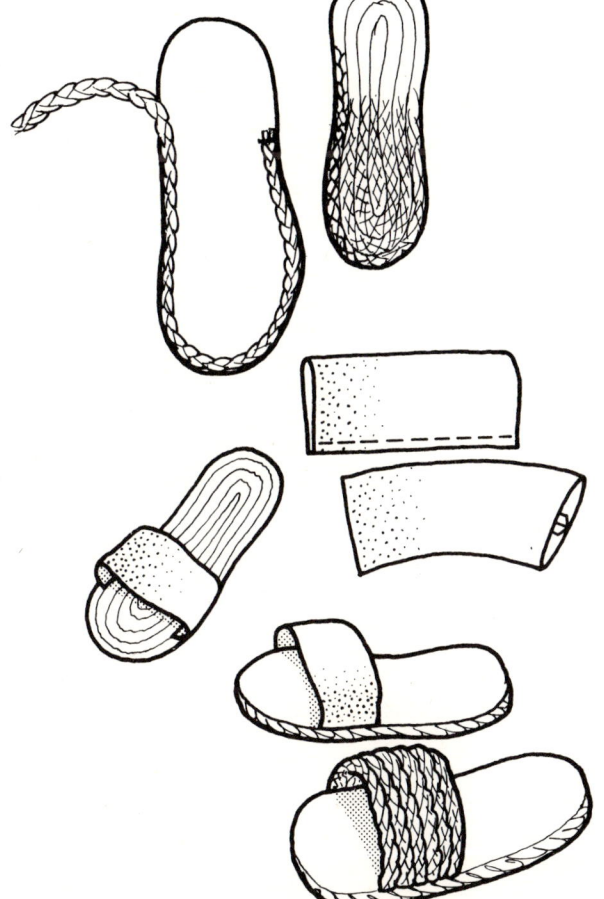

# Make Some Clothes

This poncho, made from one yard (91·4 cm) of material, can be made in cotton, towelling or woollen fabric. It couldn't be easier to make, or more prettily practical, for any time of the year. Fold the material diagonally, find the centre point (by folding again if you like) and measure 5 in (12·7 cm) each side of this point. Cut 10 in (25·4 cm) neck opening and bind it with bias tape or braid. Hem the outer edge and sew fringing to it.

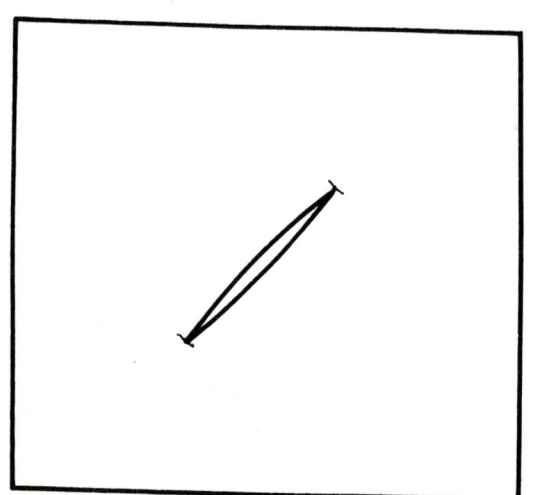
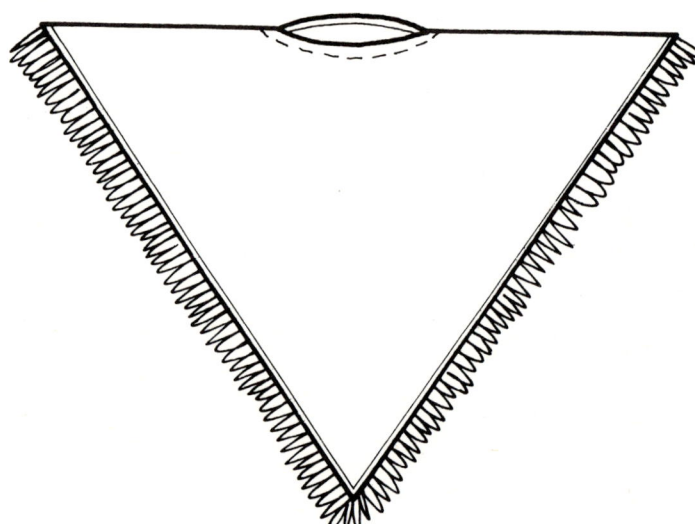

# Beach Top

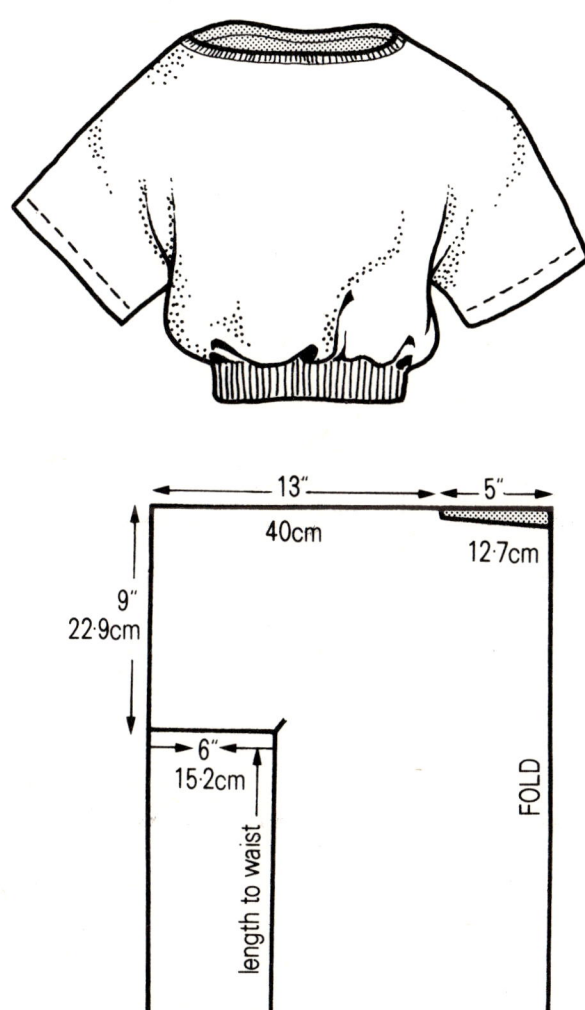

This useful towelling beach top is designed to fit an eight-year-old child. However, the pattern is so simple that it can easily be adapted to fit a larger or smaller person. Check your measurements against those given here, making any adjustments necessary. Make a paper pattern and cut out back and front. Stitch across the shoulder line and side seams, on the wrong side. Clip into the corner at underarm, and press the seams open. Hem the neckline with bias tape. Cut a strip of elasticated webbing to your waist measurement and stitch it to the top. Stretch the elastic as you stitch, to bottom edge, to gather the top. Hem the sleeve edges.

# Make a Blouse

One and a half yards (137 cm) of 36 in (91·4 cm) material makes this pretty blouse which has rickrack trim and button and loop neck fastening. The pattern is easy to make and is laid on the material, which is on the fold across, and then folded again, down, as shown. The neck is cut on the front only and the side, shaded area is cut away. Neatly hem a square of material to cover the neck opening, as shown, lay it on the right side and pin in place. Turn the blouse to the wrong side and tack round neck opening. Turn to right side and stitch neck opening. Fold the blouse at the shoulder on the wrong side and stitch underarm and side seams. Hem sleeve and lower edge and turn through. Pull neck facing through to inside of blouse, and press. The sleeves may be left straight or have elastic inserted as shown here.

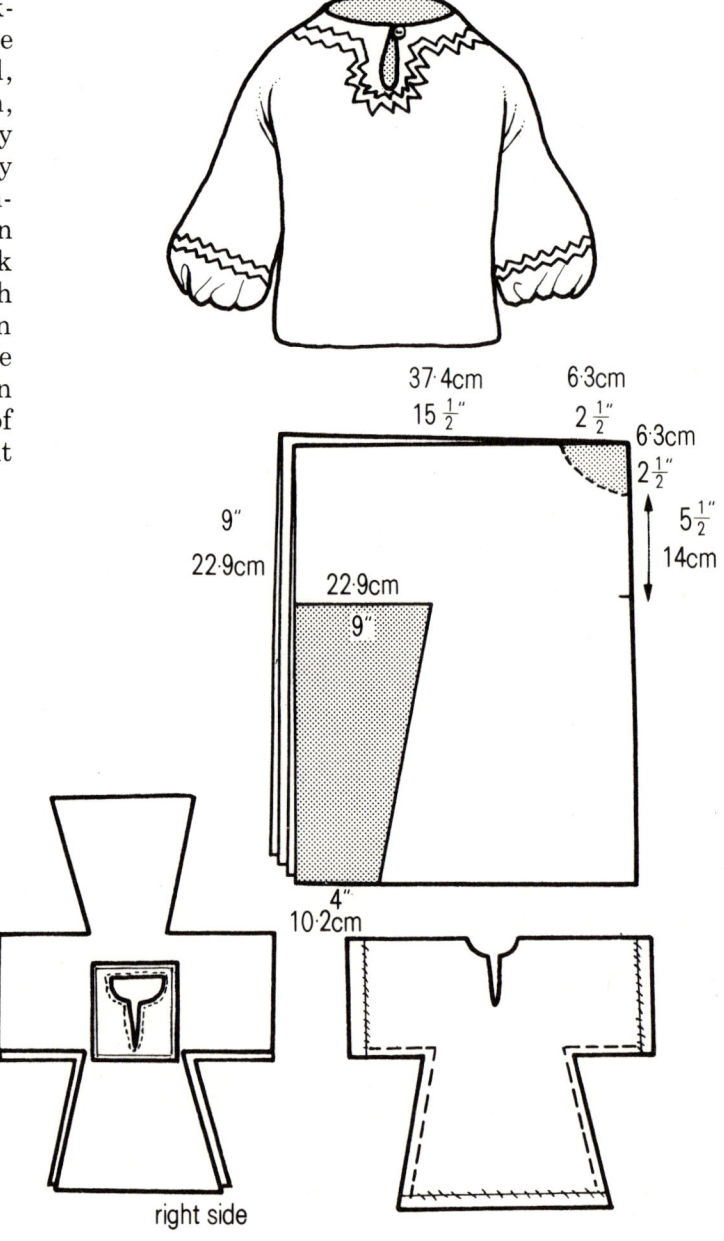

right side

# Gathered Skirt

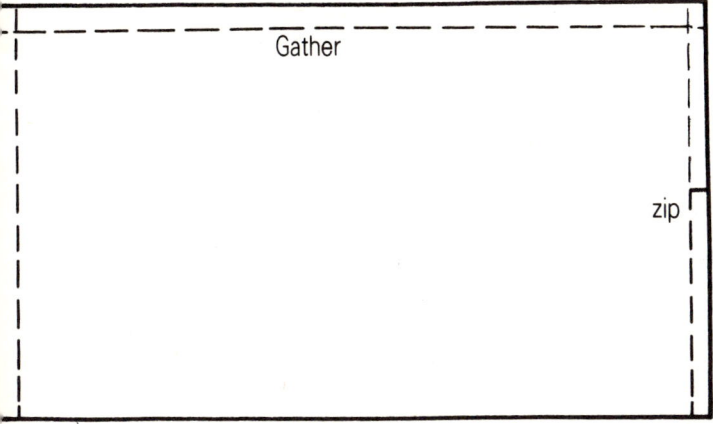

Here is a skirt which is ideal to wear with the blouse. It measures 18 in (45·6 cm) deep and requires 1¼ yards (114·8 cm) material. Buy slightly less material if you want a shorter skirt—1⅛ yards (103 cm) for 16 in (40·6 cm), 1 yard (91·4 cm) for 14 in (35·5 cm)—or more if you want a longer skirt. Fold the material as shown and cut a 3 in (7·6 cm) piece from the top. Now cut across the material in the middle. Lay skirt pieces together and stitch seams, leaving 7½ in (19 cm) open for zip. Hem the lower edge of the skirt and gather upper edge to fit waist. Cut the waistband to your measurement plus 2 in (5 cm). Lay the band over the gathered edge, right sides facing, and stitch round. Fold the band, turn the skirt through, fold under ½ in (13 mm) and slip-stitch edge over gathering. Turn in ½ in (13 mm) at each end of band and sew opening. Pin the zip into the skirt opening just below the waistband, and stitch in place. Stitch hooks and eyes on waistband.

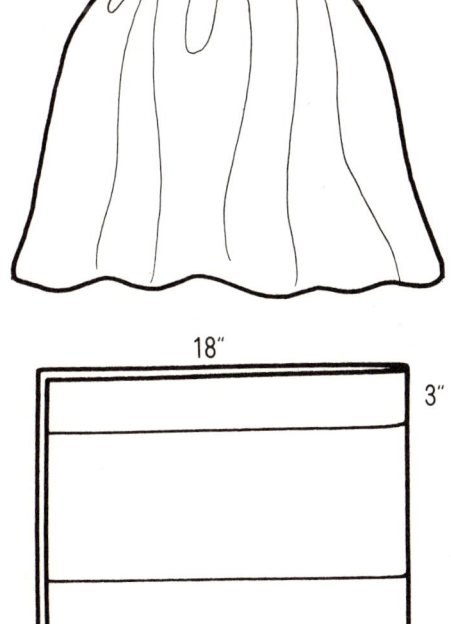

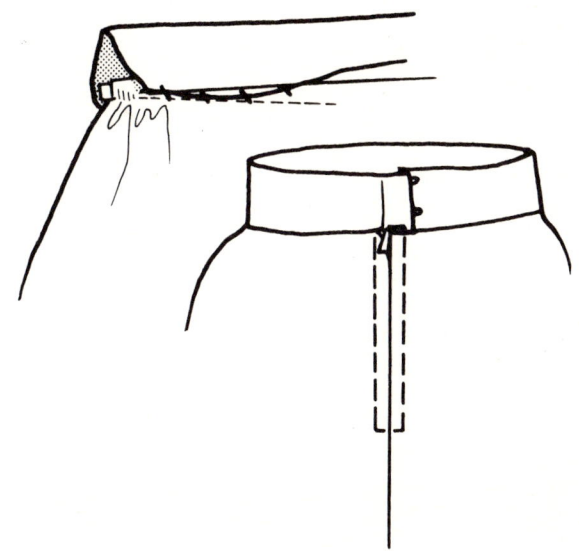

# A Simple Dress

patch pocket

waist

seam pocket

A   B

This dress is based on the pattern for the Beach Top. Check the pattern, as before, for size and fit, and allow for your length. The dress is made up in the same way as the beach top without, of course, the elastic. Hem the lower edge. Make a patch pocket as shown, binding the upper edge with the tape. The dress can be made in a bold print cotton, or you can make it in towelling and add fringing to the hem.

The second version of this dress has a tape channel stitched all round the waist inside with elastic inserted to draw in the waistline. A different pocket has been used here, which is set into the side seam. Cut a double pocket shape as shown. Before making up the dress, stitch a pocket piece to each side seam, front and back, with right sides of material facing (A). Turn the pockets to the wrong side of material and lay edge to edge. Pin to hold. When you stitch down the side seam, stitch ½ in (13 mm) on to pocket, and then round pocket shape and continue down remaining seam to hem (B). This gives a neat, hidden pocket.

# Bath Robe

The pattern for this bathrobe can be made to fit any size, and requires 2 yards (1·8 m) of 36 in (91·4 cm) towelling. Fold the towelling in half and find the centre. Measurement A is your measurement from shoulder to shoulder. Mark and cut down from these two points to the hem. On this large body piece make $2\frac{1}{2}$ in (6·3 cm) each side of centre point and bring a line down 12 in (30·5 cm) each side to the centre. Cut up centre line on front *only* and cut out the area shaded in diagram. The measurement B is the length of the sleeve x 10 in (25·4 cm) deep. Hem the sleeve edges, lay the sleeves flat on the body part on the right side, and stitch down. Now, on the wrong side, fold the robe at the shoulder and stitch underarm and side seams. Hem the lower edge. Bind all round opening with wide white cotton braid. Use the same cotton braid for a tie belt. Make patch pockets out of spare material shaded at side. You can make a sponge bag from the remaining towelling, as described earlier.

31–1

# Fun with Wool

Flowers. These flowers can be made using a bought manufactured flower maker, or you can make one yourself by sticking pins round a circle of thick card. You pull out the pins when the flower is made. Twelve pins are needed and arranged like a clock, and you work in a clockwise direction. Begin at 12 o' clock and take wool across centre and around 6 o' clock. Then back across, and wool round 1 o' clock, then back and around 7 o' clock, and so on until all the pins have been wrapped. Continue in this way until the petals are thick enough. Leave a long thread at the end, which you thread on to a needle. Sew all the loops together at the centre to hold the flower together. Sew a safety pin to the back of a flower to make a pretty brooch. The yoke of a dress would look lovely with a scattering of flowers sewn to it. Sew flowers on to a belt, a headband, a bag. Make one of the hats described earlier and trim it with flowers. Make lots of flowers and sew them all over a bedspread, or join up the flowers to make a flower-spread. You can make the flowers in any size you like, from a tiny one to sew to a felt ring, to a giant one just for fun.

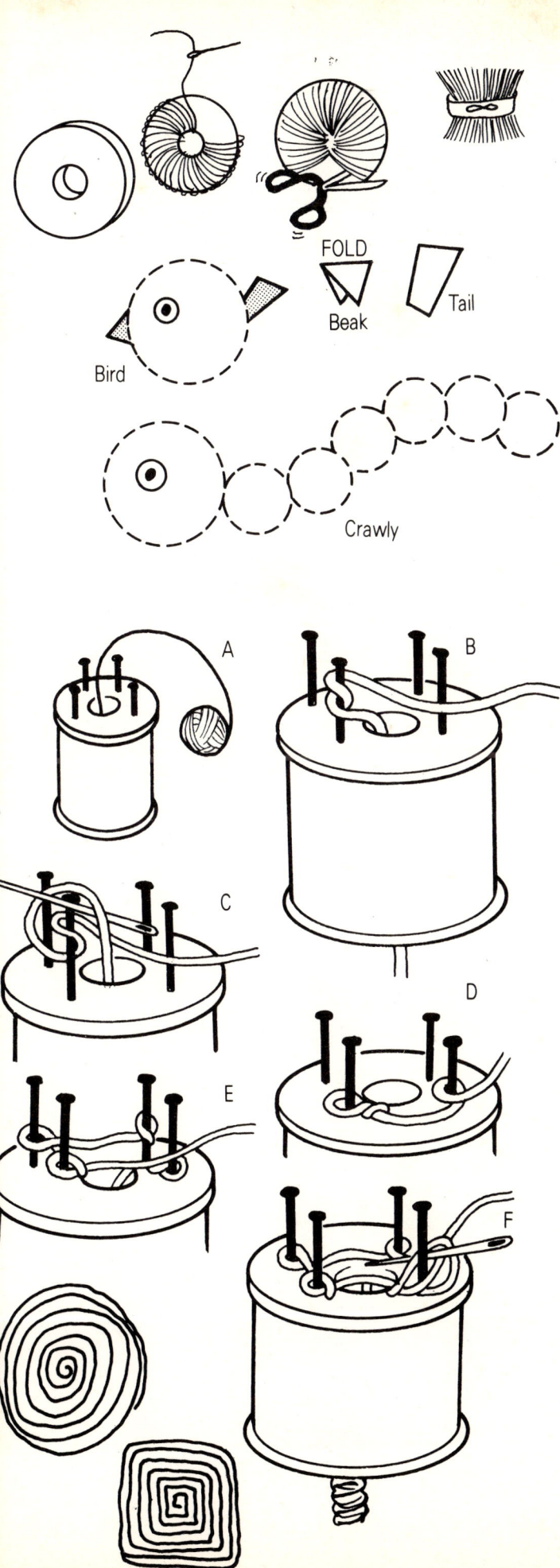

Pom-poms. Cut out two circles the same size, with holes in the centre. Using a blunt needle, thread wool through and round the circles until they are covered. Cut the wool round the edge and tie a piece of wool round between the cards. Remove the circles of card and trim the pom-pom. One pom-pom, with felt beak and tail glued on, makes a bird. Several pom-poms make a crawly.

French knitting. You will need a cotton reel with four nails hammered into it. A, pass wool down through hole with a 'tail' hanging down. B, wind wool twice round first nail, then C, with a blunt needle, lift lower loop up and over the nail. D, wind wool twice round the next nail and lift the lower loop up and over the nail. E, wind wool twice round the next nail and lift over lower nail, then repeat for last nail. F, pass wool around outside of first nail and lift lower loop up and over. Continue now with stage F, pulling the knitting through until it is the required length. Then you remove all the loops, thread wool end through them and pull tight. The knitting can be wound and stitched to form circles, or squares, or you can keep it as it is to make a belt for example.

# How to Knit

The joy of knitting is found not only in the relaxation which it brings but also in the sense of achievement felt on the completion of the article you are making. No boutique is complete without some knitted items, but first you must learn the simple basic technique. I have used plain knitting for all the items to make it easier still. Patience and practice are needed to achieve good, even knitting, and you must not despair if your first effort is less than perfect. The important things are to aim for an even tension, not pulling the stitches too tight or making them too slack and to knit the stitches on the needle *only*. It is easy, at first, to put your needle under the stitch below the loop on the needle, so take your time.

Make a loop at the end of your wool and insert a needle. Insert the other needle into the loop behind the first needle. Wrap the wool round the point of the second needle (which is your right hand needle RH), draw it down between the needles and, with the RH needle, draw wool through loop to form a stitch. Place this stitch on the left hand needle (LH) alongside the loop and you have cast on your first stitch. Continue casting on stitches in this way until you have the required number. You may find the first row of knitting into these cast-on stitches slightly awkward but it gets easier on the next! Insert RH needle point into first stitch on LH needle as shown. Wrap wool round needle (WRN) once and draw the loop through and on to the RH needle. Continue in this way to the end of the row of stitches on LH needle. Now turn the RH needle around and with the other needle knit off the stitches. Continue in this way until you have knitted the required number of rows. To cast off, knit two stitches, then lift the first stitch over the second. Knit one stitch, then lift the previous stitch over this one. Continue to last stitch. Break wool and draw it firmly through the last stitch.

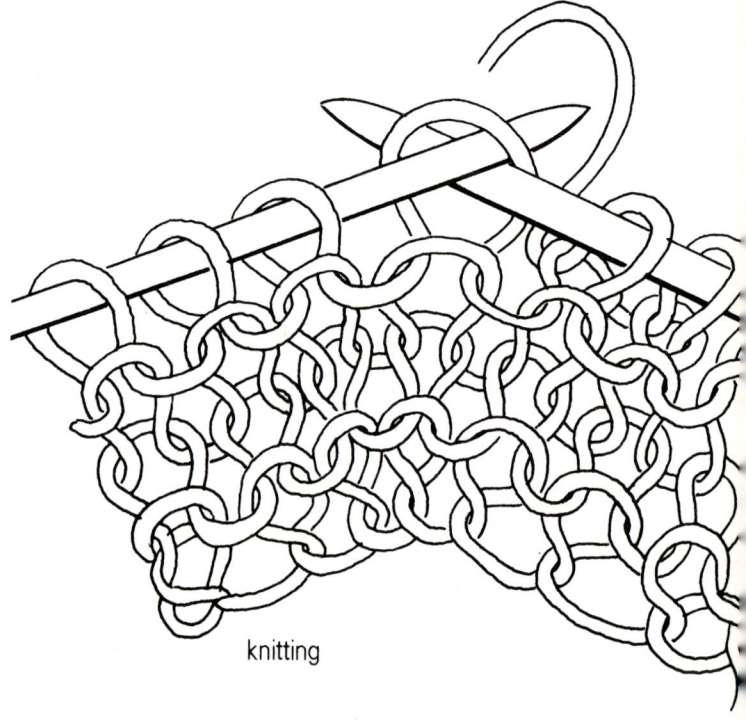

knitting

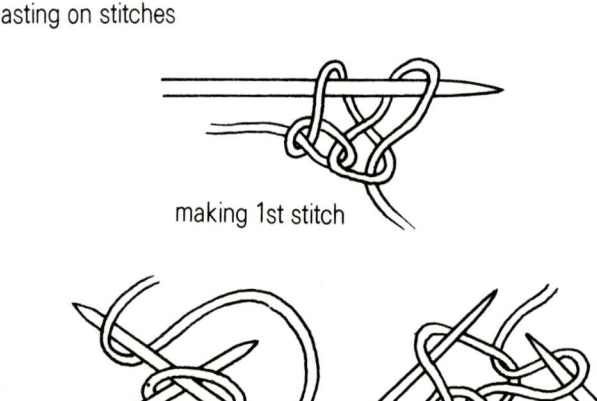

casting on stitches

making 1st stitch

1st loop

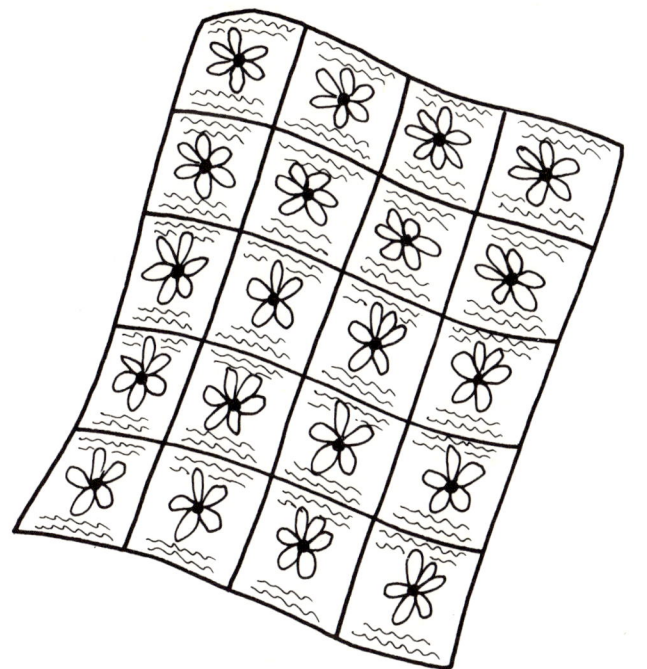

Knit plain squares to make a baby's brick, a scarf, a cot blanket. Use double knitting wool and No. 8 needles. To make the squares for any of these items, cast on 20 stitches and knit 29 rows, then cast off. For the baby's brick, knit six squares, sew them together and stuff firmly. Felt appliqué is sewn or glued to the squares. To make the scarf, knit as many squares as you need to make up the length and sew them together, edge to edge. I have made this scarf with 20 squares. The number of squares you will need for the blanket will depend upon whether it is for a doll's bed, a baby's cot or pram. Make up strips of squares, as for the scarf, and sew them together. This one is decorated with wool flowers as previously described. These squares are 4 in (10 cm) —to make larger squares, increase stitches and rows accordingly.

# Doll

Knitting squares was easy—and so is this doll, which is made of straight strips of knitting. Only her skirt is removable, but the way her body and arms are knitted gives the effect of a jumper. Her shoes are also part of the knitted legs. I have made one in red and a light beige, but you can vary her as you see in the drawings. Whichever of the dolls you make, the basic body pattern is the same. For strips, knit the same number of rows, but change over colours at the end of an even row on the wrong side. So you can have a doll with a striped top to match a plain skirt. Or leave out the skirt and make a doll with a striped top and matching plain legs to look like trousers. To make long sleeves you simply reverse the pattern. The rows for arms are knitted in the outfit colour and become sleeves, and the rows for short sleeves are knitted in flesh colour to become hands. The skirt for the party doll has 64 rows knitted instead of 32 to make a long skirt. Matching narrow strips are knitted and gathered to form collar and cuffs. You will need No. 8 needles and 4 ply wool.

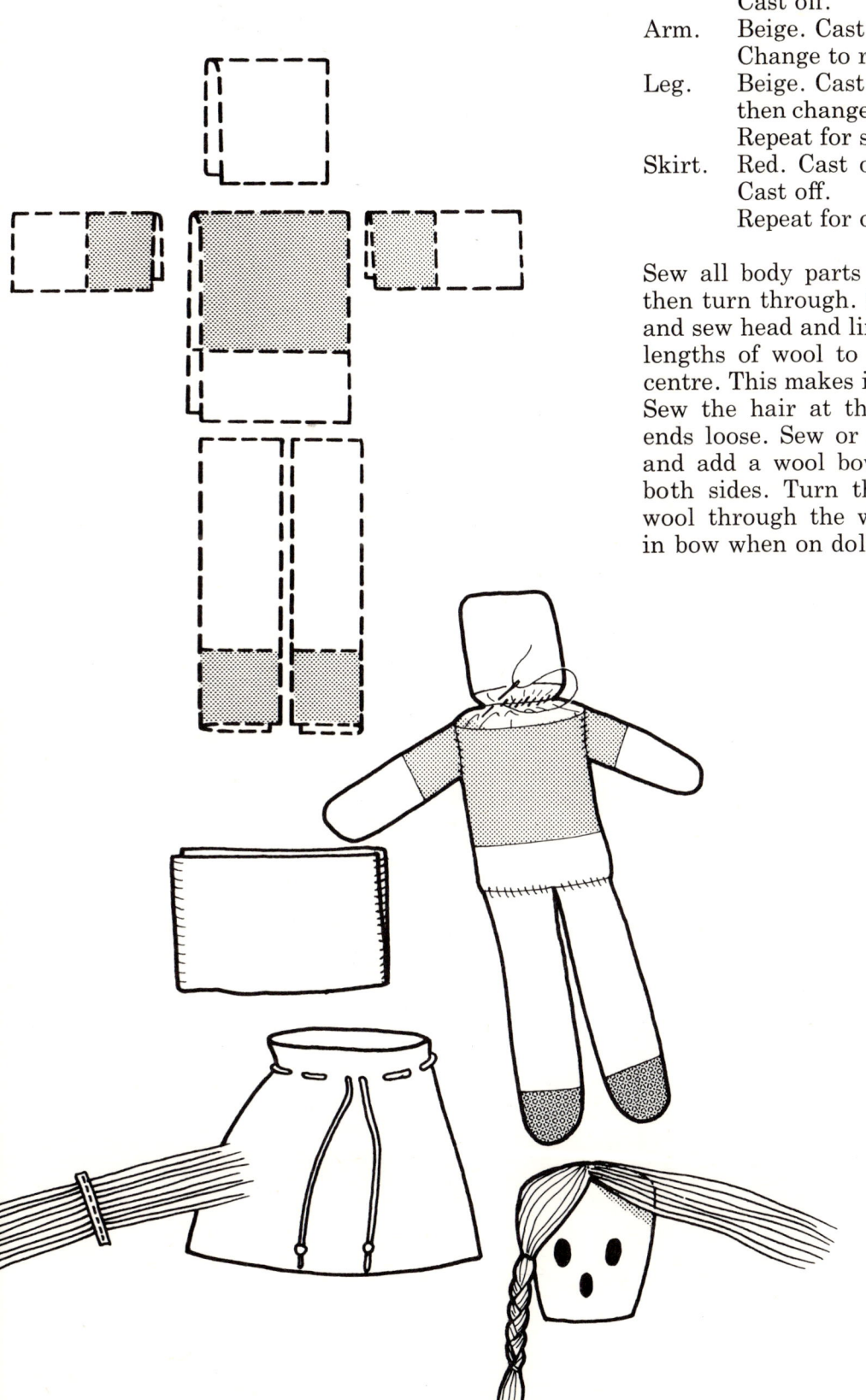

**Head.** Beige. Cast on 15 stitches. Knit for 50 rows. Cast off.

**Body.** Beige. Cast on 18 stitches. Knit 12 rows then change to red and knit 12 rows. Cast off.

**Arm.** Beige. Cast on 14 stitches. Knit 22 rows. Change to red and knit 16 rows. Cast off.

**Leg.** Beige. Cast on 16 stitches. Knit 54 rows, then change to red. Knit 16 rows. Cast off. Repeat for second leg.

**Skirt.** Red. Cast on 38 stitches. Knit 32 rows. Cast off.
Repeat for other side of skirt.

Sew all body parts together on the wrong side, then turn through. Stuff body parts with Kapok, and sew head and limbs to body. For the hair sew lengths of wool to a short piece of tape at the centre. This makes it easier to sew it to the head. Sew the hair at the sides. Then plait or leave ends loose. Sew or glue on felt eyes and mouth and add a wool bow at neck. Sew the skirt on both sides. Turn through and sew a length of wool through the waist ½ in (13 mm) down. Tie in bow when on doll.

# A Shawl

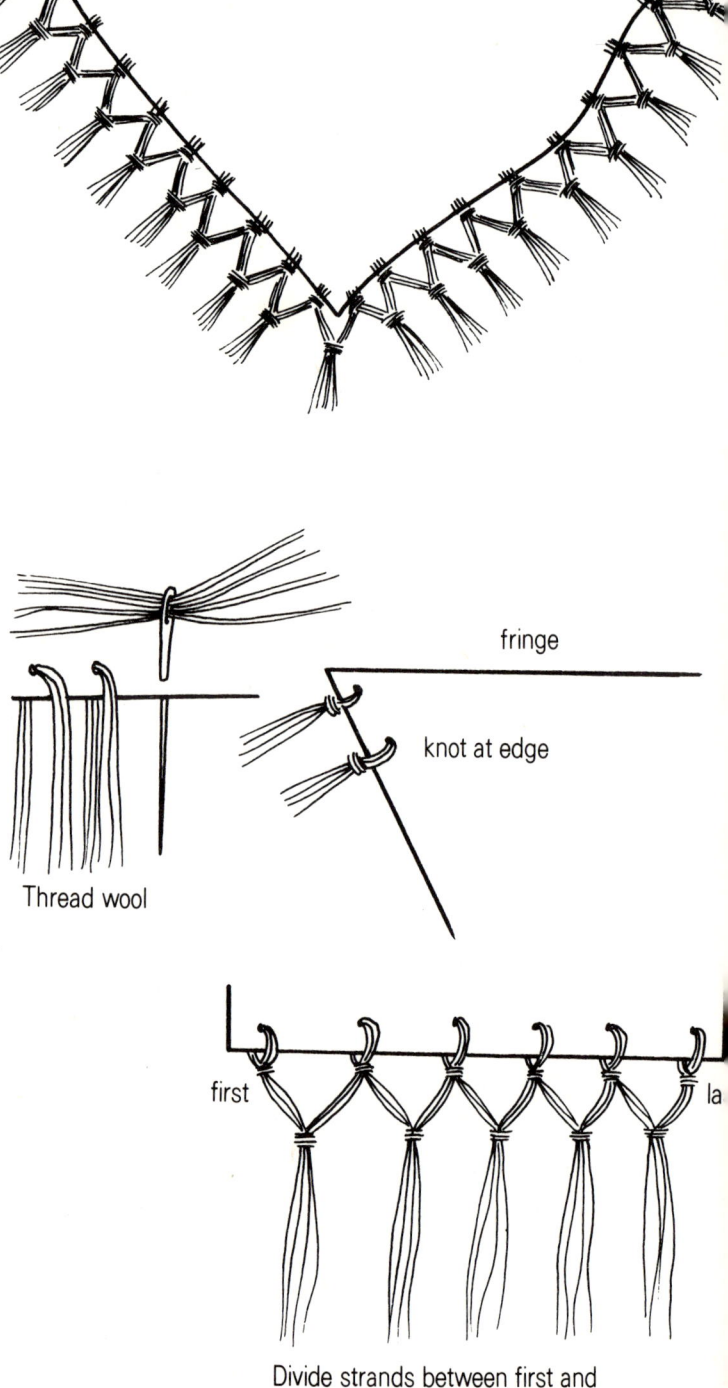

Having knitted straight pieces, you should now have the confidence to try shaping. It is very simple, and still plain knitting. And imagine how proud you will be, being able to wear a shawl you have knitted yourself. You will need four balls of 3 ply wool and No. 6 needles. Cast on three stitches and knit them plain. Increase 1 stitch at the beginning and end of what you treat as the right side (though both are the same). To increase stitches, you simply cast them on as you learned at the beginning. When the increased rows have totalled 109 rows there will be 221 stitches after knitting 218 rows. To keep count of the rows, mark them all down on a piece of paper and cross them off as you knit them. Cast off loosely. Follow the diagrams to make the knotted fringe.

Thread wool

fringe

knot at edge

first  last

Divide strands between first and last. Knot them evenly spaced.

# Knitted Hood

A pretty hood to keep you warm in winter.
Using No. 8 needles, cast on 3 stitches. Knit plain for 60 rows, increasing one stitch at the beginning and end of each row to make 123 stitches. Cast on 18 stitches at the beginning of the next two rows, making 159 stitches. Knit 36 rows, then transfer to No. 9 needles and knit 5 rows. Cast off. Turn the 5 rows over to the right side and sew A and B together. You can leave the hood plain, or embroider wool flowers on it.

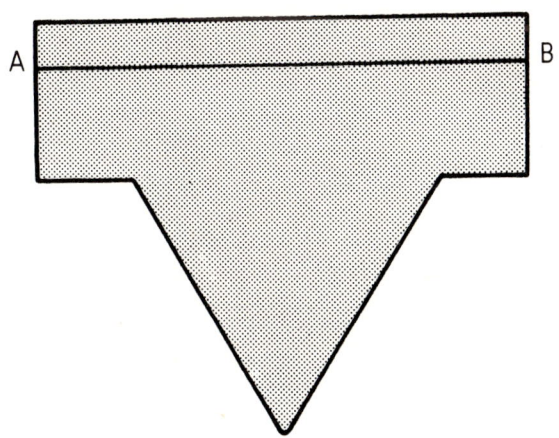

# Crochet

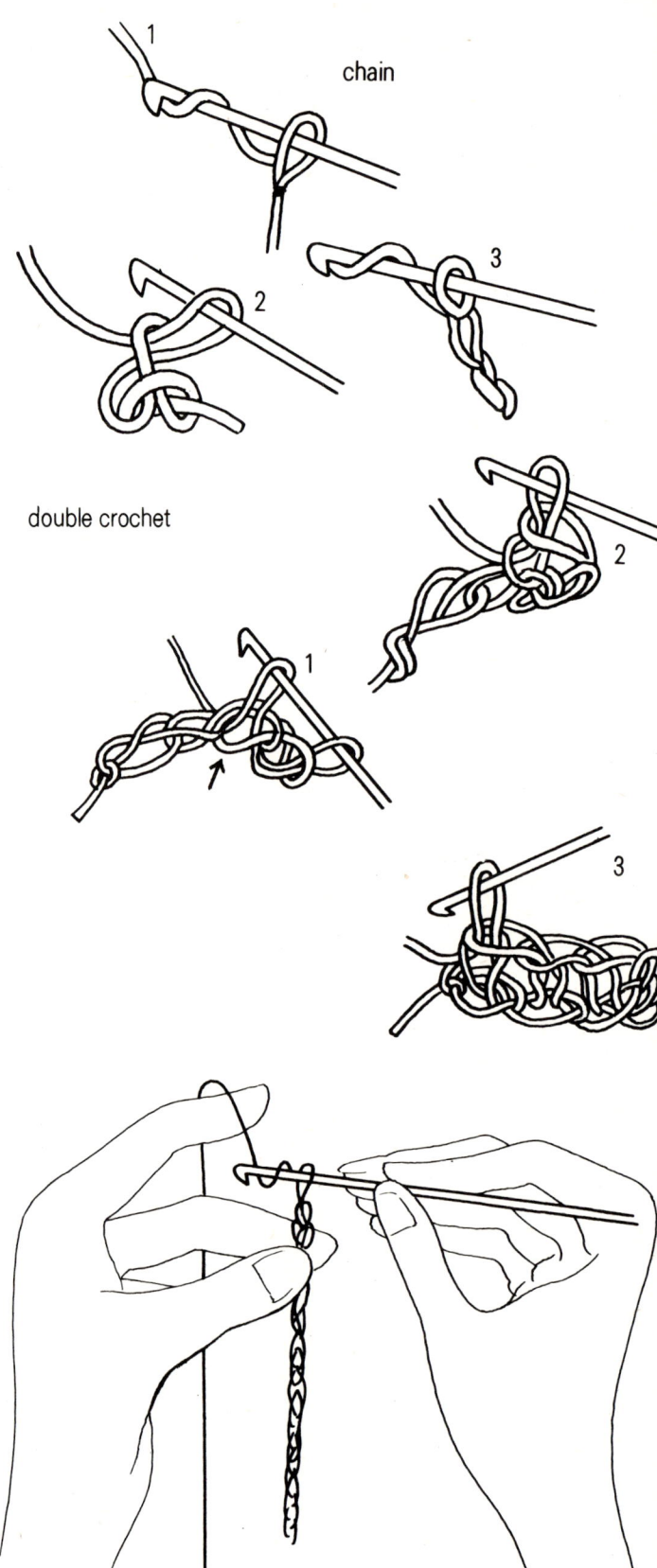

To crochet you need only a crochet hook. Look at the drawing, and practise holding the wool and hook correctly. This will help you to crochet more easily and comfortably. It is just a knack you will soon get used to, but it is important. Hold the chain with your thumb and second finger and loop the wool over your first finger. Hold the wool loosely with your second and third fingers.

## Chain

1. Make a loop and insert hook. Catch the thread suspended from your first finger (known as wool round hook or WRH) 2. Draw the loop through 3. Continue in this way until you have made the required number of chain stitches.

Double crochet. Begin with required number of chain stitches.

1. Insert the hook under the double strands of second chain, catch suspended thread and draw the new loop through, making two loops on hook.
2. Catch thread with hook and draw it through both loops on hook to make one loop. This is one double chain stitch known as D.C.
3. Continue working D.C. into each chain stitch to the end of the chain. The first chain stitch which was not worked into forms an upright stitch giving depth and a straight edge. 2nd row of double crochet. Turn work and make one chain stitch, to give depth. Do not work into this stitch, but insert hook into the first loop of the chain, which was the last stitch worked on previous row, and work D.C. as described. Continue D.C. to the end of the row. Turn work and make one chain stitch and D.C. to end of row. Continue until the work is complete, then break off wool and pull through loop on hook.

# Belt

To start you off, a simple belt in two colours—let's say blue and white. You will need double knitting wool and a No. 3.50 crochet hook. Make a chain long enough to go round your waist plus 4 in overlap. Work D.C. for 2 rows in white. Change to blue by knotting at end of row. Work D.C. for 2 rows then change back to white. Work D.C. for 2 rows, break wool and pull through loop. Fold one end over buckle and sew edge to back of belt. Sew a popper to the other end of belt to hold it.

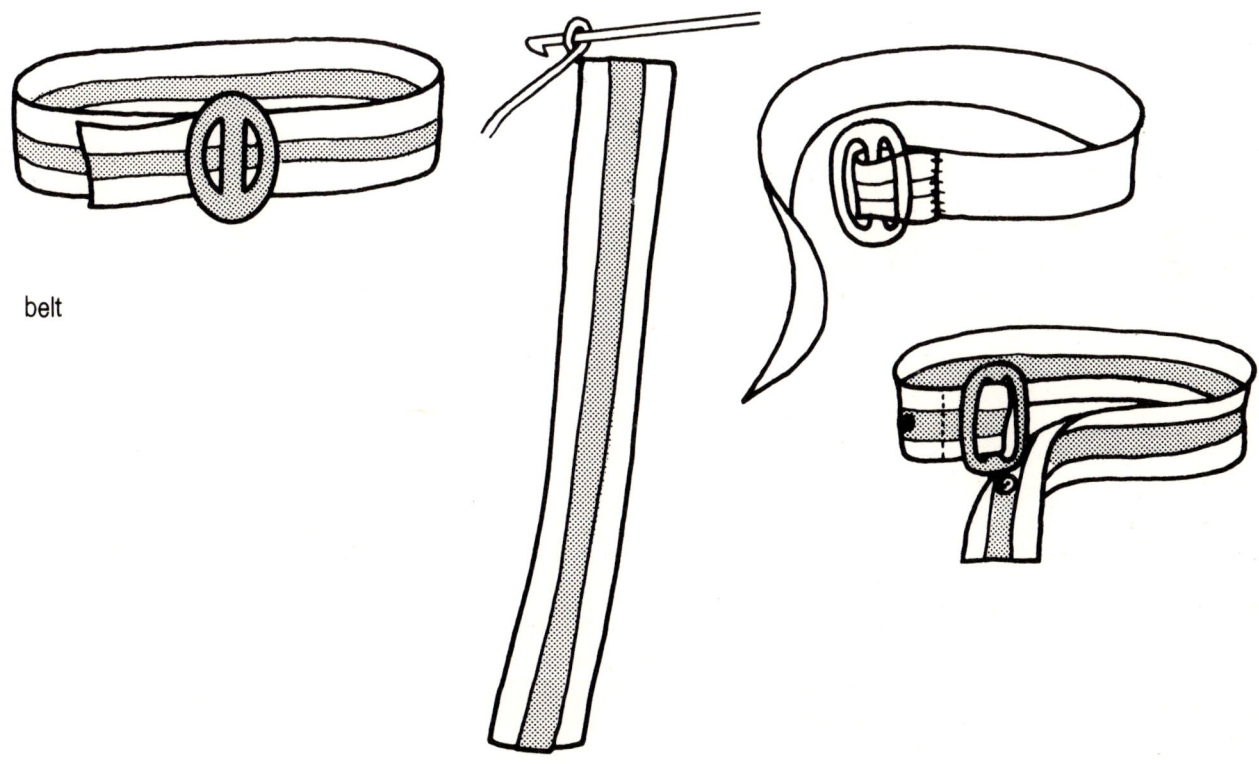

belt

# Waistcoat

To make this waistcoat you will need to know how to make treble crochet—TR. Use 4 ply wool and a 2.5 crochet hook.

Put W.R.H. then insert hook into fourth chain stitch and draw a loop through (Fig.1). Put W R.H. and draw it through the first two loops on hook, so that you have two loops (Fig.2). Put W.R.H. and draw through the last two loops, leaving one loop on hook. Repeat for number of stitches required.

To make squares for waistcoat you will need wool in four different colours.

In *first* colour make a chain of 5 stitches and join circle with a slip stitch. Work three chain stitches, then 2 TR into circle. Work 2 chain stitches to form a corner. Work 3 TR stitches into circle, then 2 chain stitches, then 3 TR stitches into circle. Work 2 chain stitches then 3 TR stitches into circle. Work 2 chain stitches and join to last stitch, with a slip stitch. Join *second* colour with a knot and begin work at a corner. Work 3 TR stitches into the space, then 2 chain stitches, 3 TR stitches, 1 chain stitch, 3 TR stitches, 2 chain stitches, 3 TR stitches and 1 chain stitch, and you have made two new corners. Repeat for remaining two corners and finish as before. Change to *third* colour as before and work 3 TR stitches, 2 chain stitches, 3 TR stitches, 1 chain stitch into a corner. Work 3 TR, stitches, 1 chain, stitch for side of square, then work 3 TR 2 chain 3 TR, 1 chain. Repeat for rest of square, and finish off. Change to *fourth* colour and repeat as for third colour but add 3 TR stitches and 1 chain stitch extra on each side. You will need 26 squares for the waistcoat. Follow the diagrams for arranging the squares and sewing them together. Finish with a chain stitch loop and button fastening at the neck.

These squares are so pretty, why not make some extra ones and make a scarf? You can make the bag by simply enlarging the squares, remembering to increase at each side. The strap and belt are worked in double crochet to the desired width.

1st colour   2nd colour   3rd colour

4th colour.

# How to Crochet Circles

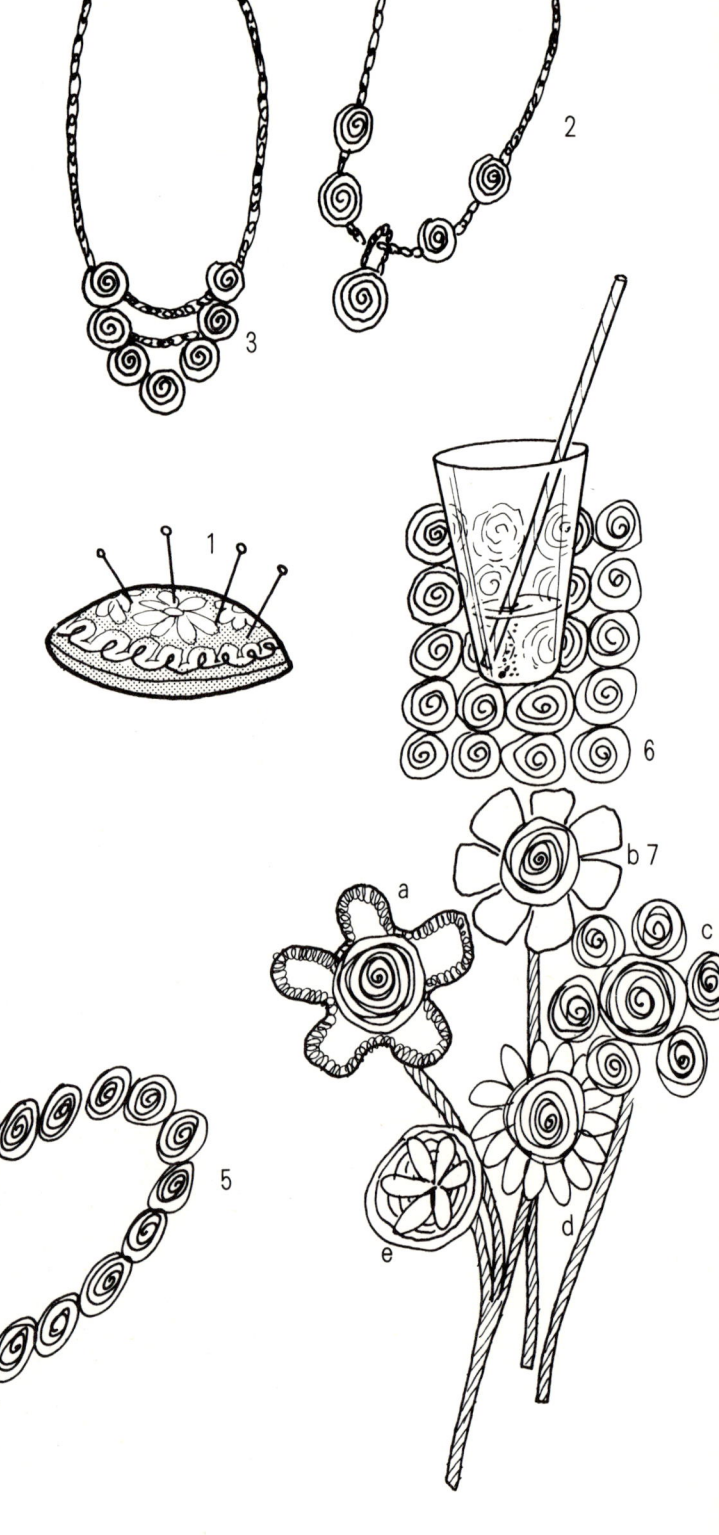

There are so many things you can make using crochet circles, and they could not be easier! They can be any size you like, to give even more scope for using them.

Let us begin with a small circle. Use double knitting wool and a 3.50 crochet hook. Work 3 chain stitches then join them into a circle by inserting the hook into the first chain stitch, W.R.H. and pull the loop through both loops on the needle—slip stitch (S.S.) Work 6 D.C. into circle, and join to first D.C. with S.S.

For the second round, work 2 D.C. into each of the 6 previous D.C. Join with S.S. The third round is the same as the second, and your circle is getting bigger now. For the fourth round, work 2 D.C. into the next D.C., 1 D.C. into the next D.C., 2 D.C. into the next, 1 D.C. into the next until the round is finished. Join with S.S.

Let us finish off at this size and see what we can make. Break the wool and pull it through the loop on the hook.

1. A tiny pin cushion. Two circles sewn and stuffed.
2. A crochet chain necklace has crochet circles sewn to it, with one circle attached by a short crochet chain as pendant.
3. Crochet chain necklace with two shorter chain loops and crochet circles sewn to them.
4. Crochet circles decorate the crochet belt previously described.
5. A belt made up of crochet circles, with crochet chain ties.
6. Circles sewn together to make a table mat.
7. Flowers made out of crochet circles. A has a crochet chain looped and sewn to the circle to form petals. B has felt petals sewn to a circle. C is made up of a centre circle surrounded by circle petals sewn to it. D has wool loops sewn round the edge of a circle. E is a circle with wool loops sewn to its centre. All have pipecleaner stems bound with green wool.

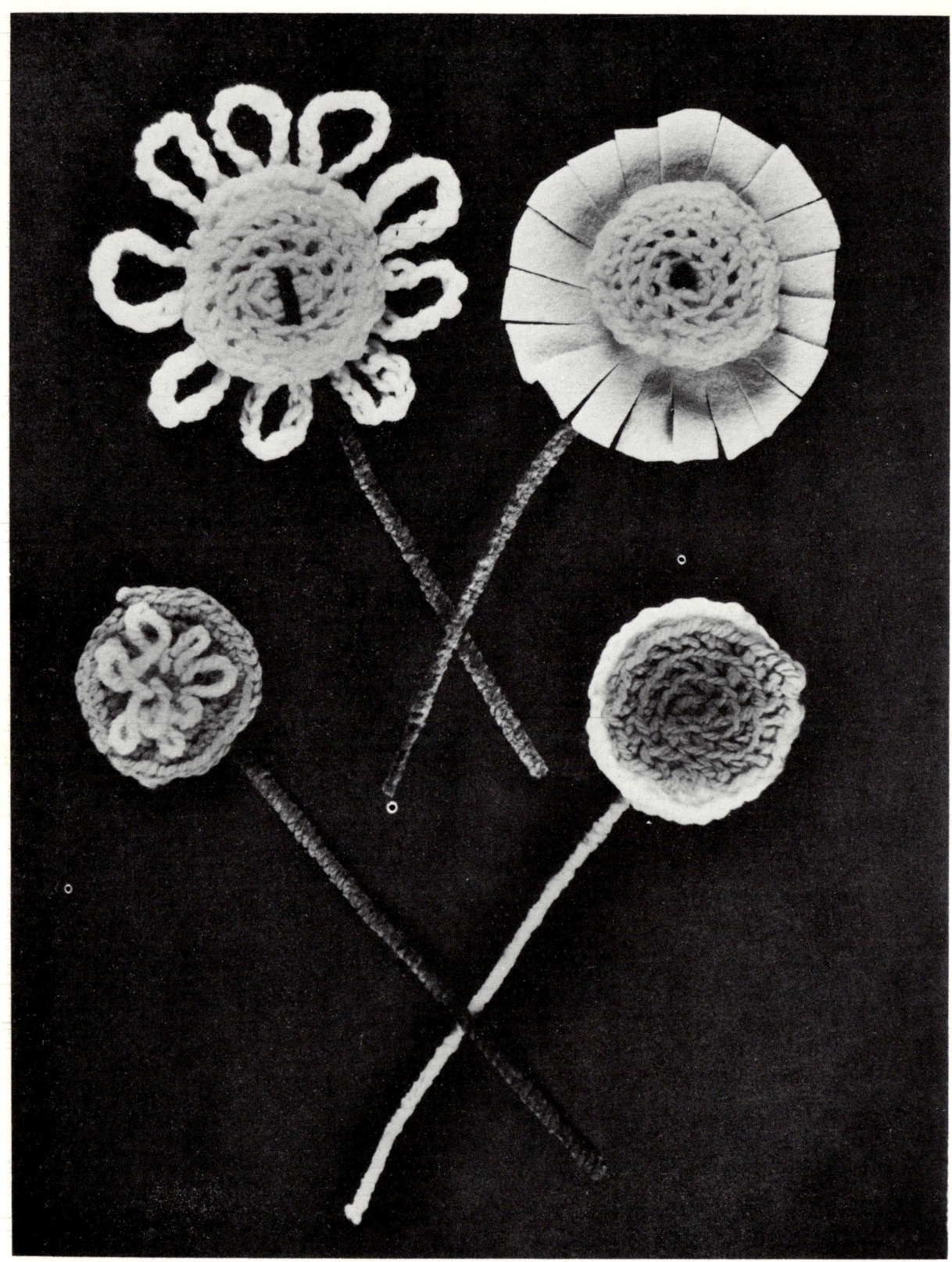

46–1

# Crochet Beret and Bag

So much for little circles. To make the beret and bag you will need to make bigger ones. You will need double, double knitting wool and a 4.50 crochet hook.

## Beret

Make a 6 stitch chain and insert hook in first chain with S.S. Work 10 D.C. into hole and join with S.S. Tie a loop of wool in a contrast colour to last stitch, work 2 D.C. into every other stitch and finish round as before. Repeat for third and fourth row. Increase one stitch into every third stitch for the fifth, sixth and seventh rounds, then work remaining sixteen rounds in D.C. without increasing stitches. Keep stitches loose so that the work remains flat. Finish off with S.S. Turn and stitch a ½ in (13 mm) hem all round and insert elastic to fit head. Make a wool pom-pom as previously described and sew it to beret.

## Bag

Make two circles as described above. Make the strap by making a chain 100 stitches long and working four rows of D.C. Sew circles to this band as shown. There are lots more things you can make in this way—table mats, cushions or, in a smaller size, a purse.

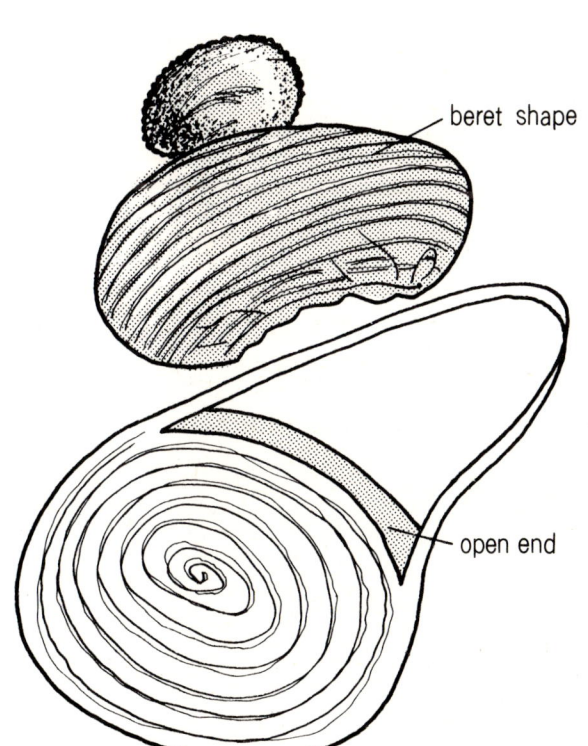

beret shape

open end

# Metrication

You will have noticed that metric measurements have been included in this chapter. Metrication need not be alarming; indeed, you can even have a good laugh about it when you take your own measurements! Because centimetres are smaller than inches, your measurements will read that much higher. Most tape measures and rulers are marked in centimetres, and you can find complete conversion tables in diaries and reference books. It would be well worth while to accustom yourself to converting from inches. Soon you will forget about inches and will think in terms of metrication, just as you now think in terms of decimalisation.

A metre equals 100 centimetres and 1,000 millimetres. A metre is about $3\frac{1}{2}$ in more than a yard. Here are some fabric widths to give you some idea:

| Width in inches | Width in centimetres |
|---|---|
| 36 in | 90—92 cm |
| 48 in | 120 cm |
| 54 in | 134—136 cm |

A 7 in zip will convert to an 18 cm zip, a 12 in to a 30 cm and an 18 in to a 46 cm zip.

Your metrication table will give far more conversions than these, and it will be useful to have it by you when you are making things. If the item you are working on requires a 7 in zip, for example, you can look up 7 in and then write 18 cm on your pattern. If you continue in this way you will soon get a mental image of metres, centimetres and millimetres. This is only a rough guide to metrication, but it seemed to me to be a good idea to include it, to give you some reassurance, and an idea about how it works. You can actually get some fun out of converting the sizes you require. Why not copy some useful size conversions onto a large piece of card, using different coloured pencils? You could have a key colour for metres, a key colour for centimetres and a key colour for millimetres.

# JEWELLERY

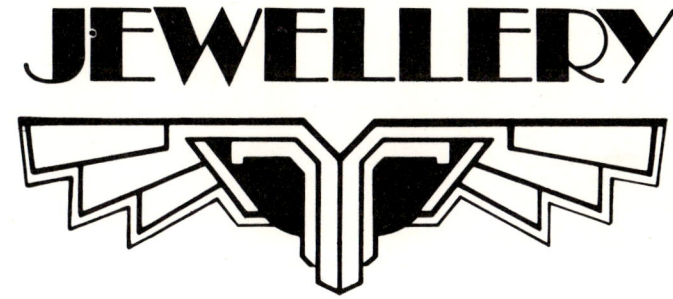

Archaeological finds have played a vital part in the search for knowledge about our past history. Much has been discovered, and is still being discovered. Almost without exception, included in these 'finds' is some form of jewellery. Down the ages, ornaments have been made and worn, whether fashioned out of seeds, birds' feathers and twigs, or precious stones set in precious metals. Our love of the decorative, and our ability to create, have continued, much of it influenced by past designs and techniques. Next time you visit a museum, an art gallery, or a Stately Home, look at the examples of fine jewellery to be seen. Take a small notepad and make sketches. You will find that many of the designs can be adapted to the methods described in this book. You may have to simplify the bead threading or silverwork, for example, but you will have captured the essence of the design.

I hope you will find jewellery designs here to inspire you to attempt new crafts and techniques. None are difficult and there is as great a variety as a book of this size will allow. There is no great expense involved, indeed you will probably find most of what you will need in your home. An old bead necklace can be taken apart and put together again with a variety of links and chains made of copper or silver wire. Nail enamel can be used to make enamel jewellery. Make your own beads, even cook your own beads. Have you ever seen bread beads? Think in terms of jewellery and you will find almost limitless sources for making it. Safety pins, scraps of wool, drinking straws, labels. You cannot string potatoes to wear round your neck, but you can make beads from apples!

Keep the jewellery you make in a jewellery box. It may be the enamelled box on the jacket, or a decorated match box. There are designs for a beaded box, covered and be-jewelled boxes, a jewellery envelope, and how to utilize cheese, cigar, pill, and sweet boxes.

Make jewellery, for beauty and for fun.

# What you will need

What you will need will, of course, depend upon the type of jewellery you have decided to make. Most of the items here list the requirements, while others are obvious. Where necessary, you will need scissors, glue for sticking, paints for painting, and so on. However, there are some tools and materials which must be listed here, in order to prepare you.

For all types of *Beadwork*, you will need thread, and it is better to use the right one than to have your efforts wasted on a thread which will break easily. Bead silk, Drima thread, strong threads like buttonhole twist, thin cords, strong wool, and fine string can all be used, depending upon the size of the bead, and the type of work. Dental floss is very good, and for some beadwork you can use thin leather thongs or macramé twine.

The type of needle you use, will again depend upon the size of bead and the type of work. Long thin beading needles are essential for small beads, otherwise any needle will do which will allow the eye plus thread to pass through the eye of a bead. Some threads, like wool, need not be used with a needle. Simply wrap clear adhesive tape (like Sellotape) round the ends, or stiffen them with glue or soap. Clasps and fastenings can be obtained from craft shops, some department stores, and mail order suppliers. In many cases you can make your own, and instructions are given for these.

A tray with a felt lining is useful to work on, to prevent beads from rolling away, and to enable you to leave the work undisturbed. Beads can be bought in various quantities and qualities. You can break up and reassemble old or inexpensive necklaces bought from chain stores. You can mix these beads with others you have. Second-hand

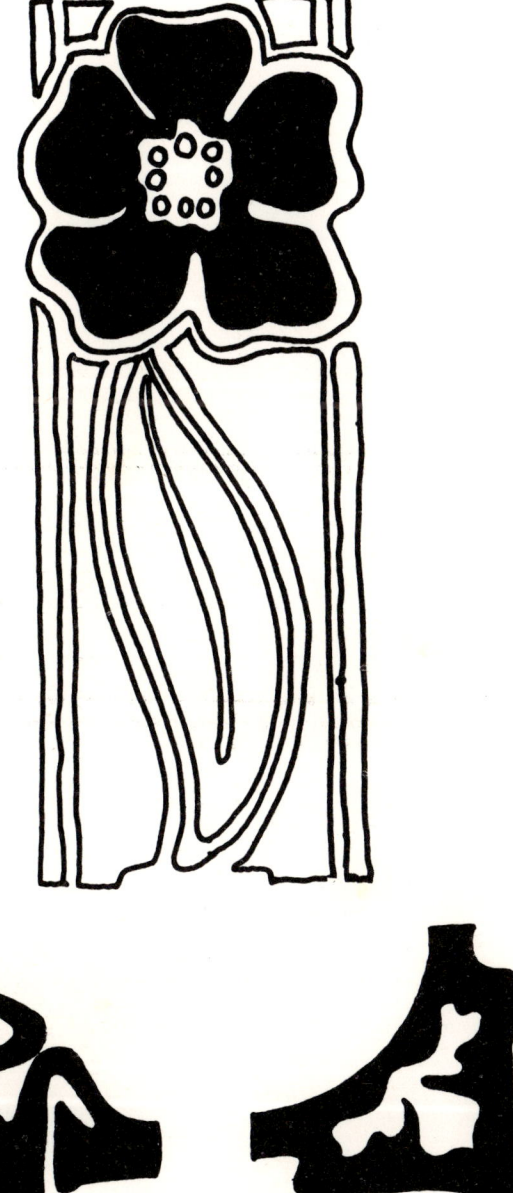

shops often have beautiful beads which can be used singly as well as together. You can make beads out of shells, seeds, bits of leather or wood. There are many methods of making beads described in this book: pieces of cooking apples, balsa wood beads, paper beads, bread beads etc.

For all types of *Metal jewellery* like silver, copper, from which you can make chains and links, you will need a little more 'hardware'. Strong sharp scissors can be used for some, but it is worth buying metal shears designed for the purpose. Round-nosed pliers are needed to shape links, and flat-nosed pliers needed for holding and shaping. For flattening you can use a small hammer with a scrap of leather or soft material tied over the head. Araldite, or any similar strong glue is a must. Anything round can be used to shape loops and links, from thin knitting needles and wood dowels, to bottles and jars. Wire for making jewellery can be the thicker gauge of fuse wire, florist's wire, brass, copper or silver wire. The thinner gauges of fuse wire are useful to practise making links and for trying out designs. 'Gauge' means the thickness of the wire, the higher the gauge, the thinner the wire.

*Copper* wire is easy to handle in 8, 10, 14 and 16 gauge, since copper wire is generally soft. Sheet copper can be bought in pre-cut shapes, or various-sized pieces. These are best in 18-20 gauges.

*Silver* wire can be round or flat. The round wires in gauges 18-24 are best to work with. Flat silver wire is obtainable in various widths—$\frac{1}{8}$ in (3·5 mm) and $\frac{1}{4}$ in (7 mm) are most suitable. Silver is sold by weight so that the higher gauges will be less expensive, as well as easier to manipulate. Sheet silver is bought in many sizes and shapes, and of course gauges. The gauges from 20-26 are the easiest to use, and again are less expensive than the lower (heavier) gauges.

For any work requiring cutting out, painting and glueing, it is well worth putting down two or three large sheets of newspaper on your work surface. This not only protects the surface of the table, but you can simply gather up and wrap all the messy bits, leaving no untidy traces of your efforts. This way, the pleasure you have derived from making jewellery will not be diminished by having a big clean-up job (and possible unpopularity!) after.

# Jewellery from Oddments

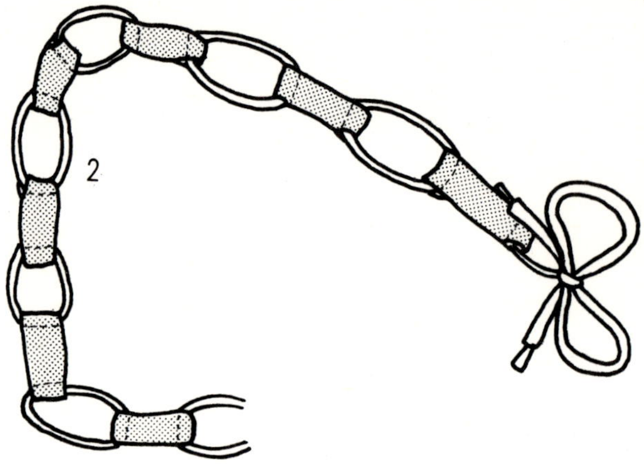

The first necklace is made from scraps of wool and a few beads. The tassels and pom-poms are attached to a length of wool which ties at the back. Wrap small pieces of Sellotape over the ends of the wool. The tassels are made by folding bunches of wool and tying round at the top to form a 'head'. To make the pom-poms cut 2 small circles of card with holes cut in the centre of each. Wrap wool over and over the outer rim of both cards together. When the ring is covered cut wool at outer edge all round, separate the card rings slightly and tie round the centre. Remove the cards and trim the pom-poms with sharp scissors. The second necklace uses scraps of ribbon and wool in different colours. Tie short lengths of wool to form circles. Fold and sew ends of ribbons over wool loops and sew across. On the two end ribbons, attach wool for ties.

If you have a button box, you will have great fun selecting a variety of buttons to thread for the third necklace. Numbers four and five, a brooch and pendant, are pieces cut from the ends of wood dowels. Both are painted, and the pendant has a ring screw fixed in the top to suspend it on a cord. The brooch has a piece of felt, with a pin sewn to it, glued to the back.

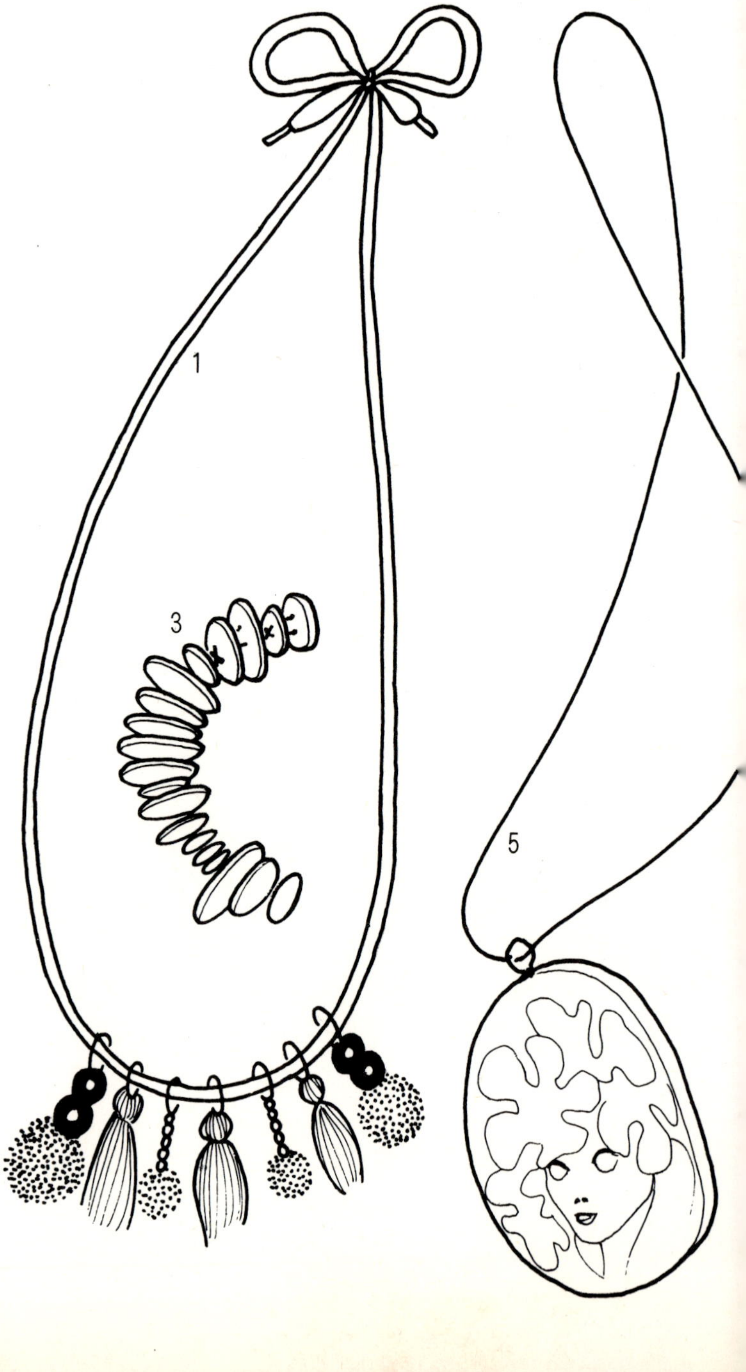

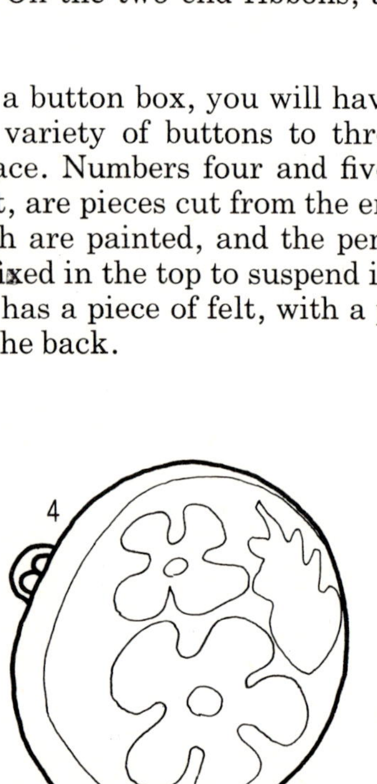

Safety pins, scraps of wool, a tiny feather which came unstuck from a toy, bits of card, and nail enamel have all been used to make the brooches and pendant here.

1. Dolly face, cut out of card is painted with nail enamel, which can be bought inexpensively in the most amazing variety of colours. She has yellow hair, blue eyes, red mouth and cheeks, and green ribbons. A piece of felt with a small safety pin sewn to it, is glued on the back.

2 and 3 in the diagram are made in the same way. The apple is painted red on the outside, with a yellow centre, and green leaf and stem. The small feather, mentioned earlier, is glued to the hat on the third brooch. The hat is ordinary enamel paint, hair is yellow nail enamel, eyes blue, lips and cheeks red.

4. This pendant is made by cutting the shape in card, fixing an eyelet at each end and glueing on tiny scraps of wool in different colours. It has a wool loop and fringe.

5. My daughter Pania (age 8) designed this little brooch made with 9 tiny brass safety pins and 36 tiny red beads. Six horizontal pins have 6 beads on each, and there are three vertical pins, one at the back for pinning on.

5—2

# Paper Beads

Cut strips of paper. Grease knitting needle and roll strips on to it. Glue ends. Paint and varnish beads and stand them in a pot to dry. Beads can be threaded on to cord, elastic or wool.
1. Straight and oval beads on wool.
2. Large straight beads painted black and white and threaded on to elastic.
3. Alternate straight and oval beads on wool. Pendant bead is attached to necklace with loops of wool which then pass through bead to form fringe.
4. Oval and straight beads on cord. Pendant is cut from card.
5. Large oval beads on cord with bow worn at front.

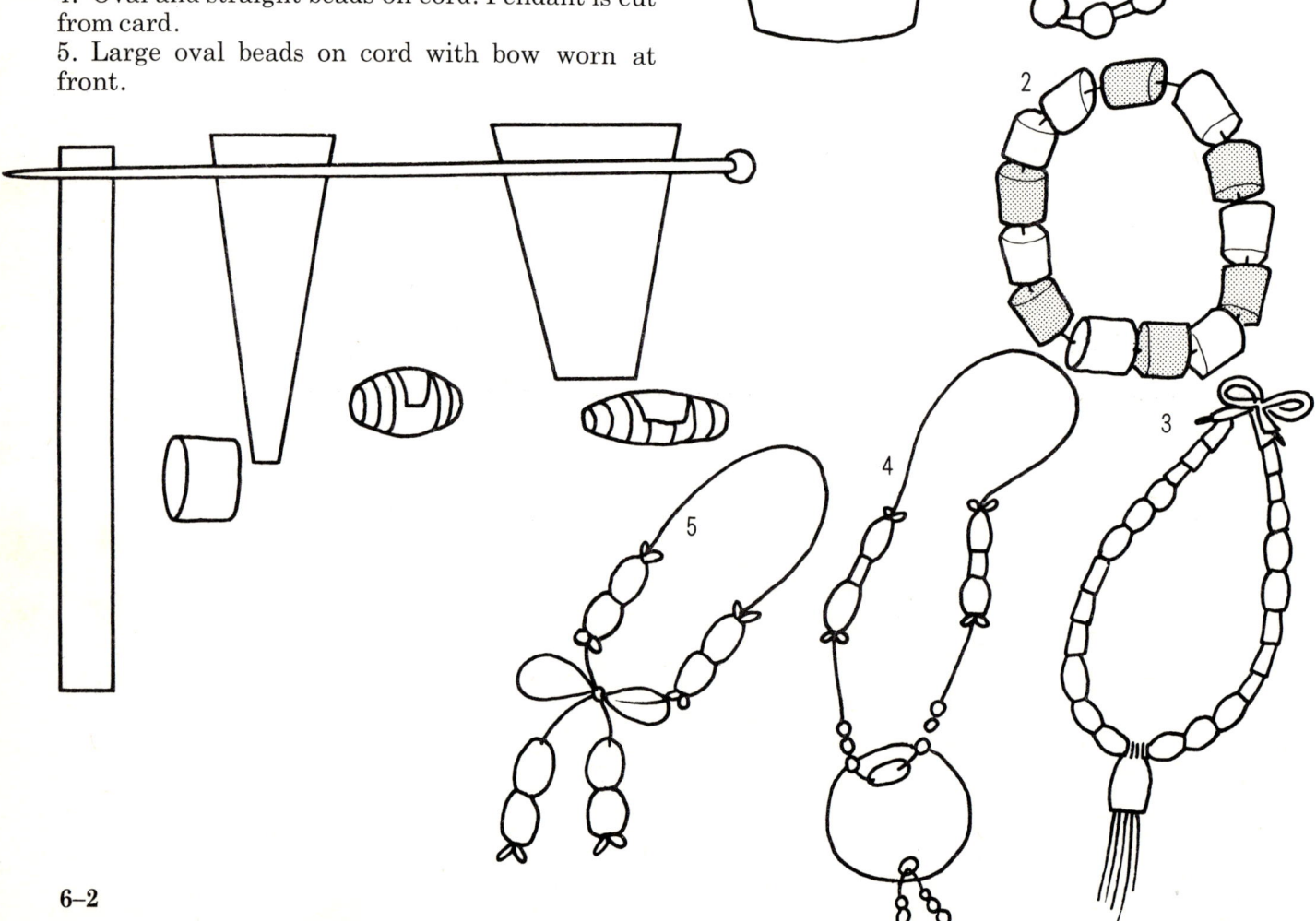

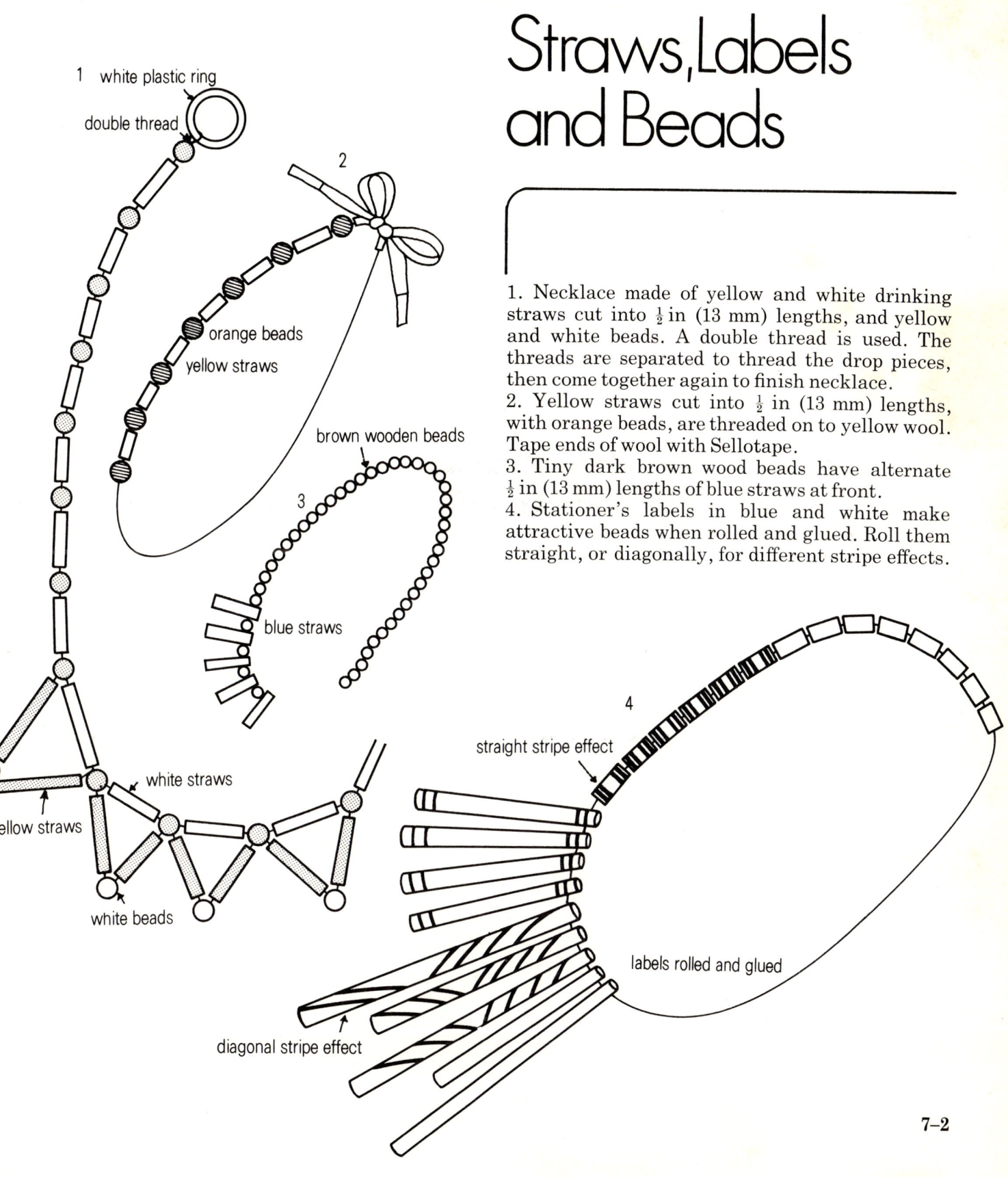

# Straws, Labels and Beads

1. Necklace made of yellow and white drinking straws cut into ½ in (13 mm) lengths, and yellow and white beads. A double thread is used. The threads are separated to thread the drop pieces, then come together again to finish necklace.
2. Yellow straws cut into ½ in (13 mm) lengths, with orange beads, are threaded on to yellow wool. Tape ends of wool with Sellotape.
3. Tiny dark brown wood beads have alternate ½ in (13 mm) lengths of blue straws at front.
4. Stationer's labels in blue and white make attractive beads when rolled and glued. Roll them straight, or diagonally, for different stripe effects.

# Paper Jewellery

All the jewellery here is made of thin card. The brooches have small pieces of felt, with small safety pins sewn to them, glued to the back.

1. A cut out cat shape, painted with black enamel paint, has tiny diamanté stones glued on to it for eyes and tail.
2. A card bow has bright nail enamel spots painted on it.
3. Star brooch is painted with silver.
4. Ladybird. Cut two oval shapes in card, and cut one shape in half. Paint the oval in black, and the two halves in red. Glue the red parts to the black, and stick on diamanté stones.
5. Card pendant has tab extension, which is folded to back and glued to make a loop. Paint the design. Thread on cord.
6. In the photograph are two bracelets and a ring. They are made of card, rolled and glued, to fit wrist and finger. The ring has a flat-based stone glued to it, and a small piece of fine string glued round the stone to form a 'mount'. Paint the card and string with gold paint. The bracelets are coated with gold-coloured wax, with string and flat-based stones glued to them. *Great care* must be taken when waxing the card. Ask a friend to help by holding the bracelet. Heat the end of the wax to make it drip on to the card bracelet. This has to be done a little at a time, but the effect is well worth the effort. Leave flat areas for stones and string decoration. When the waxing is finished, paint the string gold to match the wax. Paint inside the bracelets gold. This type of jewellery is excellent for school plays. You can use the same method to make crowns, daggers, etc. There are many coloured wax sticks as well as gold and silver.

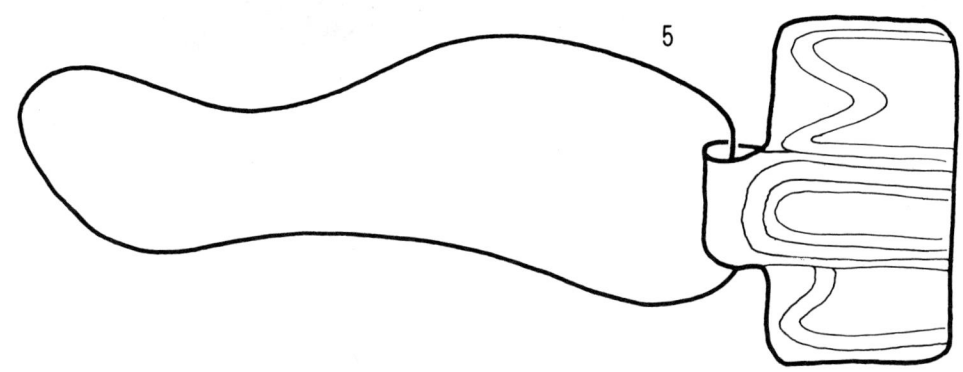

9-2

# Use of Acetate

Sheets of acetate, clear stiff plastic, can be bought in many vivid colours. Only small pieces are needed so that it is not too expensive. You simply cut out card shapes, then cut out small areas which are backed with pieces of acetate. The effect is rather like stained-glass windows. Since the acetate is not very pliable, pendants and brooches are the best things to make. For the brooches, sew pins to small scraps of felt and glue behind card parts. Here are two examples of each, brooches and pendants. The pendants would be ideal for school plays.

# Fabric and Wire

Pretty flowers can be made with wire and scraps of material. Take a piece of wire (you can use pipe cleaners too) and twist one end into a loop. Cut the loop shape in material allowing a ¼ in (7 mm) turning. Wrap the material shape over the wire loop, fold back the turning and stick with fabric glue. Make four or five of these 'petals', bunch them together and wrap the stems around with wool or green tape—florist's tape is best. Use different prints, or all the same colour. Make green covered leaves and wrap and glue them to the stem. Sew a safety pin to the back of the flower.

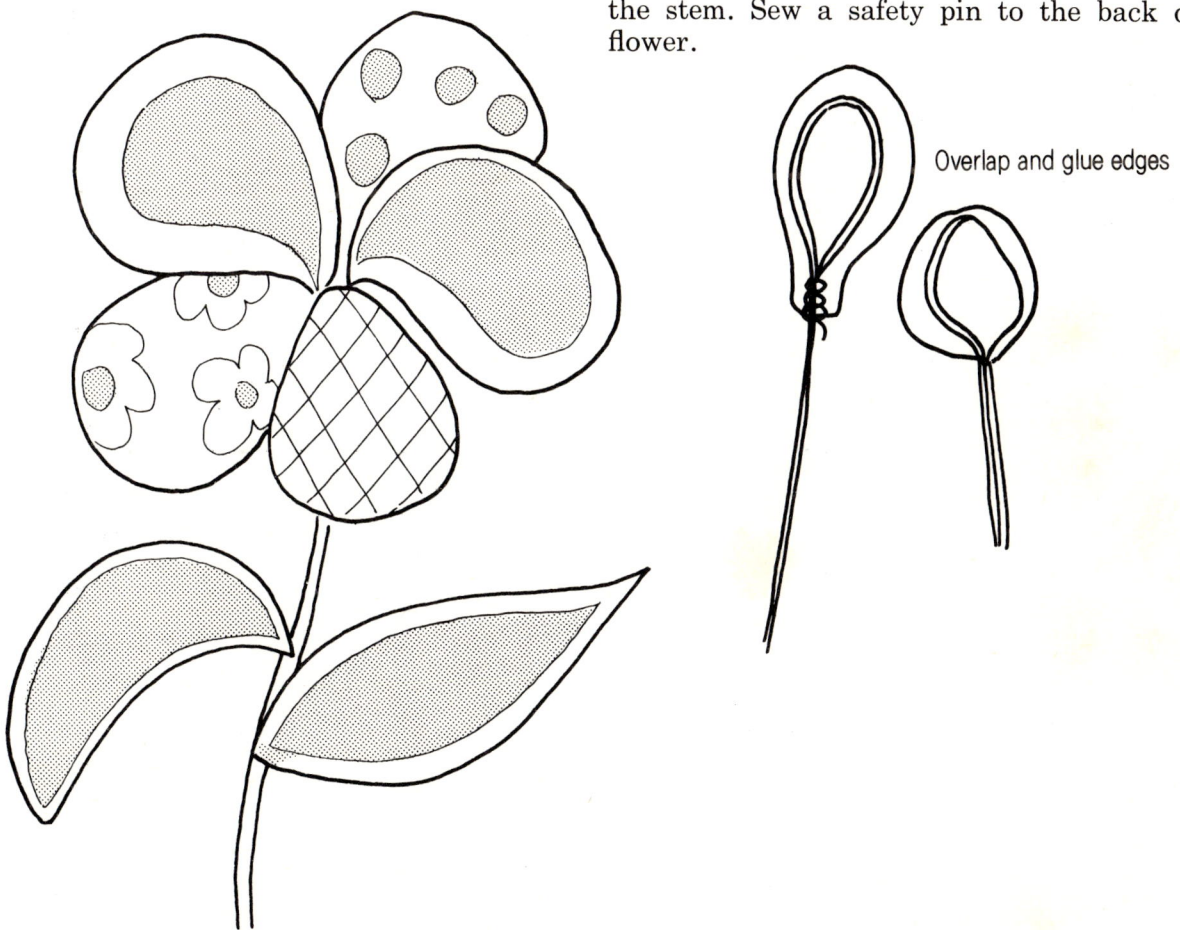

Overlap and glue edges

# Make your own Beads

Almost anything which will allow a needle to pass through it can be called a bead. Try a piece of twig, berries, seeds, tissue paper or rubber. Melon seeds make very pretty beads. Here are some beads you can make.

1. These beads are made from $\frac{1}{2}$ in (13 mm) lengths of balsa wood dowel. Mix them with coloured plastic beads for a pretty, light necklace.
2. Scoop pieces out of cooking apples and allow them to dry, to make these beads. The 'beads' will shrink as they dry, so cut large enough pieces to allow for this. Thread them with small beads between.
3. Delicate, lightweight beads can be made from small crumpled balls of tissue paper, or silver kitchen foil, sewn around with thread.
4. Chunky felt ball beads are made by cutting out six sections shown (trace pattern) and sewing and stuffing them.
5. Stick pins with coloured heads into tiny polystyrene balls to make these bright beads. Leave a space for the needle to pass through for threading.
6. Tiny scraps of foam rubber can be rolled, or folded, and threaded to make beads.
7. Tiny pebbles wrapped in bright shiny sweet papers can also become beads. Tie threads round the twists and for joining them up.
8. Tiny dried flowers can be sewn together to make delicate 'bead' bracelets and necklaces.
9. Cut a large rubber (eraser) into small squares and colour them with felt-tip pens to make beads.
10. Finally, there are all kinds of modelling materials available which can be used to make beads. Some are self-hardening and quite durable. Take small pieces of the modelling material, and roll them into bead-size balls in the palms of your hands. Pierce holes with a needle or toothpick and

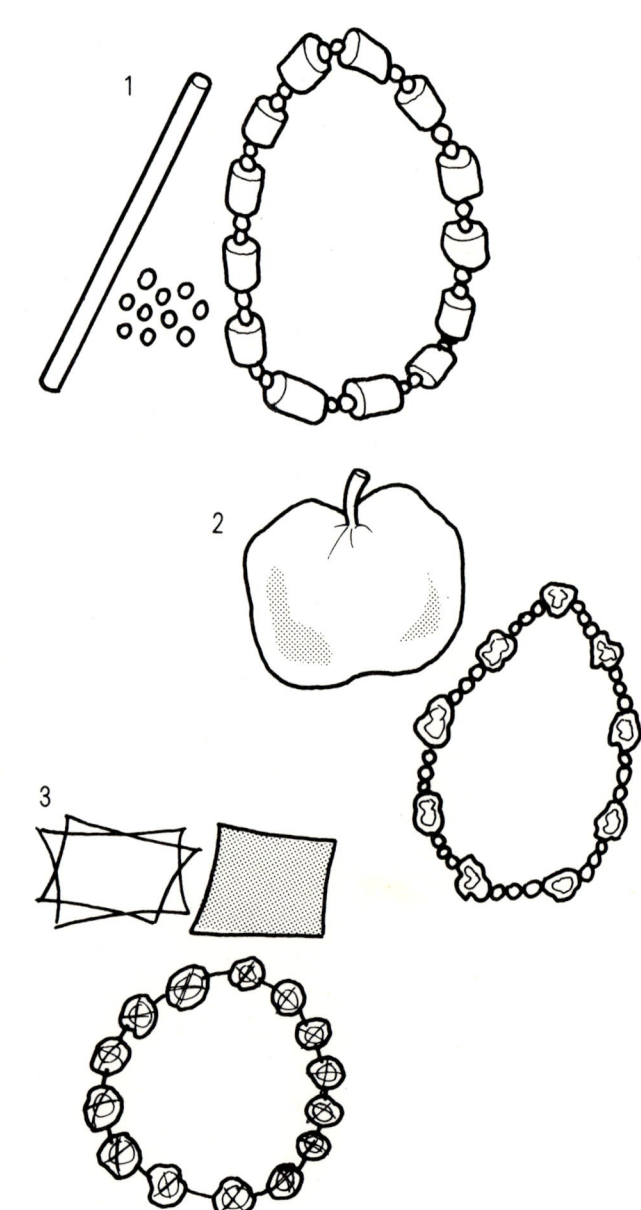

leave to dry thoroughly. When painted, these have a realistic look, and feel nice.

By the way, you can always thread jelly-type sweets on to cotton for a necklace. When you fancy a sweet, just nibble a bead off. I wonder how long your necklace will last!

13–2

# Cook your own Beads

If you are old enough to do simple cooking and enjoy it, you will enjoy making these beads. Please be *very careful* when using the cooker, won't you?

## Bread Beads

Make the dough by mixing 4 cups of flour, 1 cup of salt and 1½ cups of water. Mix with a spoon and then with your (floured) hands. Knead the dough on a floured board until it is of the right consistency. Add a little more flour if it is too wet, or a little more water if it is too dry. The dough should be baked within the hour, or it may be kept in a plastic bag, in the refrigerator. To make the beads, roll into balls in the palms of your floured hands. You can roll long sausage shapes and cut them into small sections. Pierce holes in the beads and lay them on a cookie sheet, or silver kitchen foil in a dish. Bake in the oven at 250°F (130°C) until brown. You can baste the beads with milk to get a rich colour. Re-form holes, and varnish.

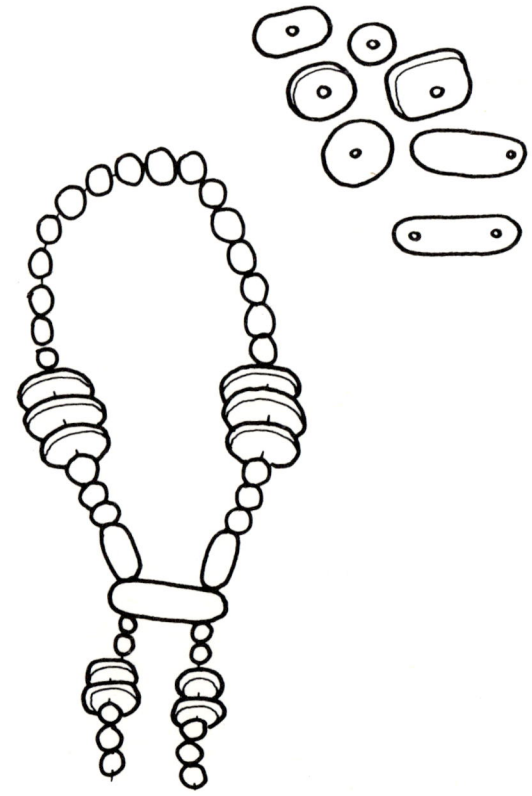

## Uncooked Clay Beads

If you are too young yet to use a cooker, you can make these beads. Mix 2 cups of flour, 1 cup salt, 1 tablespoon powdered alum, and 1 cup water. Mix ingredients and add water gradually to form a firm dough. You can colour this mixture with food colouring. Roll into beads, make holes with needle or tooth pick and allow to dry.

When you make any of these beads, remember that you can make any shape you like. You can even press a ball of mixture flat to make discs for pendants and bracelets. They look pretty between round beads. Make your beads long, flat, oval, round, square, diamond, flower shaped. You can use toy pastry cutters to get good shapes. You can paint and varnish them. You can glue flat-based beads on to them. Make them unusual.

In a saucepan, mix one cup of cornflour, 2 cups of baking soda, and 1¼ cups of water. Place saucepan on cooker over medium heat and stir constantly until the mixture is soft and doughy. Place the mixture on a plate to cool, covered with a damp cloth. When it is cool enough, turn on to floured board and knead as you would for bread.
The mixture can be coloured with dyes or cake colouring and should be well mixed in to get an even colour. Form into beads, make holes with needle or toothpick and allow to dry overnight.

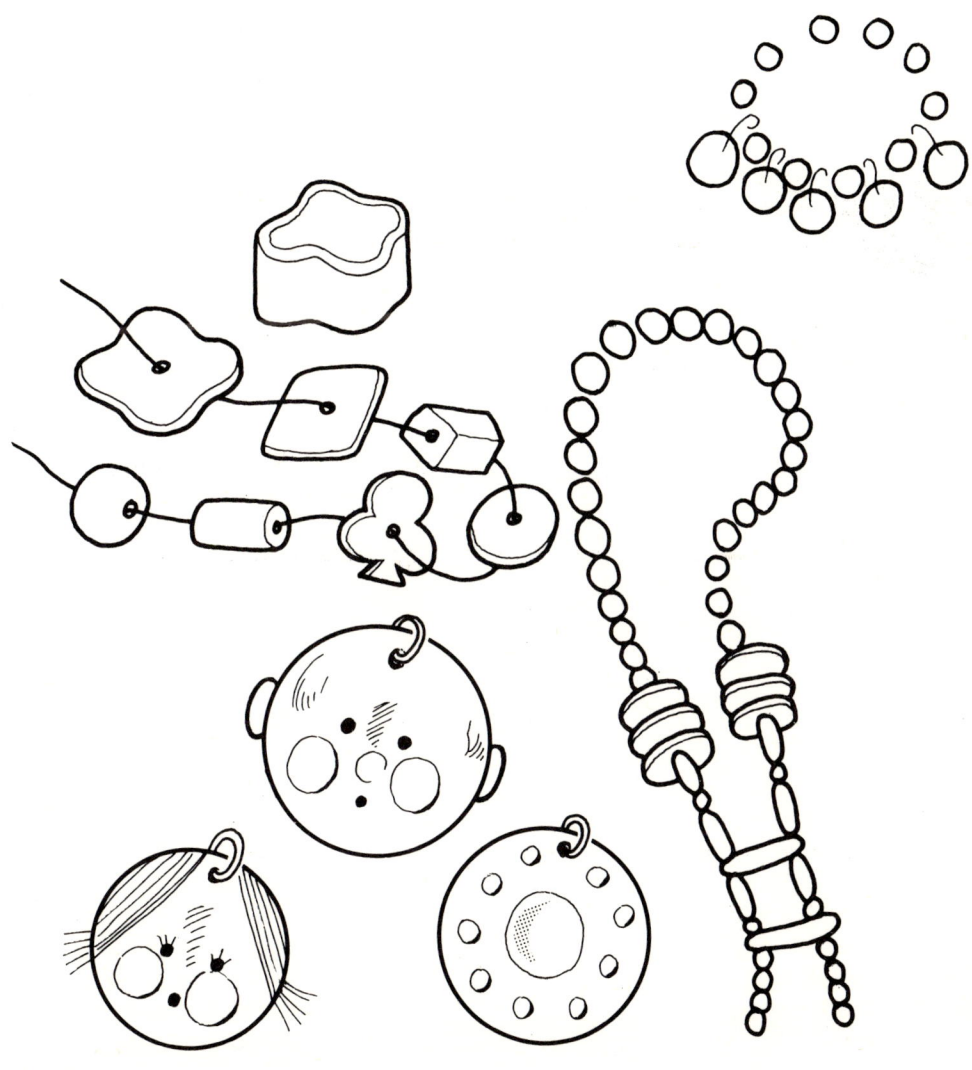

# Strung Beads

1. This pretty cascade of beads can be made for a brooch or pendant. Strands of thread are passed through a large bead, and small beads are threaded on to the strands. Knot each strand securely at the end. A thread or wire loop is run through the large bead and attached to a safety pin, or necklace.
2. Single beads are threaded for the back of the neck. The pattern is made by threading four beads, then passing the thread round and through the fourth bead again.
3. Groups of three beads are threaded and knotted on to cord. Be sure the cord is long enough to allow for knotting.
4. Simple bead necklace has a pendant which is formed by threading half the necklace, then adding three or more extra beads, and additional beads to form a circle. Pass the thread back through the three beads and finish other side of necklace.
5. Knot three cords together, then plait (braid) them, threading a bead at regular intervals on the centre cord. Make a knot and leave ends free, when it is long enough for a necklace, bracelet or belt.
6. This little chick pendant can be suspended from a necklace cord, or a bracelet, or it can be fixed to a safety pin to make a brooch. Two large yellow beads and one small orange bead make the chick. The body bead is threaded sideways. Paint the eyes and glue on tiny orange felt beak and wings. You can make several, they are so easy, and thread them, with beads between to make a necklace or bracelet. You can make other little birds or little people, or simply use the bead arrangement plain, with other beads.

16–2

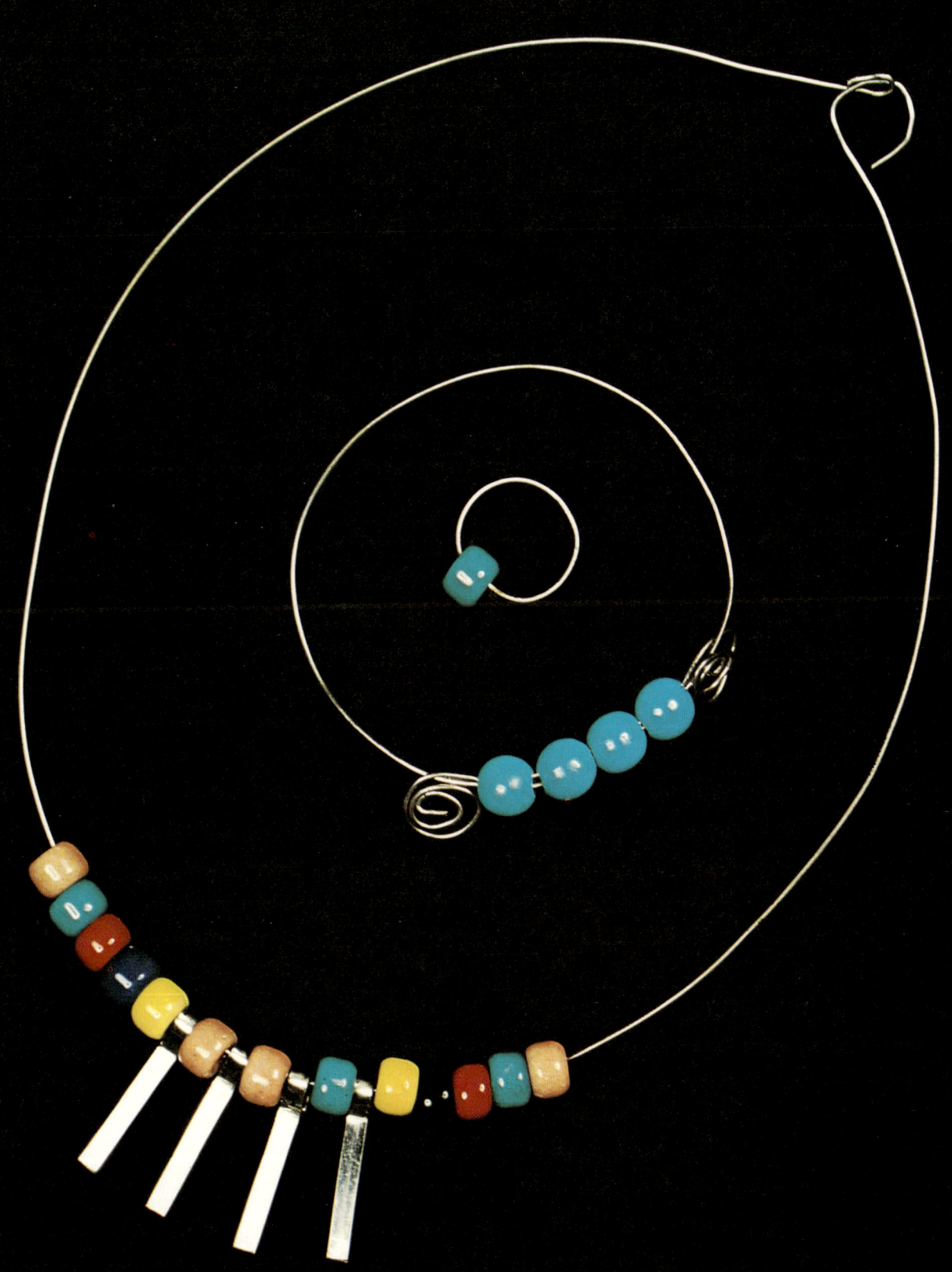

17–2

Here are some ideas for stringing beads.

1. This simple but effective necklace consists of large white beads tied on to black cord at regular intervals. The cord is tied in a bow at the back.
2. is a choker made of tiny brown, beige and orange wooden beads. A loop is formed at each end, one larger than the other. For fastening, press the sides of the larger loop gently together and pass through the smaller loop.
3. This necklace (or belt, or bracelet) requires a double thread. Thread round beads on both threads for the back of the neck. Separate the threads, and draw them through two long beads. Now cross the threads through a round bead and continue pattern to round neck beads. Knot threads through first round bead and glue the knot.
4. A magical effect is achieved here by threading the beads on fine nylon thread. Pass the thread two or three times through the small beads to hold them.
5. Bead bracelet with smaller bead loops. Thread enough beads to fit wrist, then thread enough tiny beads to form a loop. Pass the thread back through the last bead, and thread more small beads to make a loop the other side. Pass the thread back through the last bead and fasten off with a knot and a spot of glue—if you are not using a clasp.
6. In the photograph you will see a necklace which could go with the bracelet, number 5. The beads are threaded one side, then the small single loops formed, and the thread is passed back through the last bead. Thread two more beads, then repeat loop. Make five loops, with the centre one a little larger.

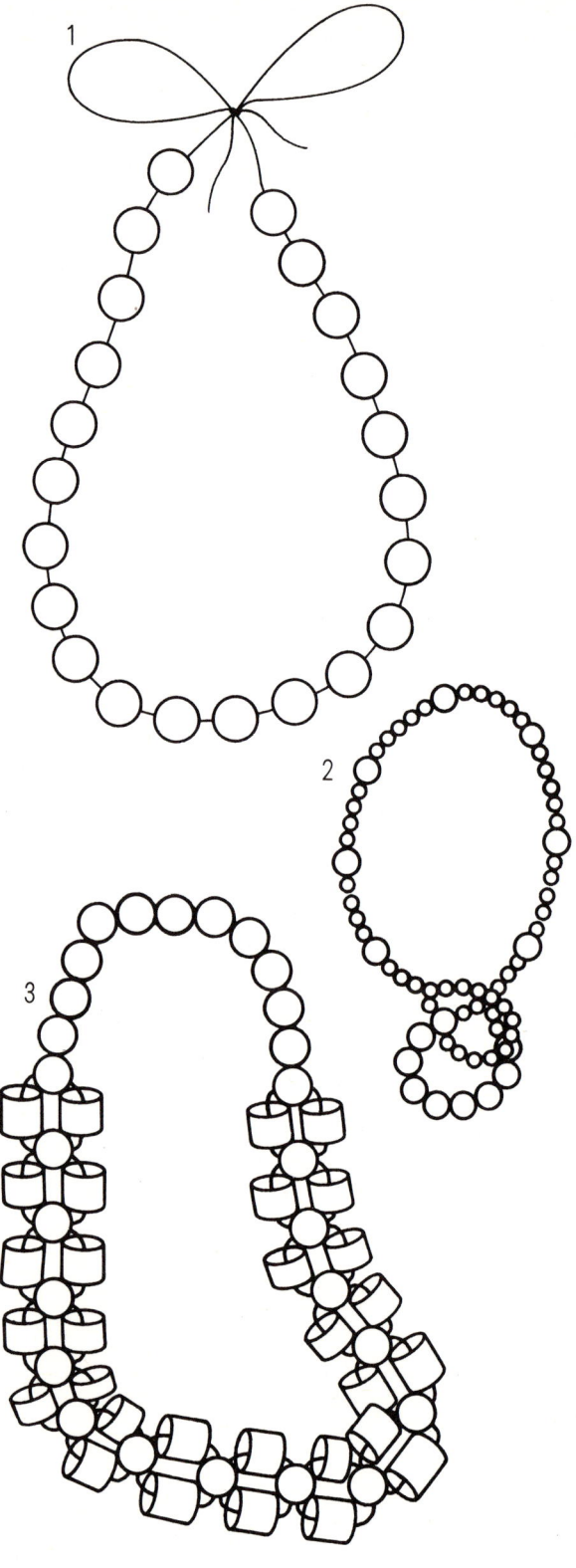

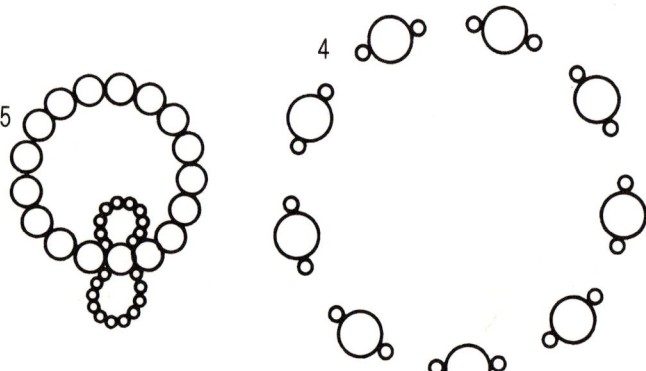

19-2

# Looped Beads

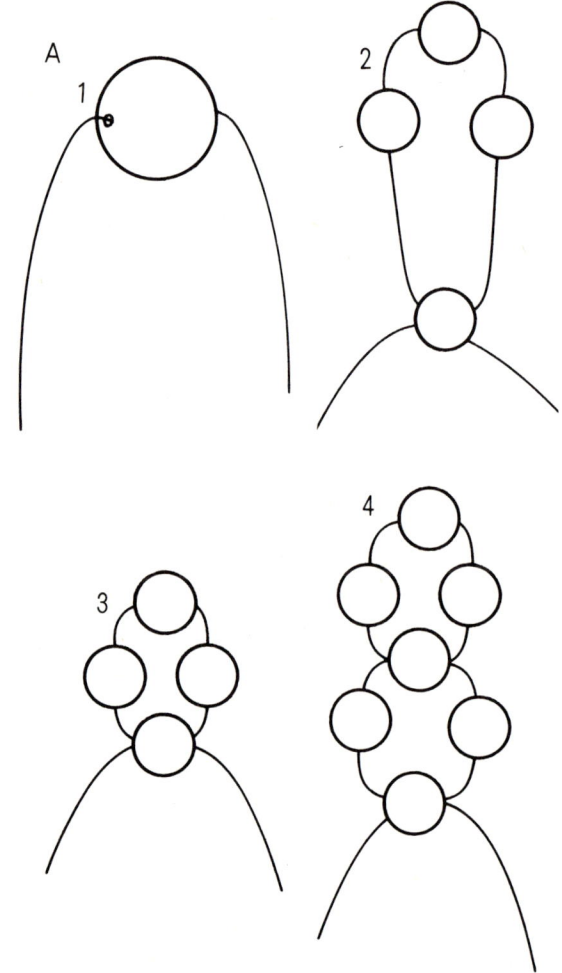

This type of bead threading is a little more complicated, but if you follow the instructions and diagrams carefully, you can make some very pretty jewellery. Diagram A shows the basic threading for this type of beadwork. A long thread and two needles are used, and the first bead is fixed to a pad as shown in A1. Now thread two beads, one on each needle, and then thread one bead with both threads crossing. Follow diagrams 2, 3, and 4 to build up the beadwork.

Sketches B and C show how additional effect can be achieved with fringing, using an extra thread knotted on to the main thread at the beginning. Necklaces, bracelets and belts can be made using this method of beading. In diagram B, the extra thread beading is part of the basic beading, and so it must be made up at the same time. The design in diagram C has the fringing made separately and can be added after the basic beading is made up. Diagram D shows a development of the basic beading known as 'matting'. Instead of the threads crossing through the single bead, they cross in the side bead, allowing more beads to be added. Two or more rows can be made up in this way to make bracelets, 'chokers' and belts.

Diagram E, a pendant for necklace, brooch or earring, shows how you can shape this type of beading. It is very easy to make. Thread one bead, using two needles (as described above), thread two, then three, and so on, until there are six beads on the final row. Make and glue a knot at the end. The needles pass through all the beads on each row, crossing the threads and forming the edge.

Keep beadwork even, keep designs simple, and only tackle the ones you feel you can manage. Try the pendant E first perhaps, before making the more elaborate designs B and C. Choose the right beads for the right piece. The pendant can be made in wood or plastic beads, while the necklaces would be more effective in crystal, jet, or pearl beads. You can also mix beads—pearl and crystal together for something special, wood and glass or plastic for everyday wear.

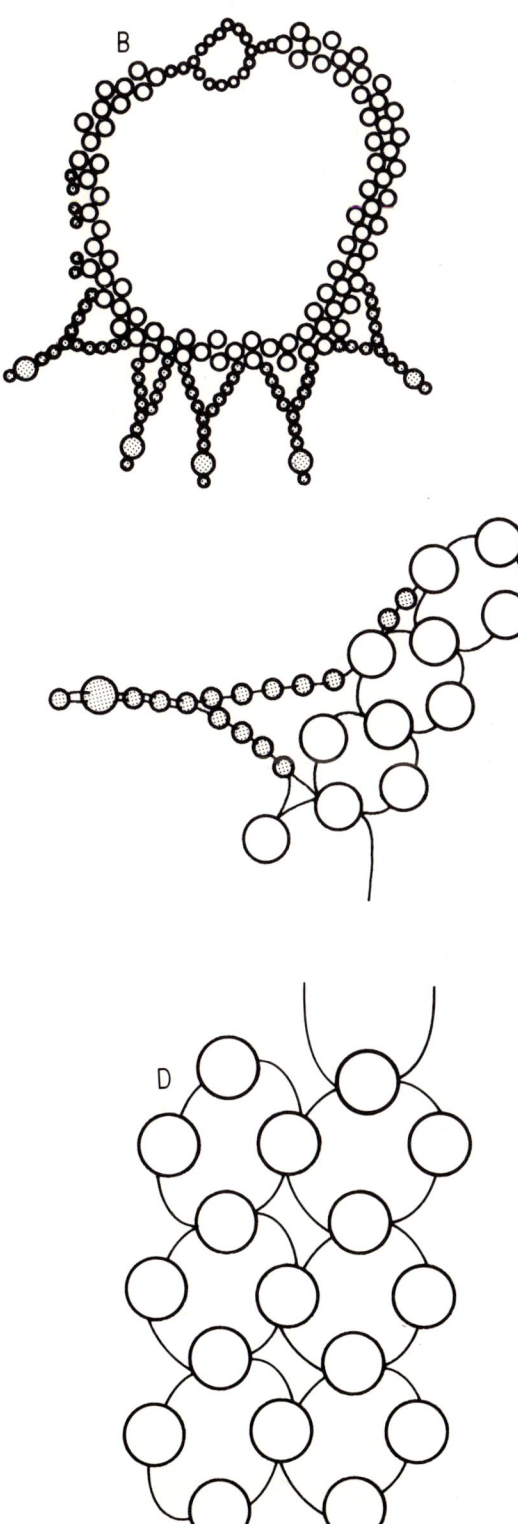
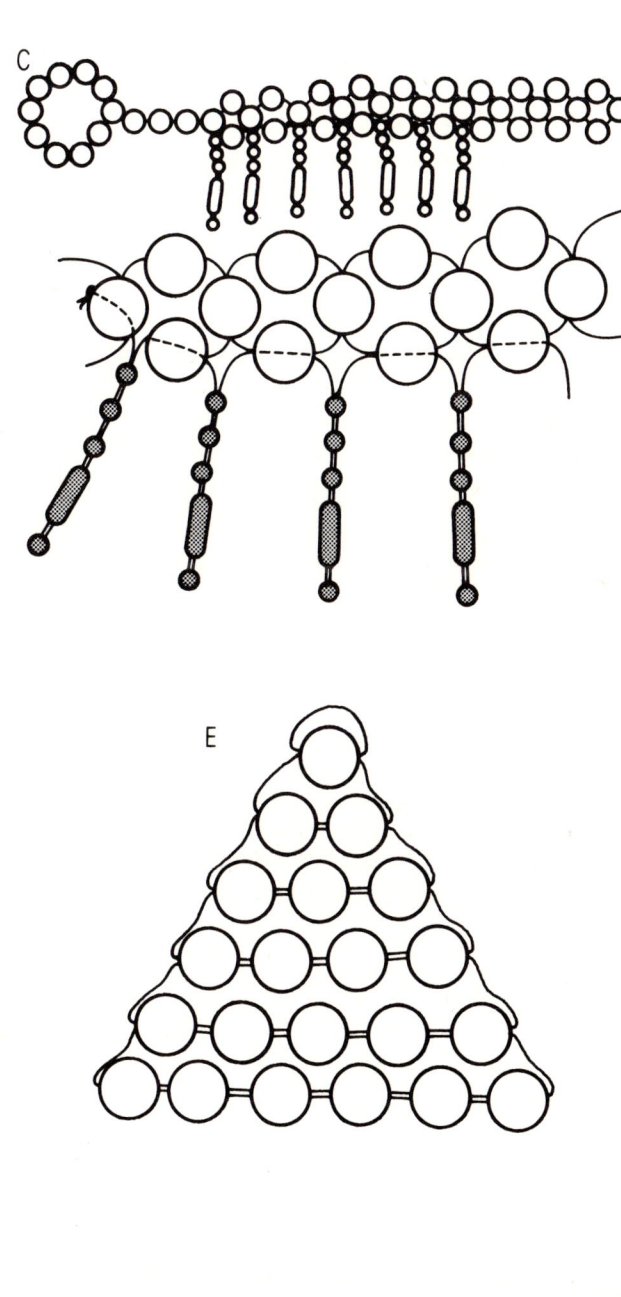

# Indian Beadwork

This type of beadwork requires very small beads, a fine beading needle and waxed thread. Use a very long thread, doubled, and drawn through beeswax to strengthen it and prevent tangles. The basic threading for the flower necklace and bracelet in the photograph, is as follows: Make a knot at the end of the double thread, thread six beads, then insert needle between the knot and first bead to form a circle. These are the petals and we will call them red. Now thread one bead (the centre bead we will call white) and pass the needle through the fourth bead of the circle, pressing the white bead into the circle. Draw the thread tight all the time, to keep the beads close. Now* thread 2 red and 1 white and pass needle through the bead next to the one that the thread comes out of. Thread 2 red and pass the needle through the red bead next to the white bead. Repeat from * until desired length. You can see this more clearly in the diagram. Then finish off by running the threads back through some of the last beads, and make and glue a neat knot. The necklace in the photograph has five beads threaded between each flower motif.

Fringing is made with a separate thread attached to point where the fringe is to begin. Thread the number of beads for the required length of fringe, then pass the needle through the fourth beads from the end and back up through the other fringe beads. Pass needle through the next bead and make the second fringe. Repeat in this way until you have the number of fringes you want. This type of beadwork uses a very definite pattern and the colours of the beads you use should complement the pattern, not confuse it. Straight rows of these small multi-coloured beads are very pretty. But for this type of work, two colours are best, three at most.

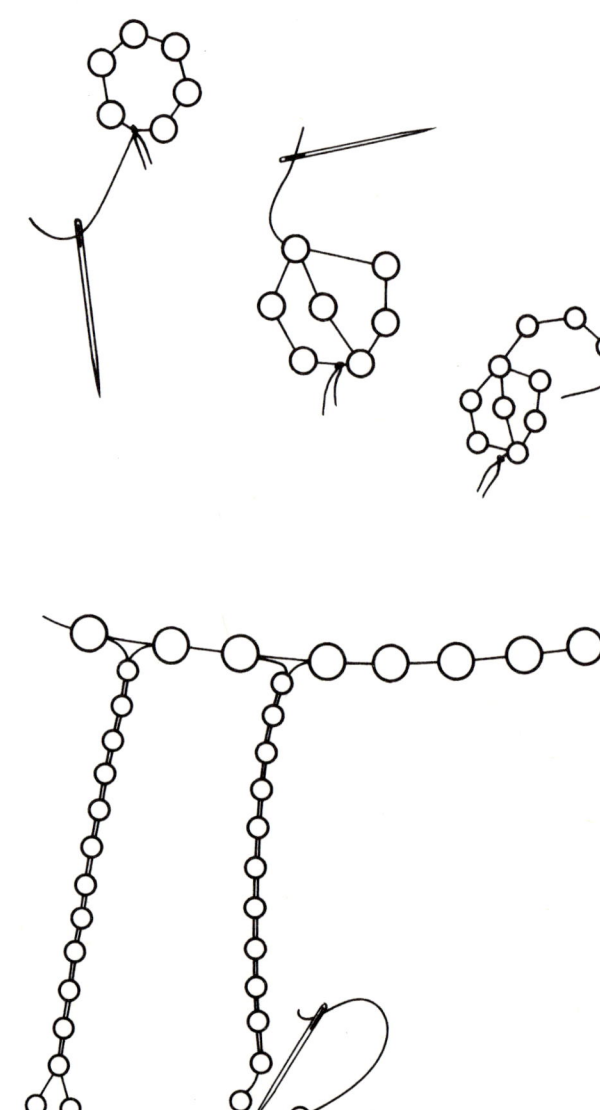

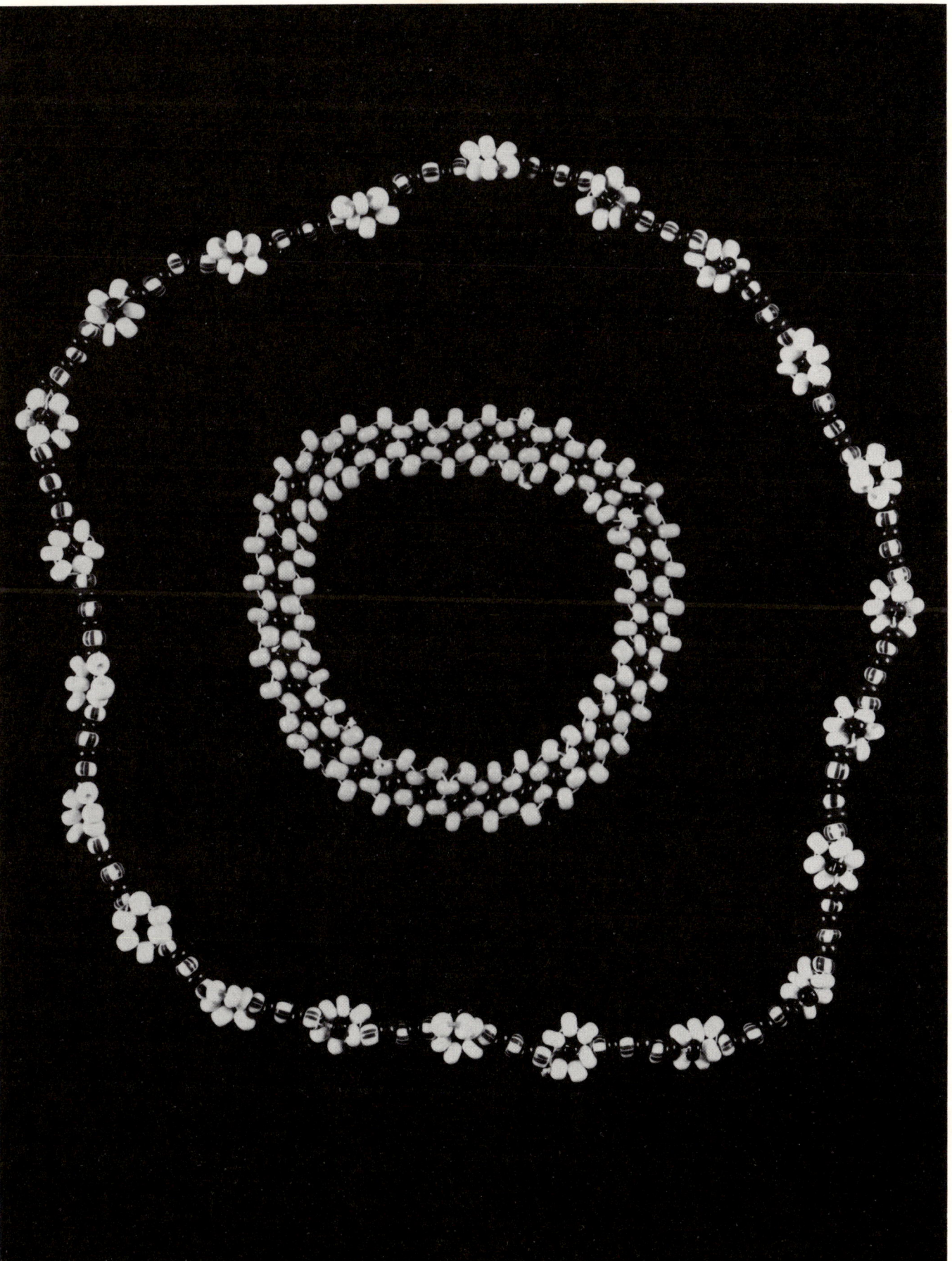

# Bead Weaving

The craft of beadweaving is much easier than it might appear to be. A simple loom is essential and you can buy one, or make one. A cardboard box, with notches cut into both ends to hold the warp threads will do. The number of warp threads will depend upon the number of beads used for width. Tape the ends of these threads under the box as shown.

Tie the end of the thread in your needle to the warp thread on the left, and weave back and forth four times without beads to strengthen the end, finishing on the left. Thread first row of beads and place *under* the warp threads, pressing the beads between the threads. Pass the needle back through each bead to the left again. Push the beads up, and pull the needle thread, to keep tension even. Continue in this way until you have the desired length. If the item is longer than the loom, allow enough length in warp threads and as you finish the length of the loom, lift the warp threads off. Move the finished work up and retape. To finish off make four rows of darning as at the beginning and thread needle back through last row of beads. Make a secure knot and cut thread.

When weaving a design it is best to have a chart to work by. Small squared graph paper is ideal for this purpose, each square representing one bead. Colour the squares and make patterns simple. When you have completed a pattern, it helps to write the number and colour of beads beside each row. Let us take the butterfly motif as an example. 1st row—10 white beads (w.b.). 2nd row—10 w.b. 3rd row—2w, 2 red (r), 6w. 4th row—1w, 5r, 1w, 1r, 2w. And so on. The graph designs shown here are as they look, but the edge marked top is the 1st row across the loom.

You can make necklaces, bracelets and belts using this method of beadwork, and you can see some examples here. Loops and fringes are added after the item is made, and these are described in Looped Beads and Indian Beadwork respectively.

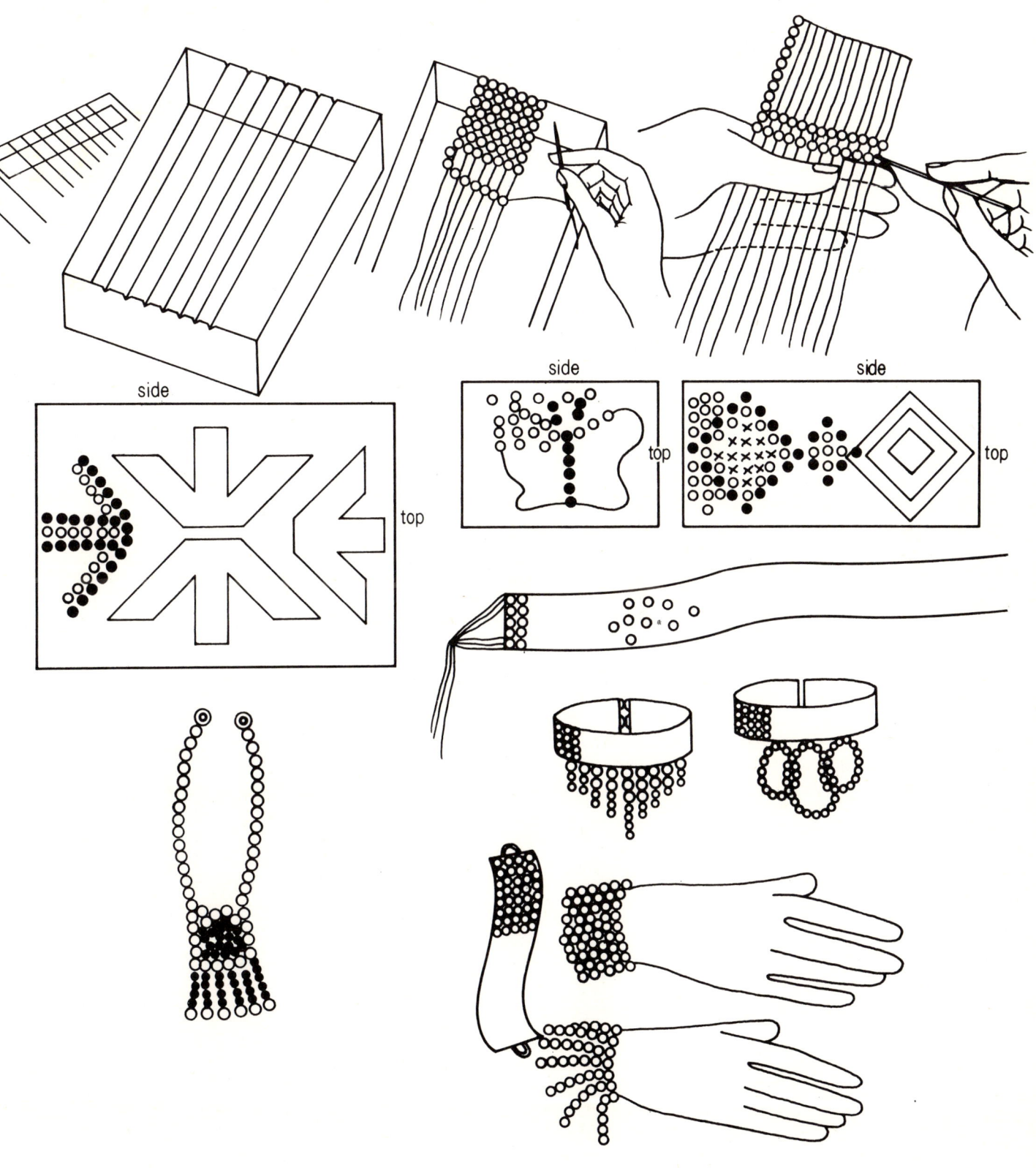

25-2

Here is another example of bead weaving which requires no loom. The number of strands used depends on the width required. We will work on 4, doubled to make 8. Knot four strands of thread on to a length of cord, using macramé knots to form double strands. Attach cord ends to something steady, like a chair. Follow the diagram for the first example. Thread beads on to each pair of strands for the first two rows. Row 3—Thread a bead using one strand (on the left) and take the second strand over to second line to make a pair with one of its strands, and thread second bead. Take second strand of second line over to the third line and make a pair with one of its strands. Thread third bead. Take second strand of third line over to fourth and thread fourth bead using all three strands. Using the threads as they are thread beads for rows 4 and 5. Row 6—Take one strand from right (thread bead on two remaining strands) across to 3rd line, making a pair with one of its strands, and thread bead. Continue in this way to line 1. Rows 7 and 8 are repeats of rows 1 and 2. Row 9 is a repeat of row 3. Continue to desired length and knot ends of strands securely.

The second example is very easy, if you follow the diagram carefully. The first row has four beads threaded on each double strand. The strands are divided for the second row to thread eight small beads. The third row has five beads, the fourth row has eight small beads, the fifth row has four beads, sixth row eight small beads, seventh row five beads and so on. This gives a bobley edge to the work.

Even with these two simple examples, look at the various things you can make, and variations on them. 1a is a pendant using two colours for design and effect. 1b is another pendant with the strands divided to form fringing. 1c is a narrow belt with bead fringing threaded on to ends. 2a is a pendant with bead loops. 2b is a bracelet, and 2c is another pendant with hanging fringe. 2d is a belt with hook and eye fastening.

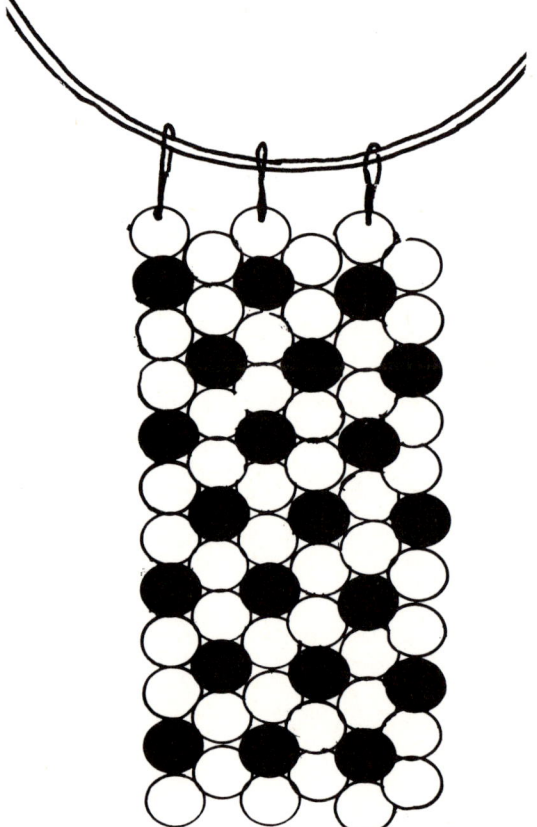

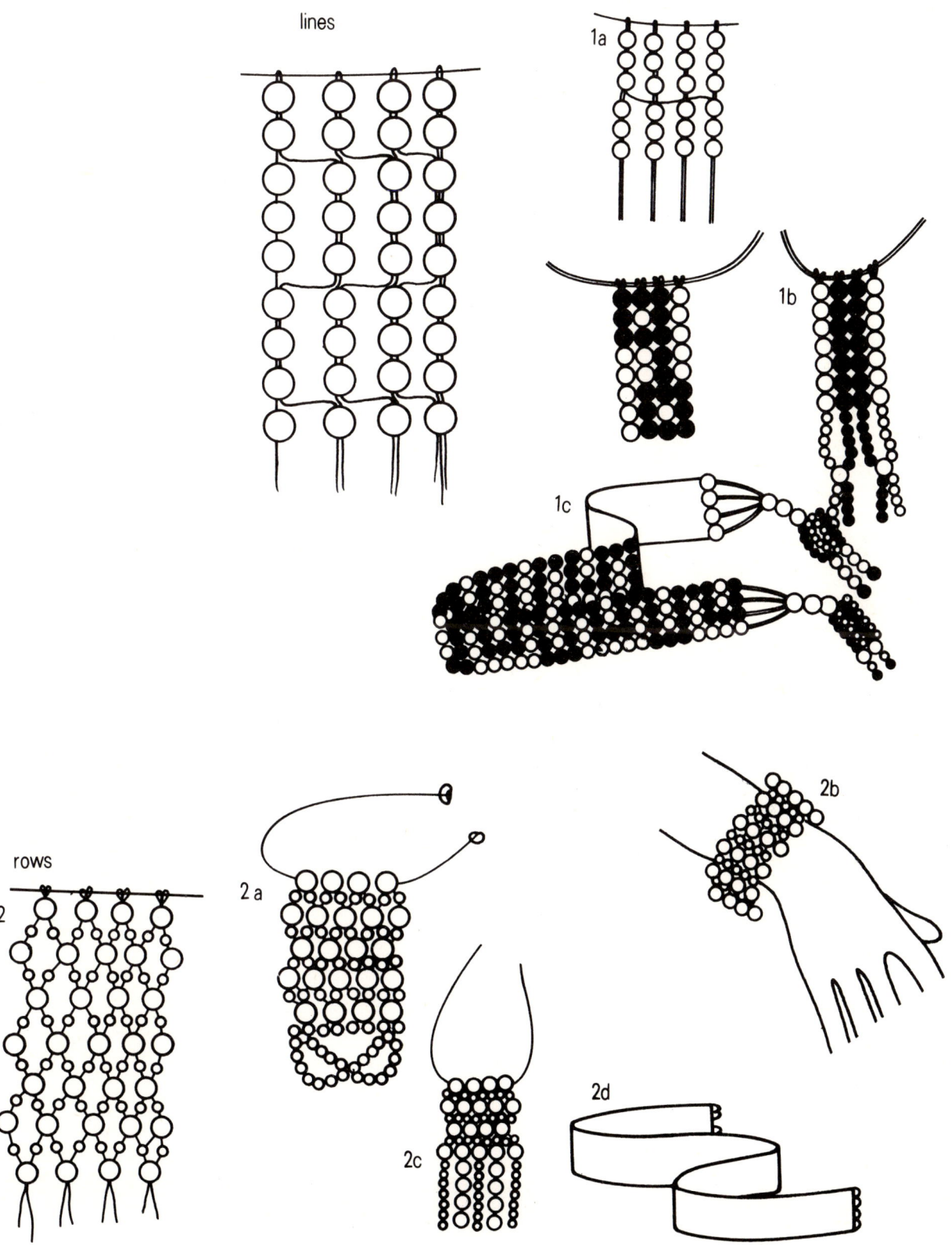

# Chains

You may already have some chain necklaces which look a bit dull, or you can buy chains like the white plastic one, or inexpensive gilt chains. Here are a few ideas for cheering up chains.

1. A white plastic chain, bought from a hardware shop, has had some of the links gently opened and white plastic rings inserted. Gives a very lightweight chain a more chunky look.
2. This one is a gilt chain, and again, some links have been opened and brass rings inserted between. This kind of thing does not look 'expensive' but it does have a more designed look—and it is fun.
3. Another length of chain has been opened. Three rows of wire links with small pearl beads and red glass beads on them have been inserted. See making links and chains (page 31), to see how to make links for this necklace and number 5.
4. A long gilt chain has groups of four large beads threaded on to it. The chain is loosely knotted between the beads.
5. In the photograph opposite—a really cheered-up chain. It was a bought chain, and I have made lots of wire rings and links with beads to go on it, as well as blue plastic rings, and yellow, red, orange, light and dark blue large beads. The small beads are orange, brown and white.

# Copperwire Jewellery

Soft, rounded, copper wire shapes make bright, expensive-looking jewellery at little cost. You will need wire cutters and round-nosed pliers. Also, round objects like jars and bottles will be needed to shape the wire. And, of course, you will need copper wire. As you know, wire comes in various thicknesses called gauges. For these pieces you will need 8, 10, 14 and 16 gauge wires.

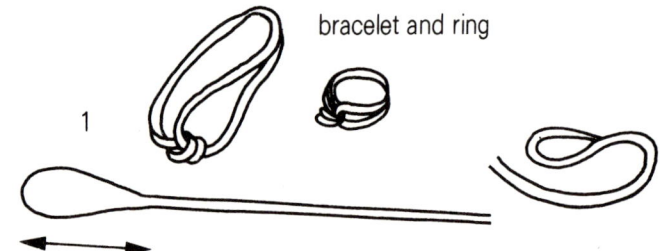

bracelet and ring

It is practical to begin with something simple, and the attractive looped bracelet and ring could not be easier. To make the bracelet you will need 8 gauge wire, about 20 in (50·8 cm) long. Bend the wire, forming a curved loop at the bend. Squeeze the wires together about ½ in (13 mm) from bend of loop. Wrap the two wires around a jar to make the curve, then pull the wires through the loop and bend them over, using the pliers. The ring is made in the same way, using 10 gauge wire.

The looped necklace requires 10 gauge wire. Cut a length to go round your neck with allowance for fastening loops at each end—about 20-22 in. Shape the loop round a very fat jar and, with the pliers, fold over the end loops for fastening. Cut 4 pieces of wire 6 in (15·2 cm) long to form the four loops. Curve these round a small jar like a little meat paste jar, and with the pliers fold back ½ in (13 mm) loops each end, but do not quite close them. Push the loops over the necklace and squeeze them closed with the pliers.

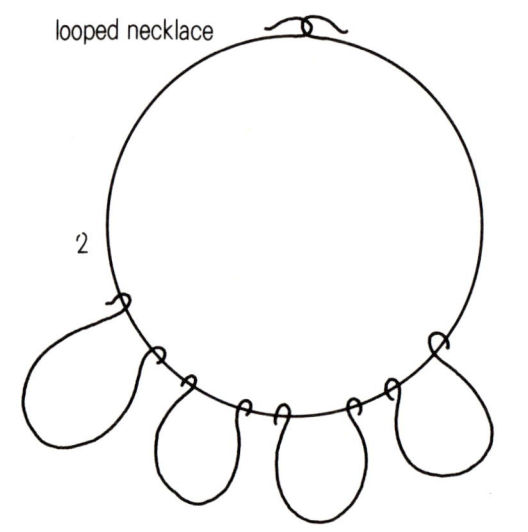

looped necklace

The third item is a necklace made up of copper wire 'beads' and round jump links. The jump links can be bought or you can make them by wrapping 14 gauge wire evenly, round a knitting needle several times, slip off needle and cut between the rings. Make as many as you will need for joining the beads. Measure round your neck with a piece of string for the length you like, and so that it needs no fastening. Make enough jump rings and 'beads' to measure this length. To make the beads, cut 10 gauge wire into 4 in (10 cm) lengths. Bend each end to the centre to make a small loop at each end. Wind 14 gauge wire round the centre to cover. Join the beads together with jump links between as shown. The fourth design is a form of chain which can be used for a necklace or bracelet, or a belt. Two rings are formed, one smaller to fit inside the other, with a long narrow jump link to join the rings together. See drawing. To make the jump rings narrow, squeeze gently with the pliers as shown. Close the jump links once the rings are in them.

In the silver wire section you can find other ideas for using copper wire.

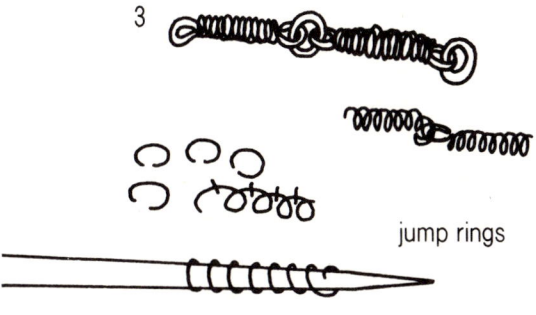

jump rings

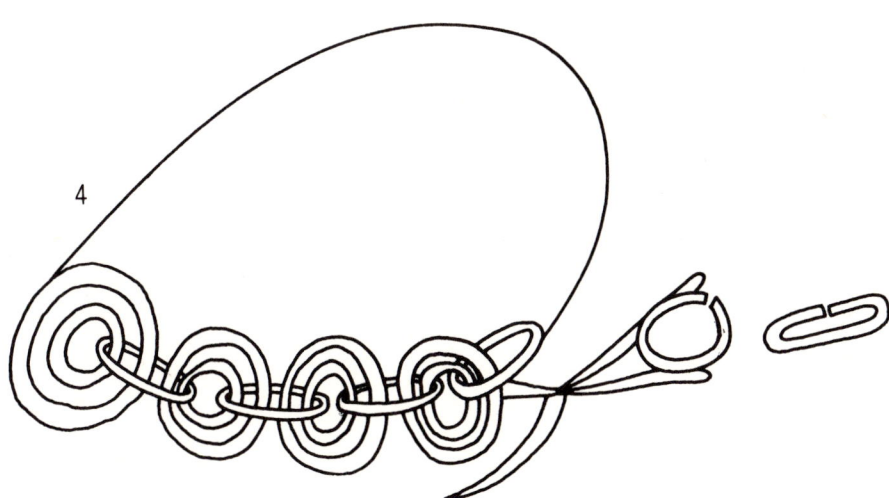

# Simple Enamelling

The beautiful, distinctive look of enamelling can be achieved without the use of a kiln or even enamel powder. Earlier in this book, in Jewellery from Oddments, you found that nail enamel could be used to paint on card, giving a bright, glossy, finish. Nail enamel is now used to decorate the items on the following pages.

You will need nail enamel in various colours plus white pearl nail enamel and clear nail enamel. These can be bought cheaply at inexpensive chain stores. If you prefer, you can mix just two or three drops of coloured ink with clear nail enamel, or white pearl enamel. Colours should always be mixed in a small bottle with screw-on cap. Paint direct from the bottle—the enamel hardens on exposure to air. You will also need acetone, which is the basis of nail enamel remover and can be bought cheaply at any chemist's shop. Copper blanks, copper wire and pieces of sheet silver can be bought from craft shops. The sheet silver can be cut into shapes as you will see, and pumice stone, dampened, is very good for smoothing edges. Emery-cloth and emery-paper can also be used wrapped round a ruler or something similar. Almost any metal can be used, though gold cannot be bought without the Treasury's permission, and would be too expensive anyway! But silver and brass are good, and you can even enamel tin cans and coins. Toothpicks and fine-point brushes are useful for dripping tiny drops of enamel or acetone on the work, or for swirling the colours together.

The items described on the next few pages are mainly for copper. The surface of the copper must be absolutely free of dirt and grease. You can clean it with alcohol, or use damp French chalk which is then washed off with water and dried.

You must not touch the piece with your hands once it has been cleaned. If you prop it on the edge of a coin, you can use a thin steel ruler to lift

it and so avoid touching it. When you enamel it, lay it on a piece of card or a tray, which can be lifted and placed somewhere safe for the piece to dry. Never touch the piece while the enamel is wet or you will leave finger marks which cannot be removed. Since you are going to use a little acetone with the nail enamel you must be very patient, and allow the piece to dry thoroughly.

When the blank has been cleaned, as previously described, paint the surface with acetone, and then a coat of the base colour nail enamel. Before this has dried, using the toothpicks, or a brush, drip another colour enamel on to the surface to make small spots which will quickly blend with the base colour. Unexpected patterns and colour changes will occur which is half the fun of this method. To make the colours 'run' more, a tiny drop of acetone can be dropped on to the enamel, using the toothpick or brush. Do not use too much acetone, however, as it slows down the drying considerably, and thins the enamel. The ground enamelling can consist of two or more colours and if you then apply white pearl enamel, you will achieve subtle blends of colouring and texture fascinating to watch. You can also drip colours on to the surface and blend them very gently with a fine brush. You can paint a flower and allow the edges to blur softly into the background. Many effects can be achieved by experiment, and you will no doubt make some discoveries yourself.

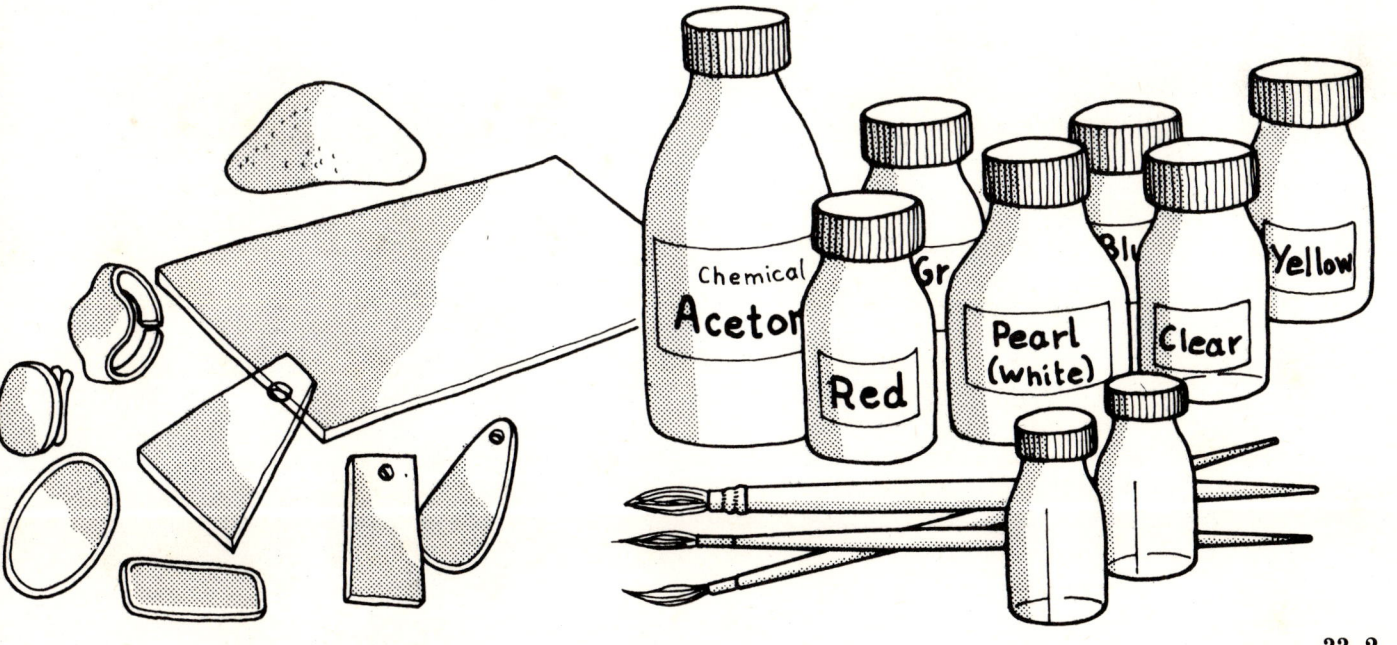

# Wire and Loops

Soft thin silver or copper wire is formed into loops on a knitting needle. The coil is then cut into separate rings and these are glued to the blanks, forming a design. Straight pieces of wire can also be used, to form enclosed areas. A tiny drip of nail enamel is placed around the rings, using a toothpick or fine brush. The areas around the rings are then painted with nail enamel. The rings and straight wires are glued on with Araldite, and small tweezers help to place them. Round-nosed pliers can be used to form shapes. The first bracelet is cut from sheet copper and formed round a jar. The second bracelet (or ring) will need to have a paper pattern made first, which is then cut out of the copper. It is a pretty enough shape to cut out in silver. The brooch with the initials would make a very attractive gift, and any initials can be used, of course. The wire strips and loops can also be fixed to the blank with clear nail enamel.

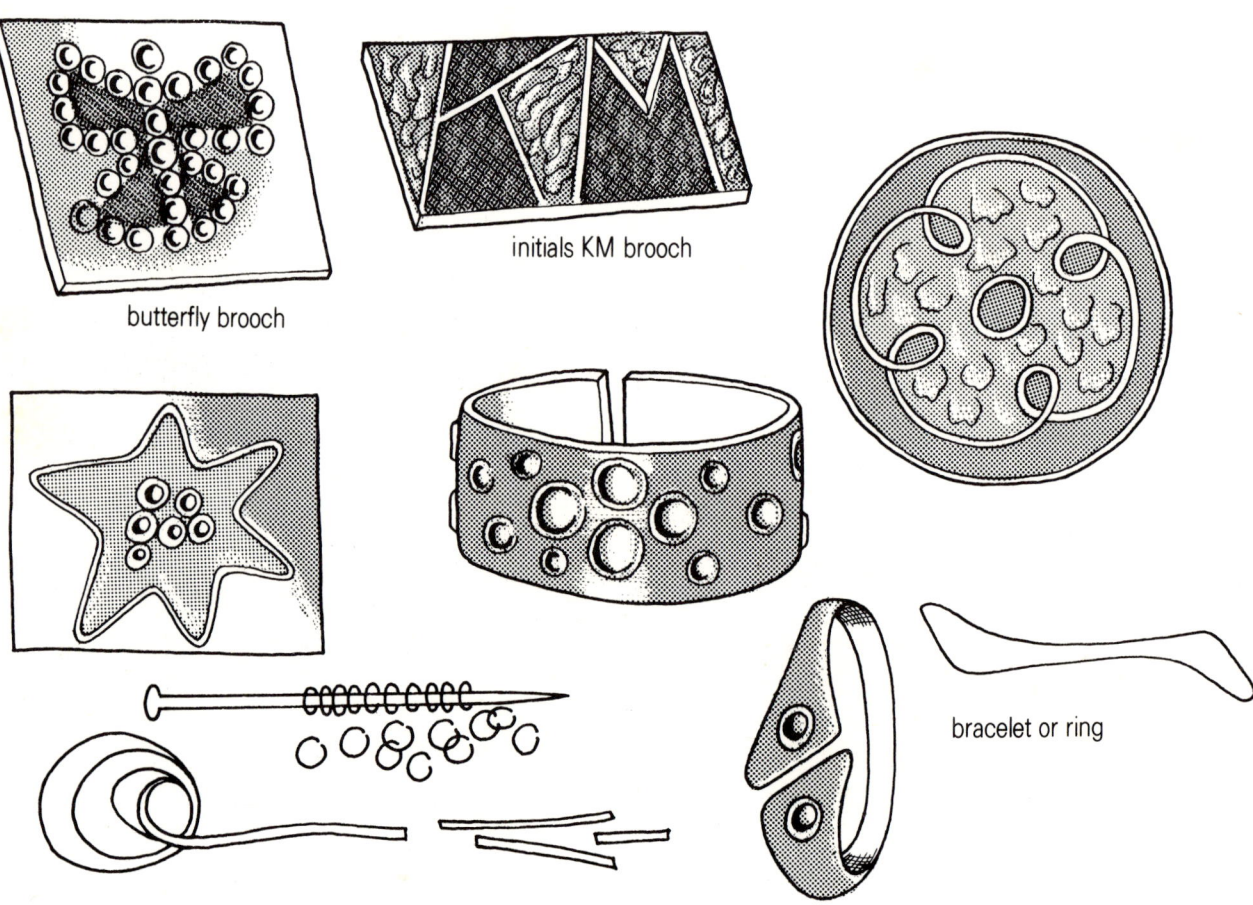

butterfly brooch

initials KM brooch

bracelet or ring

# Rings and Things

Brass buttons, copper or brass farings (that is, the mounts to which the decorations are affixed) of rings, earclips and brooches, can all be made beautiful. Here are twelve designs which can be adapted for any of the farings. Shaped and straight wire, and wire circles have been glued to most of them. The copper shapes can be bought, or cut from sheet copper. The edges are rubbed smooth before preparing them. Some of the designs can also be used for cufflinks, like numbers 2, 4, and 8. Numbers 1, 9, 10, 11 and 12 are brooches. Number 12 has small shapes of silver, odd scraps from silverwork, glued to it, and is then very carefully enamelled round them. The lighter areas, the centres of numbers 2, 3, and 4, and the outer edge of 11, are white pearl. It is impossible to give the full effect of colour and texture in drawings, but the enamelled jewellery box on the jacket shows this clearly.

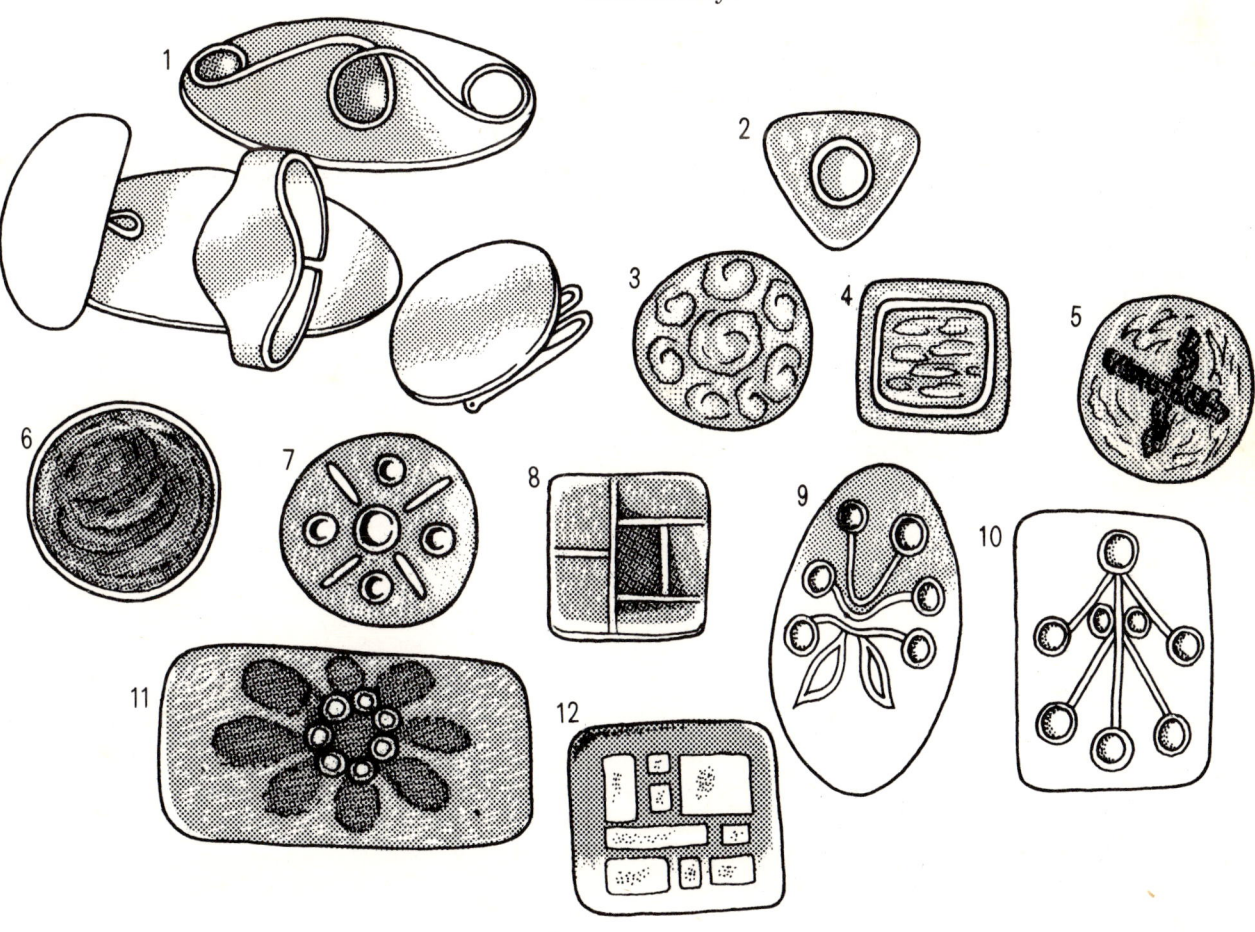

# Making Links and Chains

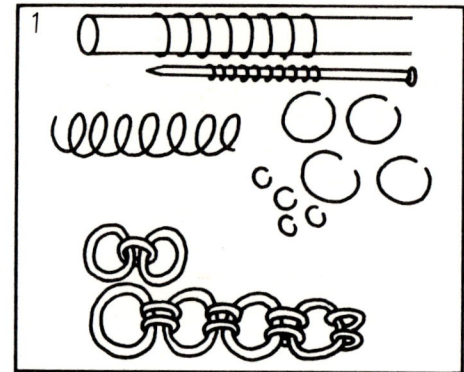

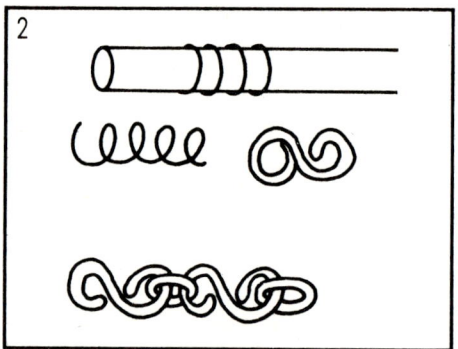

Links for chains can be made of almost any wire, from fuse wire (the heavier gauges) to silver wire. The gauge of the wire and the size of the links will depend upon the item you wish to make. To keep all the links equal in size, you will need a 'former'. Knitting needles and wood dowels in various sizes are ideal for this purpose.

The first example is the plain round link. The wire is wrapped tightly and evenly around the 'former'. Remove the spiral and cut through the top of the links.

No. 2. Wrap the wire round the dowel 'former' to make four loops. Remove the spiral, and fold two rings out and away from the other two so that they lie flat.

No. 3. This link can be used alone or with beads. Use round-nosed pliers to bend and shape the end loops—follow the dotted line.

No. 4. This is a figure 8 link, so called because of its figure 8 shape. Follow the dotted lines and shape with the pliers. You can see how pretty this can be combined with other links and beads.

No. 5. Spiral links can be simply made by wrapping the wire round the 'former', then shaping the ends into loops.

No. 6. This link is more effective in one of the thicker wires which are at the same time pliable. Soft copper wire is good. Make a fairly large link, then gently squeeze it to form the second shape. Now fold the narrow curved end up and over. It is like the hook of a hook-and-eye fastening.

No. 7. When you have made your link chain you will need to fasten it. Here are two simple fastenings for you to make. The first is a hook-and-eye type, the hook being shaped in a similar way to number 6. The eye is a triangle shape. Small links

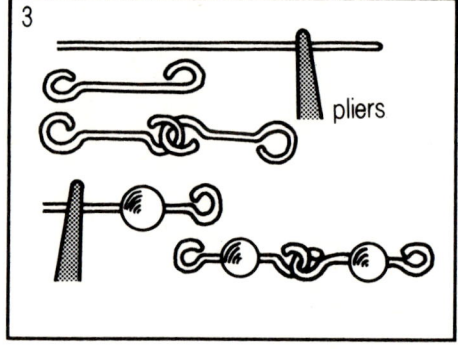

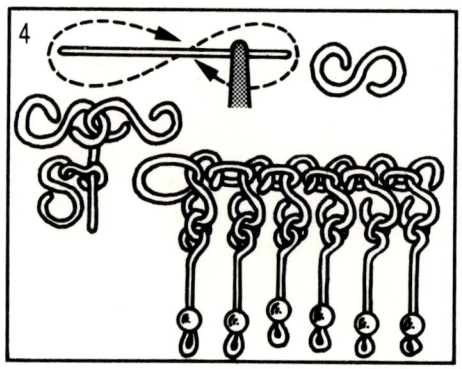

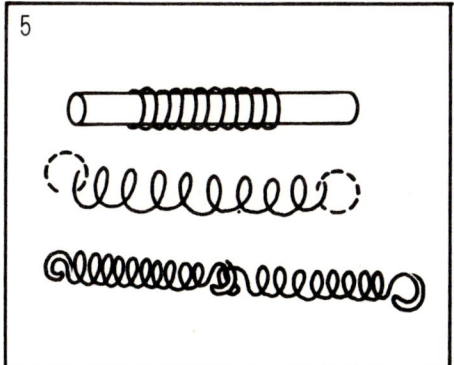
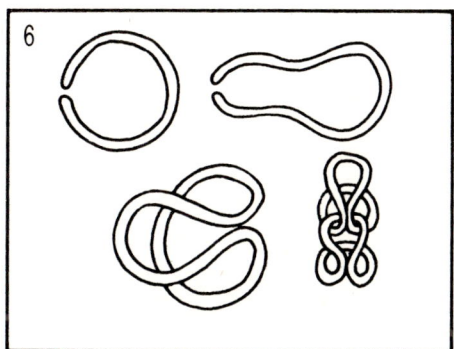
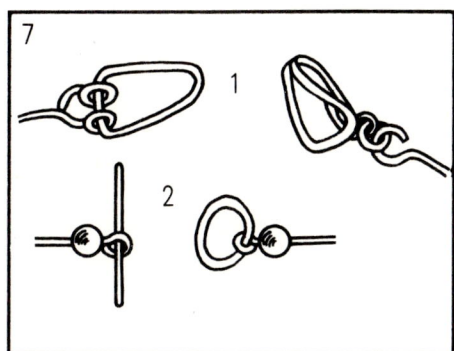
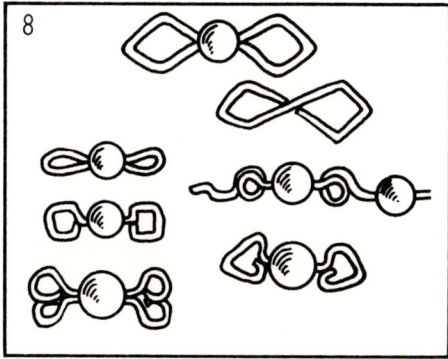

attach them to the chain at each end. The second is a loop-and-bar fastening. Links with small beads are used at the end of the chain, and one link holds a short piece of straight wire securely, while the other holds a round link.

No. 8. Links with beads can be made in many shapes and sizes, diamond, square and heart-shaped as well as round. You can even use two wires, with a bead with a large enough hole for the two wires to pass through. Curve the loops over for the top loops and under for the bottom loops, so that they meet at the centre.

Any or all of these links can be joined to make delicate or chunky chains. Thin cheap fuse wire is ideal to practise making links with. You can use it to try out designs which you can then copy in the wire of your choice.

# Silver Jewellery

Silver is one of the loveliest of metals, and very easy to work with. You will need little in the way of equipment, and there are no dangerous or difficult materials or techniques involved.

You will use silver wire mostly and this can be bought in various gauges. The higher the gauge number, the finer the wire. The 16 to 24 gauges are the most suitable. It is also worth noting that silver is sold by weight—another incentive to use the thinner wire which is lighter. Sheet silver is also sold by weight in gauges from 10 to 28. The lighter weights are again better suited for jewellery. Metal shears or very sharp scissors, round-nosed and flat-nosed pliers, and link 'formers' are all you need for these designs.

No. 1. This is a necklace made up of the variety of links shown on page 37, No. 8. Use light and dark beads for the different links, say pearl and dark red glass.

No. 2. This attractive link design can be used individually for a pendant or earring, or linked together to form a necklace or bracelet. The large ring is formed in the usual way with round wire wrapped round a 'former'. The head of a small hammer is covered with cloth and then the two sides of the ring beaten flat. Figure-eight links are attached.

No. 3. The flat-nosed pliers are used to hold the wire, while the round-nosed pliers are used to form it. Here are two shapes of coiled wire; the square one has a bead at the centre. They can be linked to form necklaces and bracelets.

No. 4. Two beads and two wires are used to form this attractive link for a necklace or bracelet. The drawing shows clearly how the wires are curved and the links formed.

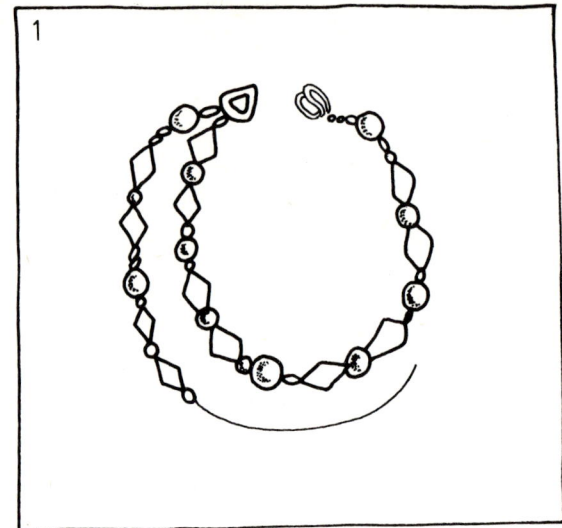

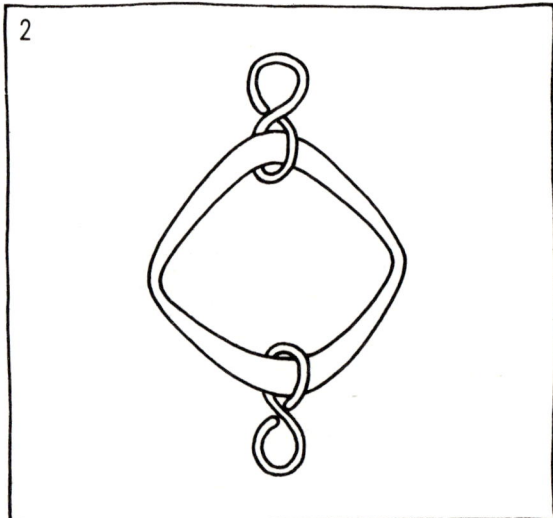

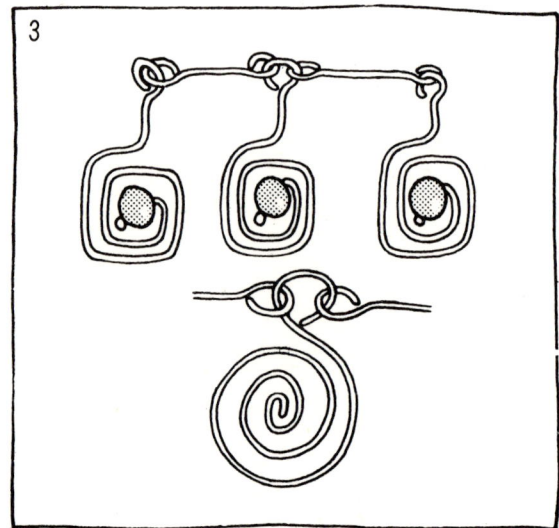

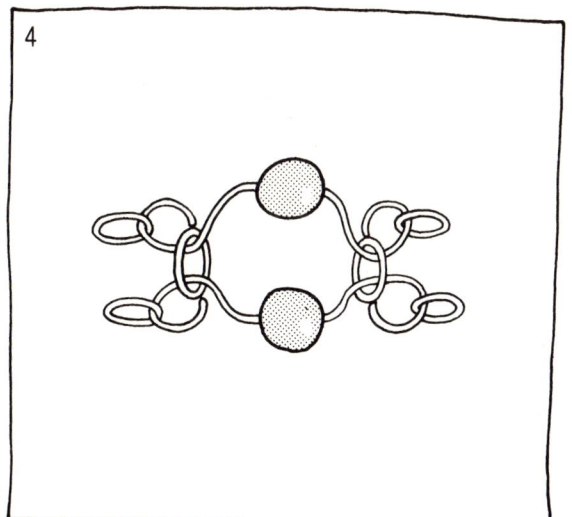

4

In the photograph is a lovely silver link necklace with an interesting arrangement of various size and shape beads all in dark green. The four large, long, beads are placed at the front and flanked by two beads slightly larger than those which make up the remainder of the necklace. The beads came from an ordinary threaded necklace of mixed beads which was a little too heavy for comfort. One necklace of beads can make two or three new ones when linked in this way.

Just to show that wire can be twisted and bent into many forms, here are six more designs, each quite different from the other. The first is a wire neckloop with the ends bent back to form a single clasp. Beads are threaded onto the wire with a bead on each, then finished off with links and attached to the neckloop between the threaded beads. The loops of number 2 are twisted after the bead is threaded and then links formed. The simple link with the bead is attached between the twisted links.

No. 3 can be a necklace or bracelet. A loop of wire has a fastening like the one on page 37, No. 7. Wire is linked at one end to fix to the loop, a long bead threaded, then a small round bead, and the wire taken across and glued with Araldite into the next bead. A little tricky but well worth the effort. No. 4 is a simple beautiful ring. The ring is based on the link No. 6 on page 37. A link with a fine bead is fixed through the loops of the ring. No. 5, a pendant, is made by twisting the wire as you thread the beads. The end of the wire on the left is then twisted round the first loop, a bead threaded onto it and the wire formed into a link beneath the bead. Glass beads in blue or red would look very fine on this silver pendant.

No. 6 is another pendant. The centre is a larger version of the diamond link No. 8, page 37. Wires with beads threaded onto them are then bent, and the ends formed into links to attach to the diamond link. A tiny spot of Araldite in the hole of the beads will keep them in position.

The pendants can be repeated and linked to form necklaces or bracelets. Or they can be attached to a bought chain, or one you have made. Practise all the designs first with cheap fuse wire to get the knack of bending and twisting, and for measuring lengths of wires needed. You will probably want to try designing your own silver jewellery, and it helps to draw the designs on paper first. Keep your designs simple, remembering that the silver of the wire is beautiful and decorative in itself. Also, a single good bead is better than a lot of cheap ugly beads.

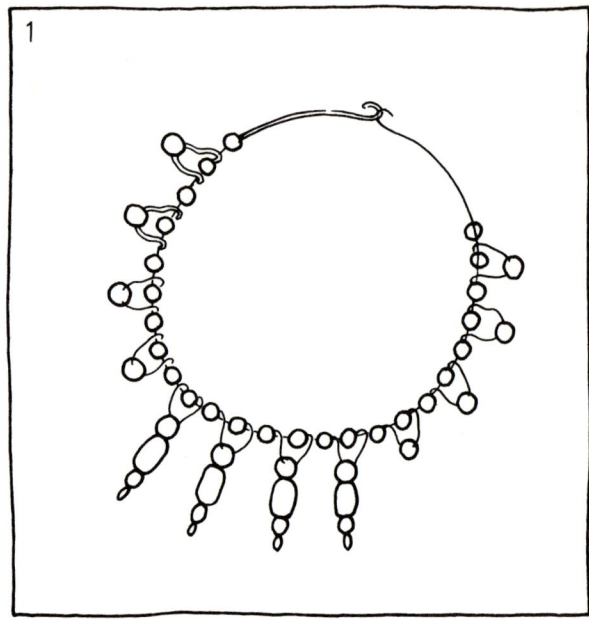

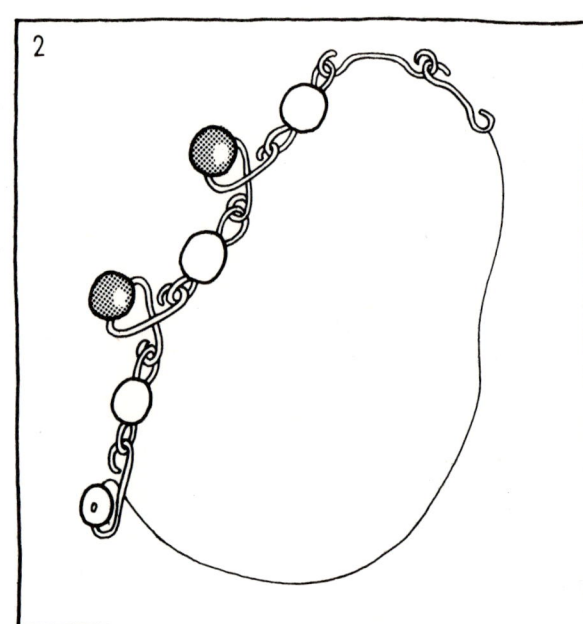

3

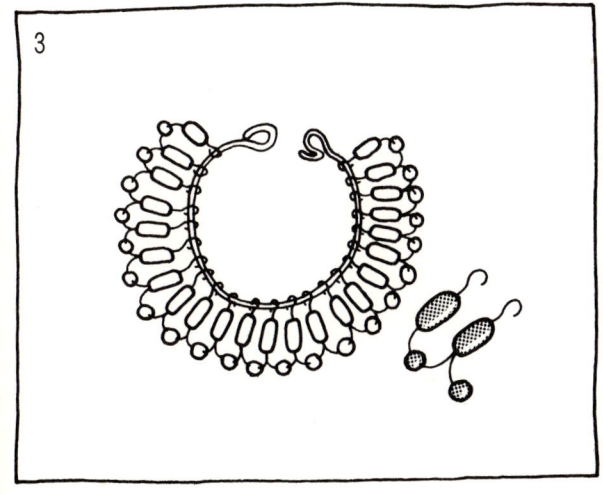

4

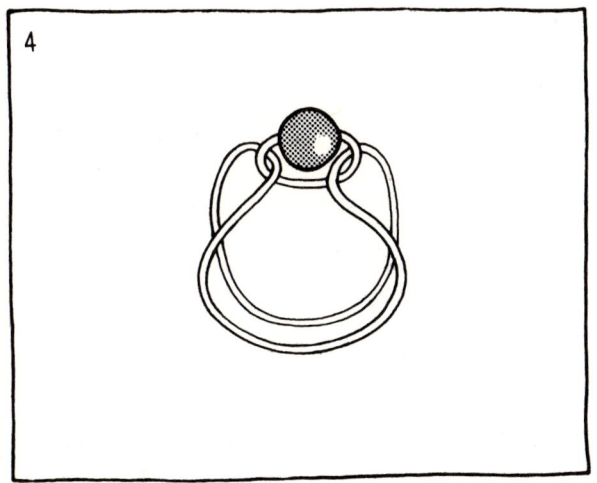

5

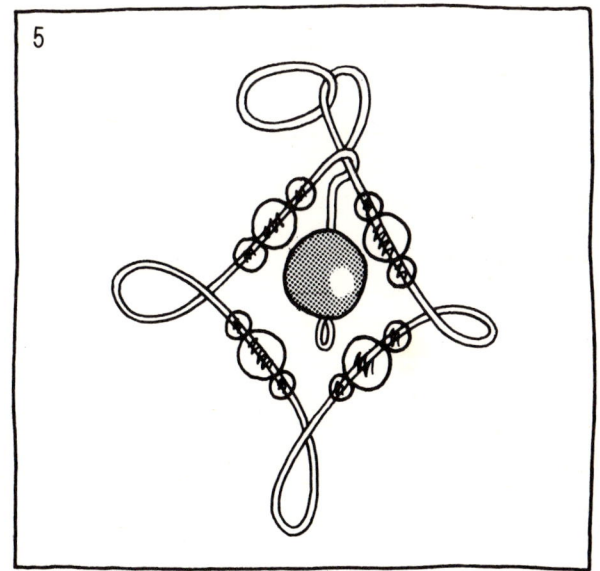

6

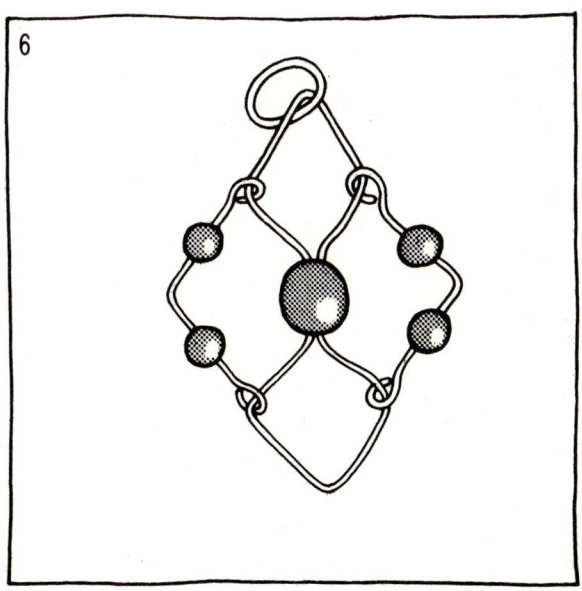

Here the items use round wire, flat wire and sheet silver. Metal shears, or very sharp scissors, are needed to cut the sheet silver. All glueing is done with Araldite. In the photograph is a simple wire bracelet with four blue beads.

No. 1. A pin, an earring and a ring, all made using coiled wire.
No. 2. A bracelet using flat and round silver wire—cut the round wire longer to allow for curves. Wrap small pieces of flat wire round to hold.
No. 3. Pendant in sheet silver has a hole cut at centre—a very sharp craft knife is used for this. Holes are made for links, and a bead link in the large hole.
No. 4. Two more pendants, cut from sheet silver. The first has tiny scraps of sheet silver glued to it. The second is made up of a square and oblongs, all linked together.
No. 5. A pear pendant, and P initial. The P has a flat-based stone glued to it, with a circle of wire glued round it. A pin can be glued to the back with Araldite.
No. 6. An owl pendant will usefully and decoratively use up all those tiny off-cuts of sheet silver. The eyes are two flat-based stones.
No. 7. Circles of sheet silver, linked together to form a necklace or bracelet, have flat-based stone and wire surround glued on each.
No. 8. Sheet silver fish pendant, with silver wire glued round the outline, and around the flat-based stone.

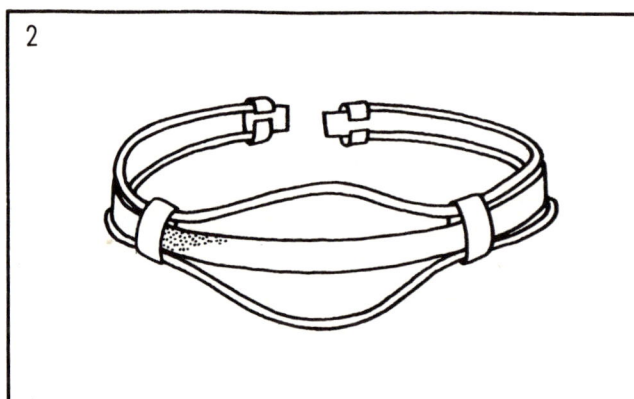

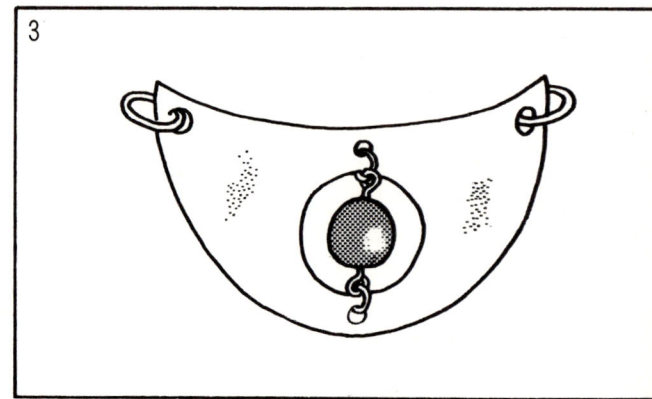

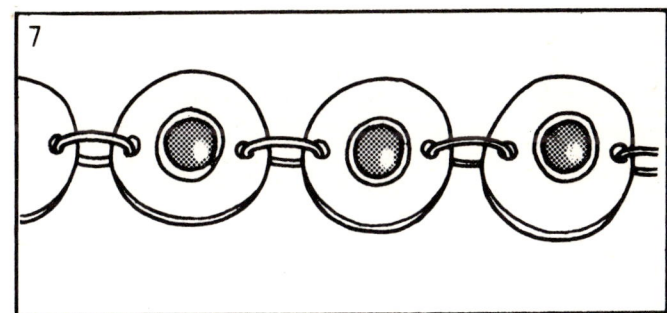

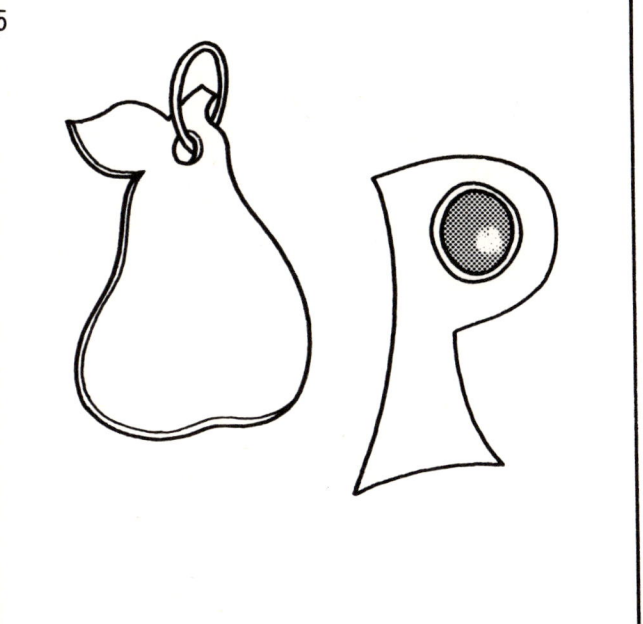

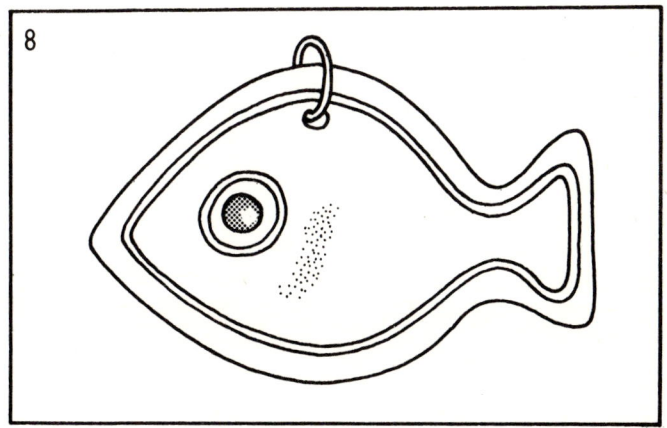

43-2

The necklace in the photograph is made of silver wire with a pendant cut out of sheet silver. A strip was cut in one with the shape, to fold back and act as link. A flat-based silver flower button has been glued to the pendant, with cut out leaves and a wire stem. Below are some more ideas for round and flat silver wire, and sheet silver. A simple heart on a neck loop is pretty, and the elephant is fun. Two of the rings are made with flat wire, the first has the edges covered with two 'diamanté' stones, while the second has a bead. The first round wire ring is made in the form of two loops and has two small beads threaded first. The second has the wire ends looped and tucked into the beads. The single bead pendant, and the flat link and beaded wire neck loop are easy to copy.

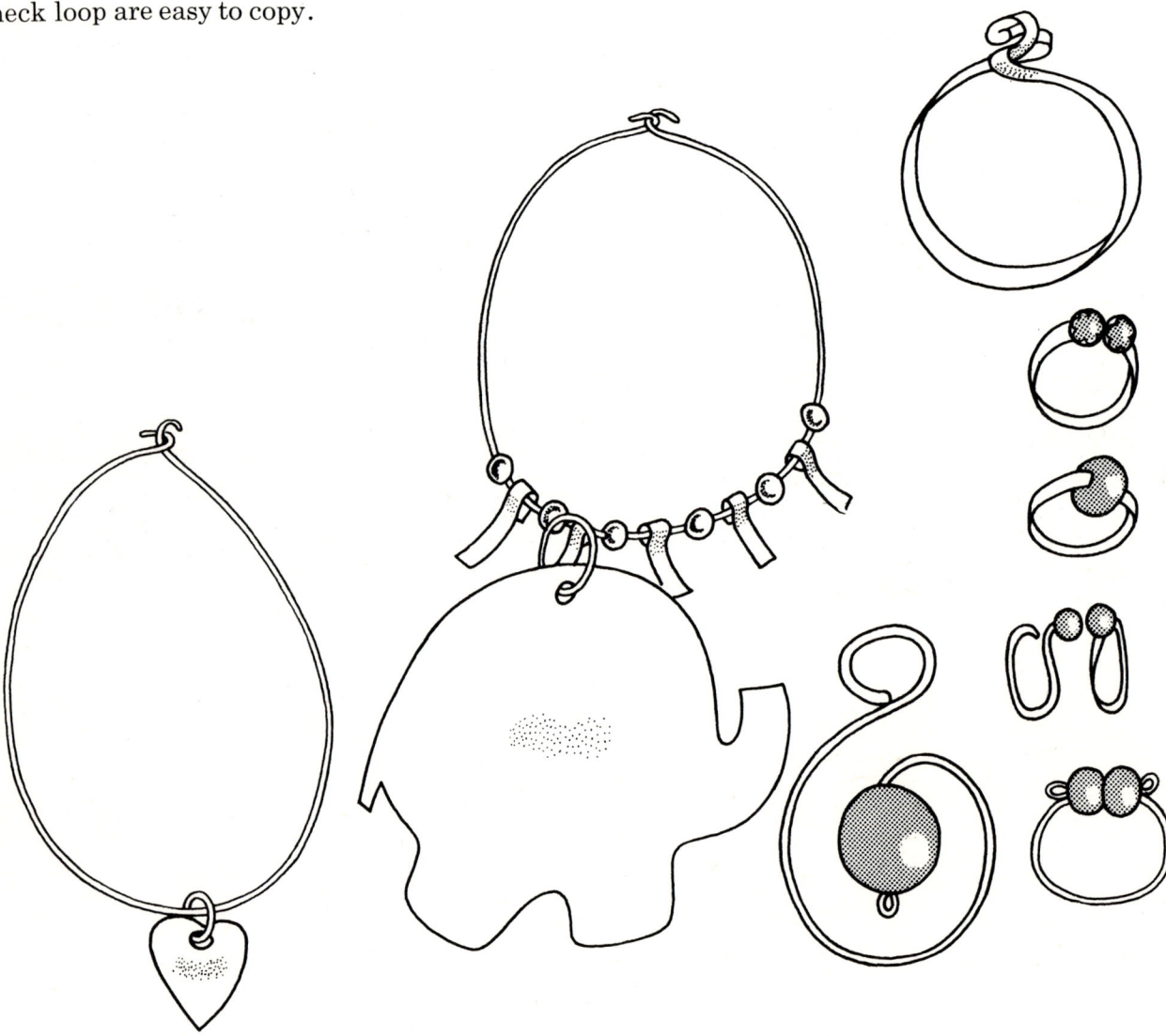

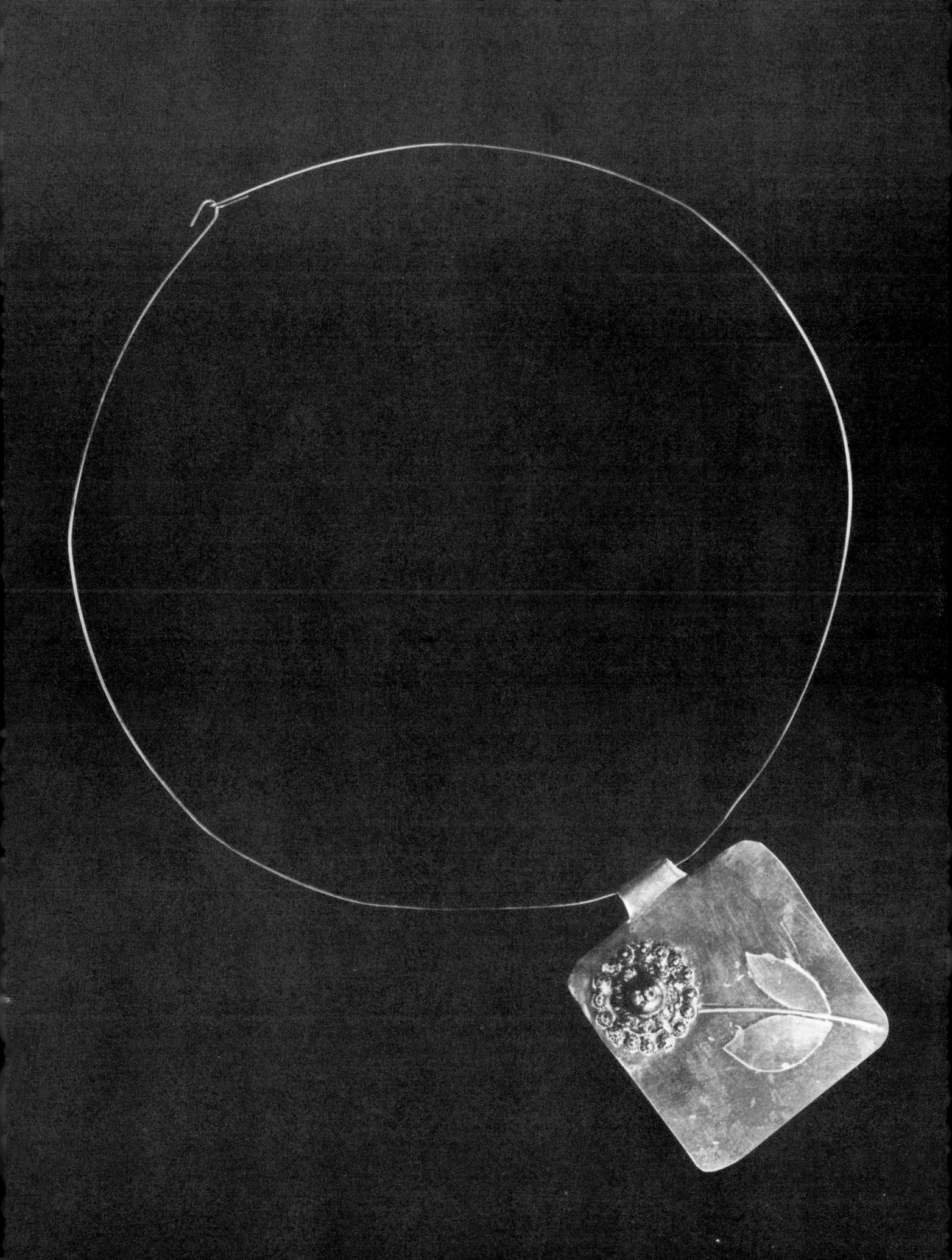

# Jewellery Boxes

Covered boxes are easily made and very pretty to hold the jewellery you have made. Instructions given are for a 4 in (10 cm) square ring box, but you can make the box in any size, in the same way. Cut out the three card patterns shown—box, lining and lid. Score along the fold lines with a knife. Cut one piece of outer material for box, one piece of lining material for lining, and one of each for lid. Box. Sew corner seam of outer material, seams inside. Sew corner seams of lining material, seams outside. Tape corners of box and box lining card edge to edge. Insert card box into outer material, fold in ½ in (13 mm) all round and glue to card. Place lining material into lining box, and fold out ½ in (13 mm) turnings and glue to card. Put a spot of glue to base of box and insert lining box. Glue quilt wadding square to lid, and tape corners. Sew corners of outer material, seams inside, and corners of lining, seams outside. Place card lid into outer material and lining into lid. Turn under edges and neatly hem. 1. uses a variety of linked beads (see links and chains) to decorate it. They must be neatly sewn so that stitches are as discreet as possible. 2. 1 in (2·5 cm) braid has been used for the sides of lid and box, and a braid bow sewn to plain lid. 3. has a bead embroidered panel, which is wrapped over card and glued to lid. Box No. 4 is a bead box using 'matting' technique described on page 27. Make squares all the same size and oversew edges together between beads. Sew lid loosely so you can open it.

Box No. 5 is an old tin box decorated with wire links and flat-based stones, to give a precious look. Copy the jewellery method described in Links and Chains. You can cover or decorate cheese boxes, cigar boxes, firm card sweet boxes, pill boxes etc. Even a box neatly covered with newspaper and then varnished looks interesting. Line boxes for a better finish where possible—felt glued inside will do.

Carefully unstick an envelope and use it as a pattern. Cut out in felt, embroider with beads, and sew it together to make a pretty jewellery container. Having made some jewellery, cherish it, wear it, and keep it in a jewellery box.

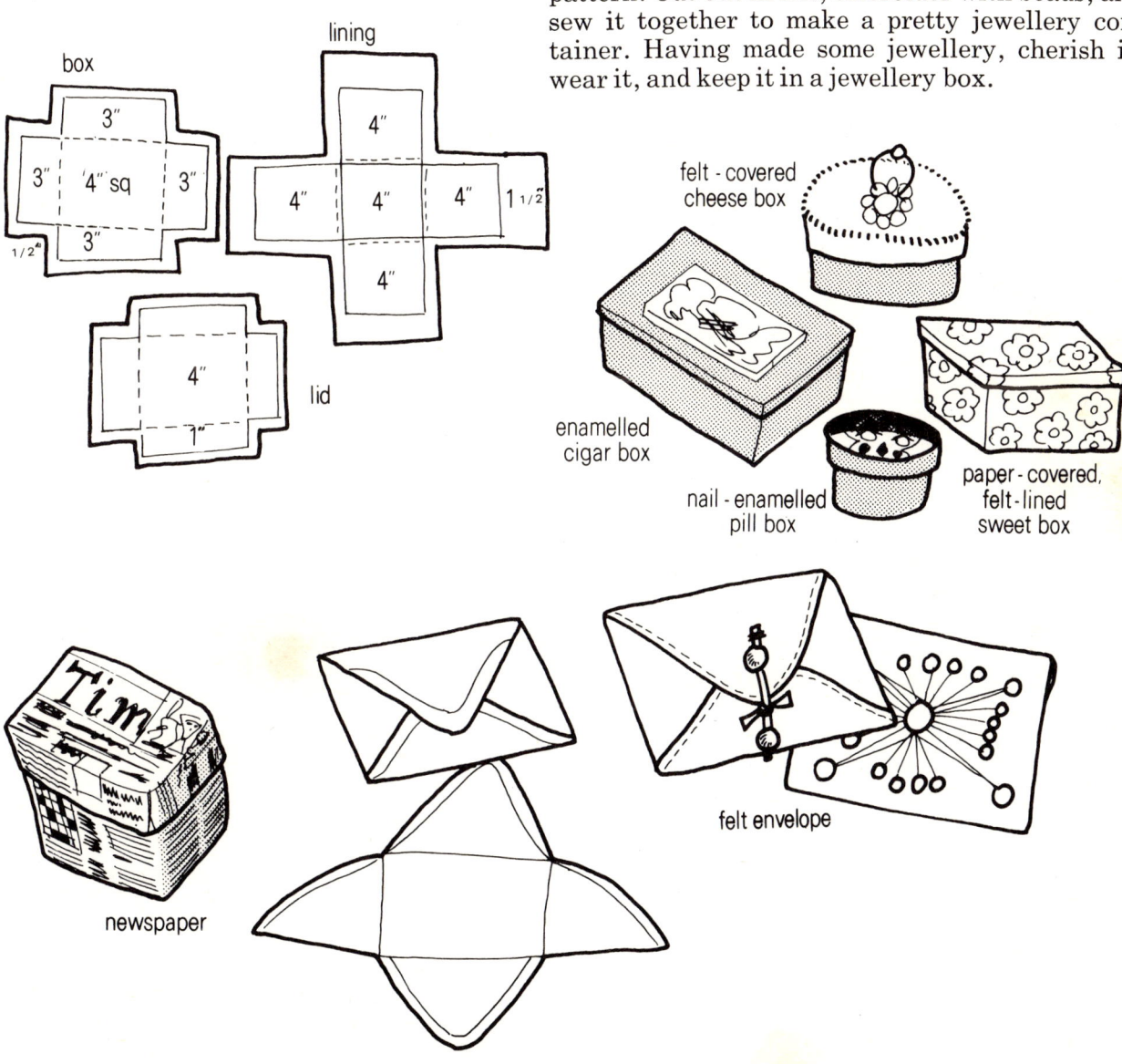

The pretty enamelled box on page 47 may be the one you would like to contain the jewellery you have made. It is simply a cigar box with a piece of enamelled copper glued to the lid. See simple Enamelling for the technique. If you would like something easy, large, kitchen size matchboxes can be the answer. Remove the drawers from four boxes and glue them together carefully. Paint the inside with a bright nail enamel and leave to dry. Cut a lid to fit the top of the box, make it fractionally larger all round. Paint inside and cover outside with patterned paper, turning under edges all round to give a clean line. Slip a piece of paper between the card and patterned paper to form a hinge, which is glued to the box side. Cover outside of matchboxes with pattern paper. You can make a small one using a single box. Neatly score and wrap card all round lid. Paint drawer with bright nail enamel or paint. Glue pressed flowers on top and add your name.

# PATCHWORK & APPLIQUE

Patchwork and Appliqué are two of the most practical as well as decorative crafts. I wonder how many knees and elbows have been patched to make clothes last that little bit longer. How many pieces of carefully hoarded materials have been sewn together to make beautiful patchwork quilts. Appliqué, originally used to decorate clothes, has found its way into the nursery, the kitchen, and the bedroom. The uses of both crafts are many and varied and are more popular today than ever before. They can be delicate or bold, ornamental or practical (or both), amusing or formal. Gifts made using either craft have a uniqueness which no factory can reproduce.

Because the combinations of materials used for patchwork and appliqué have an immediate visual impact, designs should be kept simple and bold. Shaped tiles can often inspire a patchwork design. Greetings cards and story-book pictures can readily be adapted for appliqué. It is important to match your project with your degree of patience. If you prefer to see your work develop and finish quickly, leave the larger items, like patchwork or appliqué quilts, to someone else. Choose instead one of the smaller, simpler objects. A finished pot holder is far more satisfying than a half finished quilt.

# Templates for Patchwork

Patchwork templates can be bought in a variety of sizes and shapes—in metal, plastic or card. I have drawn some here which you can use. Trace them and transfer them to firm card. Be sure you cut them accurately.

The smaller size patches are used for toys, jewellery and small items. The octagon cannot be used alone. A square of the correct size must be used with it to fill in the inevitable spaces.

I have not drawn squares, rectangles or triangles as these are easy to draw yourself.

The pentagon is used for such toys as balls and dolls.

Use the template to cut out the papers, or linings, over which the material pieces are sewn. Cut the material itself $\frac{3}{8}$ in (1 cm) larger all round, to allow for turnings.

The size and shape of the template you use will, of course, depend upon the size of the item, and the size of the fabric pattern. It is a good idea, before cutting up precious material, to draw the design on paper, using the actual size template you are going to use. Colour it with crayons if you like, since the relationship of colours is as important as that of shapes.

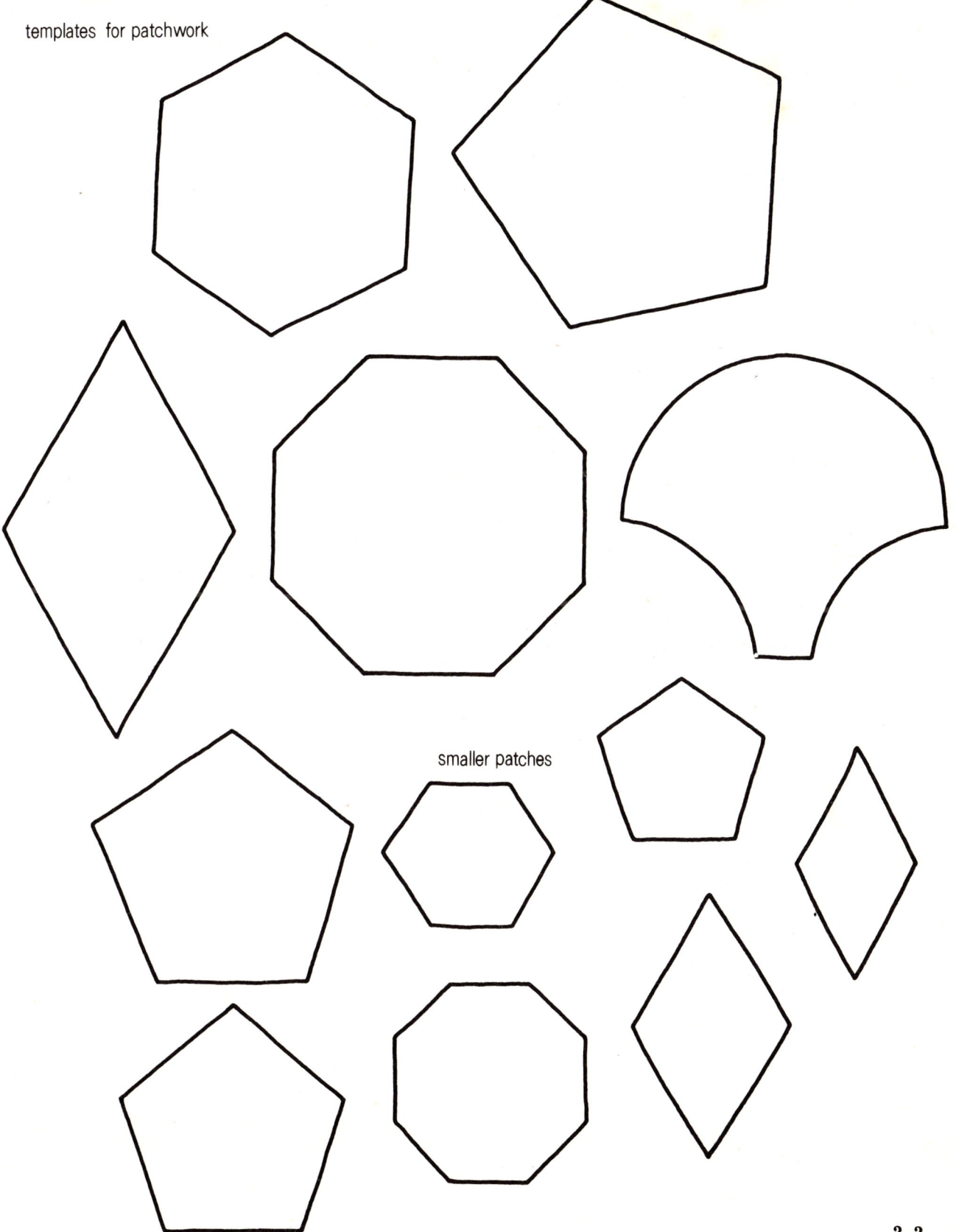

# Assembling Patches

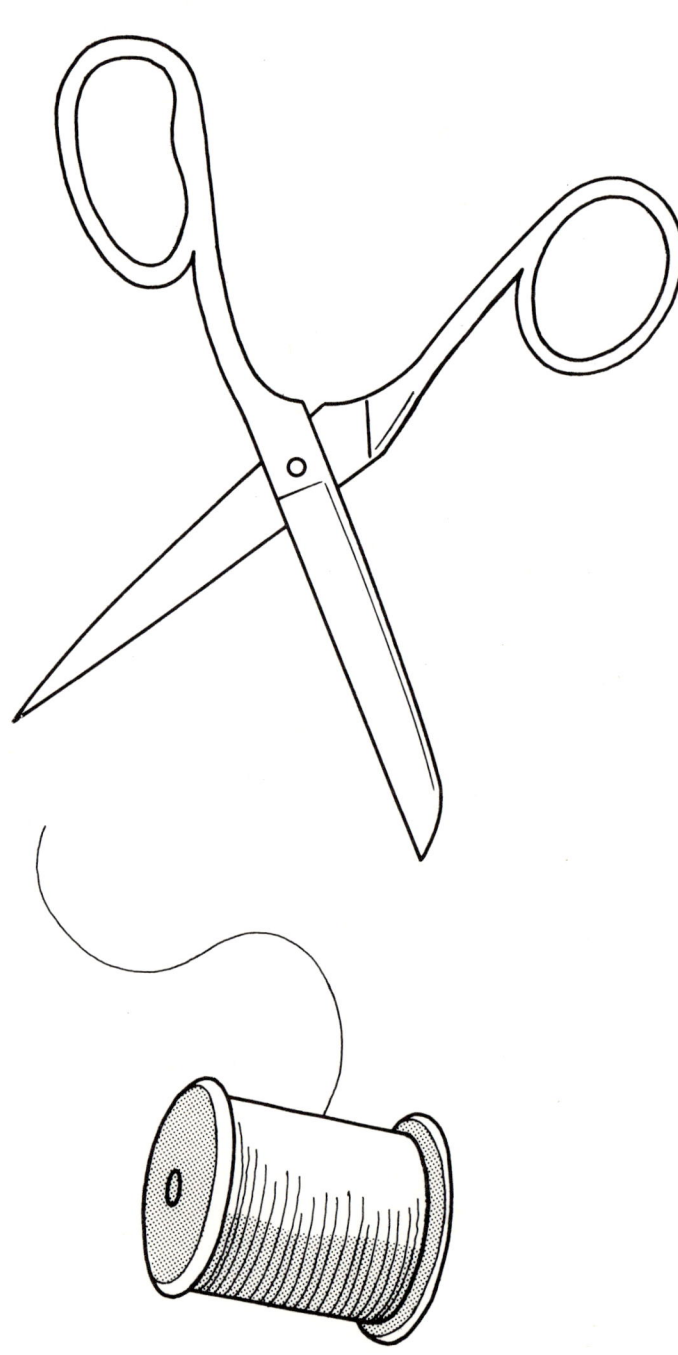

Cut papers, or linings from Vilene or Pellon. Pin a paper to the wrong side of the material and fold over the turnings, tacking them in place. Sew patches together by oversewing the edges. You can see all these stages in the diagrams opposite. Diagram 1 shows the hexagon patch being made up. Diagram 2 shows the diamond patch being made—note the way the very pointed ends are folded three times through stages a, b, and c.
Diagram 3 shows the clamshell patch being made up. The turning is folded over the curved edge, making tiny tucks in the fullness as you go. You can see how these patches are laid out and stitched to a background fabric.

Perhaps the main source of supply for patchwork pieces is scraps left over from dressmaking or home furnishing. Dresses that the children have grown out of are anouther source, and, of course, you can buy new fabric by the yard.

Whatever the source of your patchwork material, there are just a few simple rules to observe to achieve the best results. The weight and texture of material patches in one piece of work should be as similar as possible. New materials should be washed before making patchwork to remove dressing and allow for shrinking. The grain of the fabric should all go the same way. If you are making a large item, such as a quilt, make small groups of patches and then join them together.

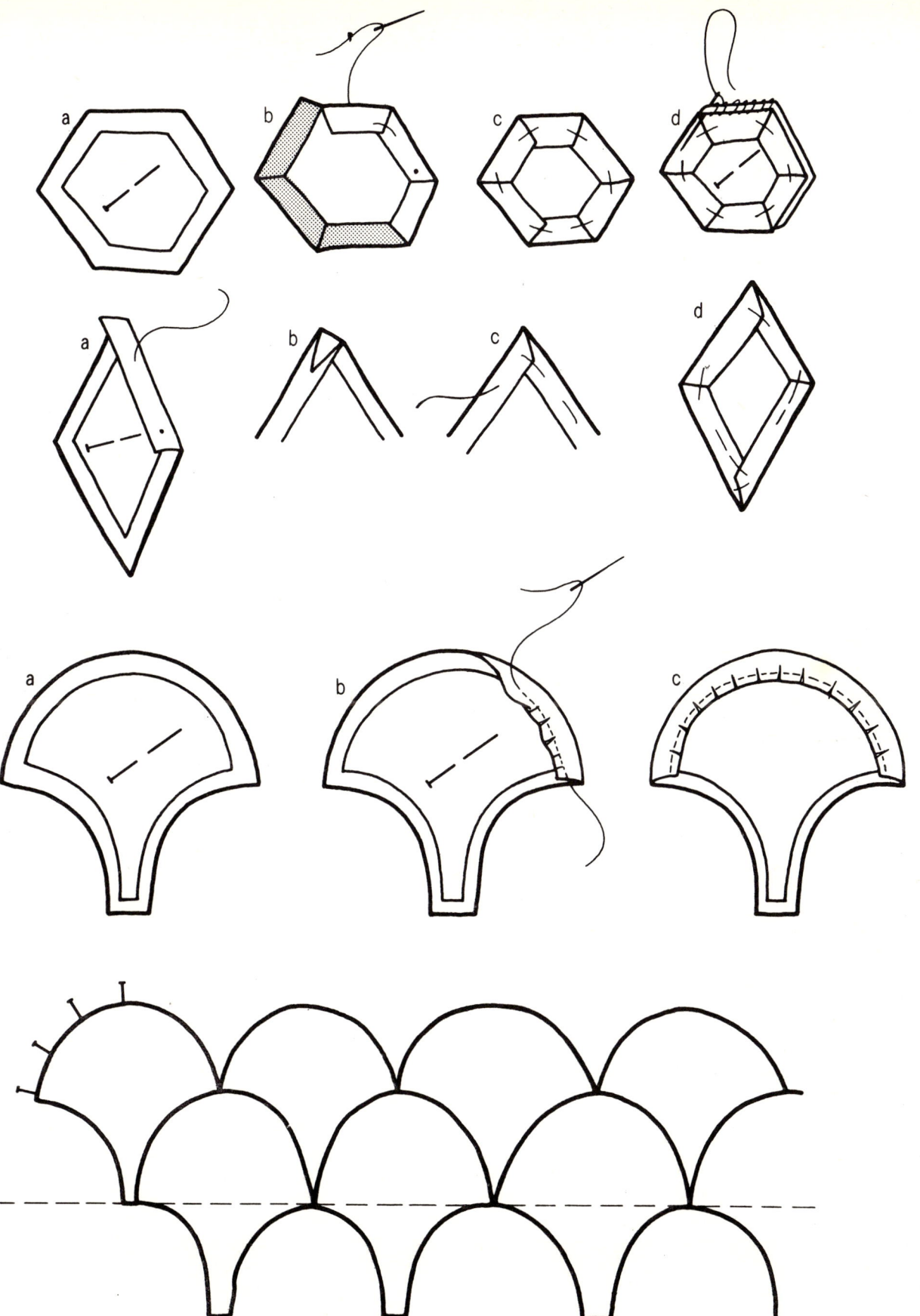

5-3

# Techniques of Appliqué

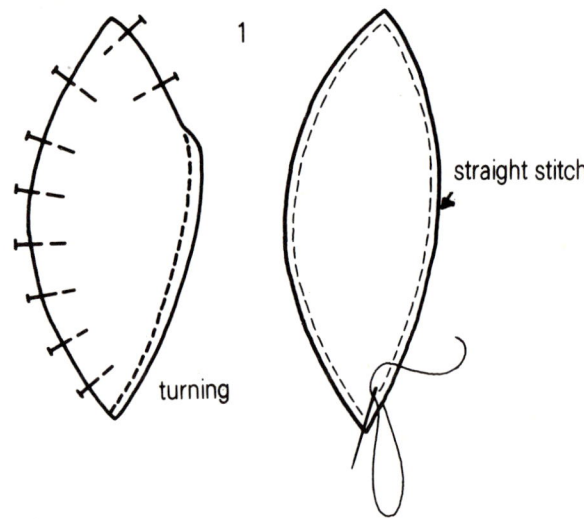

To begin appliqué you need, of course, a project—that is, the item you wish to make and the design you wish to apply to it. I hope you will find some inspiration in this book.

You will need plenty of material, a variety of colours, patterns and textures. While, in patchwork, it is advisable to keep texture and weight similar in one work, in appliqué, you can combine, happily and effectively, as great a variety of fabrics as you like.

The shapes can be applied to the background fabric by turning under the edges and sewing them down with running stitch, or slip-stitch, blanket stitch, or machine stitch etc. Or the shapes can be cut without turnings and applied to the background fabric with embroidery.

When you have made a drawing of your design in the required size, you can cut out the pieces to use as patterns for cutting the material. You may find it helps to draw the design on the background material. Cut the material shapes and sew down with the straight grain running in the same direction as that of the background material.

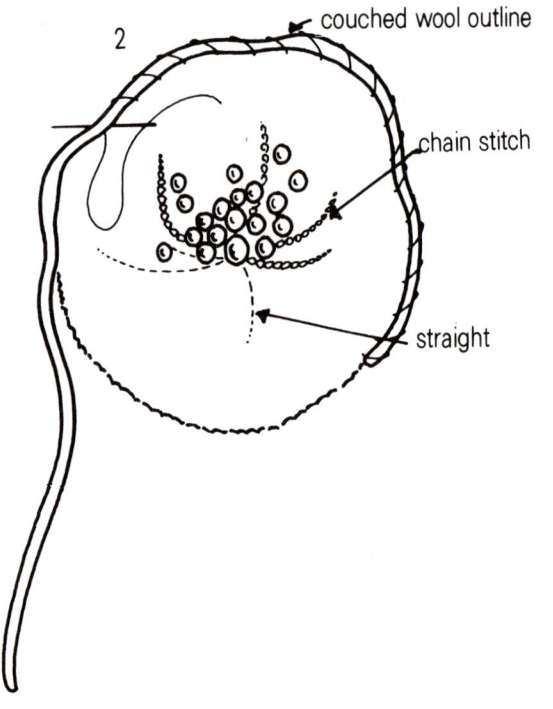

Diagram 1 shows hemmed and flat-stitched leaf.
Diagram 2. An un-hemmed flower is bordered with couched down wool.
Diagram 3. All pieces are felt and glued to backing.
Diagram 4. All pieces are made up before being slip-stitched in place. The figure is developed in layers.
You will find more about these on page 44.

hidden stitching

# Some Small Patchwork Items

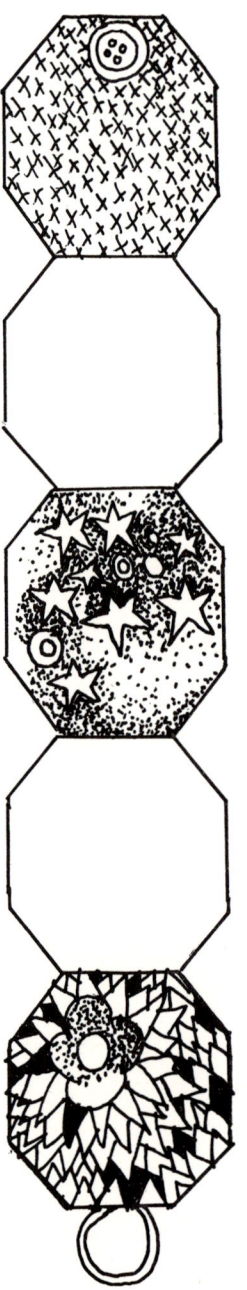

Here are some small patchwork items to start you off. The first is an octagon patch bracelet. Each patch is cut double, sewn round, right sides facing, then turned through. Close the turning and sew the patches together. A small button is sewn on one end patch, and a cotton, button-hole sewn, loop at the other. Make the patches on one side plain and those on the other side print. Sew buttons on both sides and you have a reversible patch bracelet.

No. 2 is a hexagon brooch. A "window" was cut in the material to give an interesting detail. This was placed over a firm card hexagon patch and the turnings glued down. The back is covered with a felt hexagon with a pin sewn to it.

No. 3 is a bracelet made up of felt patchwork shapes embroidered with small beads. They are overlapped and sewn together and fastened with a bead and cotton loop. A bracelet for special occasions this one.

No. 4 is a perky little pendant. Three yellow felt diamond patches have been sewn together and lightly stuffed with cotton wool. A small loop is sewn at the point. Tiny black felt eyes and orange felt beak are glued on.

No. 5. This smart pendant is a larger diamond shape cut from firm card and covered with a fine linen. The back is finished as for No. 2. Small beads have been sewn to the linen and a small silk loop sewn to the point. These two pendants can be worn on a chain, a length of cord, wool, or plaited embroidery silk.

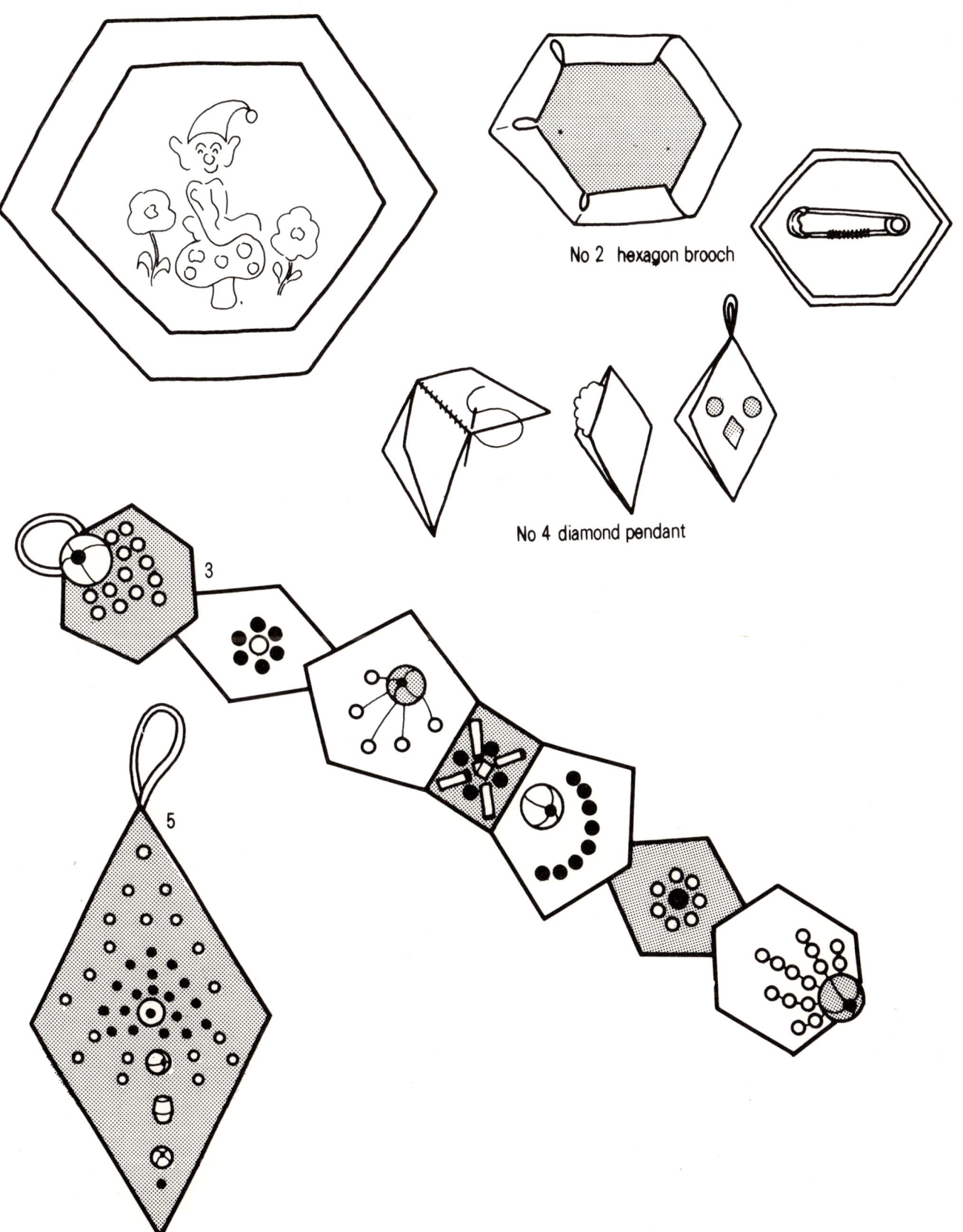

# Toys from Patches

## Diamond Fish

Our first toy is a diamond fish. Satin or shiny cotton, or brocade material would be ideal for it. Cut eighteen diamond patches and four triangles. Assemble the diamond patches in threes as shown —nine for each side—and the triangles for the tail. Sew all the patches of one side together and then the patches of the other side. Now sew round, leaving an opening. Turn through and stuff firmly. Close the opening and sew on felt circles for eyes.

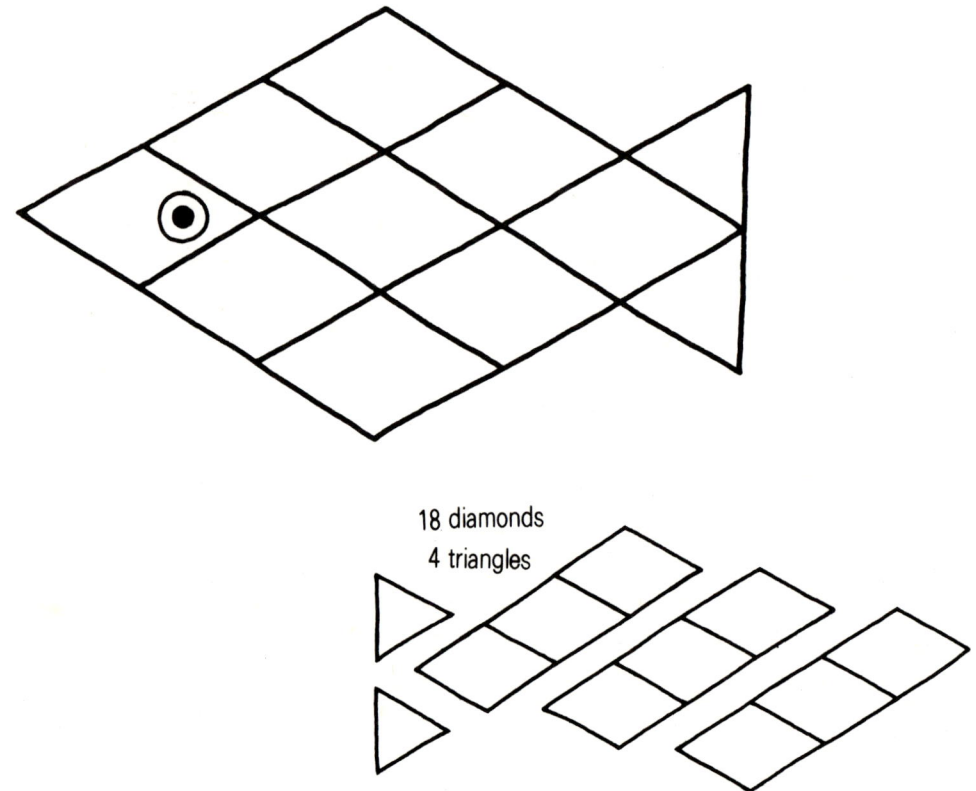

18 diamonds
4 triangles

# Square Duck

This bright duck is made of plain and flowered square patches. Draw a duck in the size required and divide it up into squares as shown, four for the head and twelve for the body. Double this number to make thirty-two squares for the two sides of the duck. Now sew the squares together, first one side, then the other. Place the sides together, right sides facing, sew round and turn through. Sew up the opening. Sew on felt eyes, beak and tail.

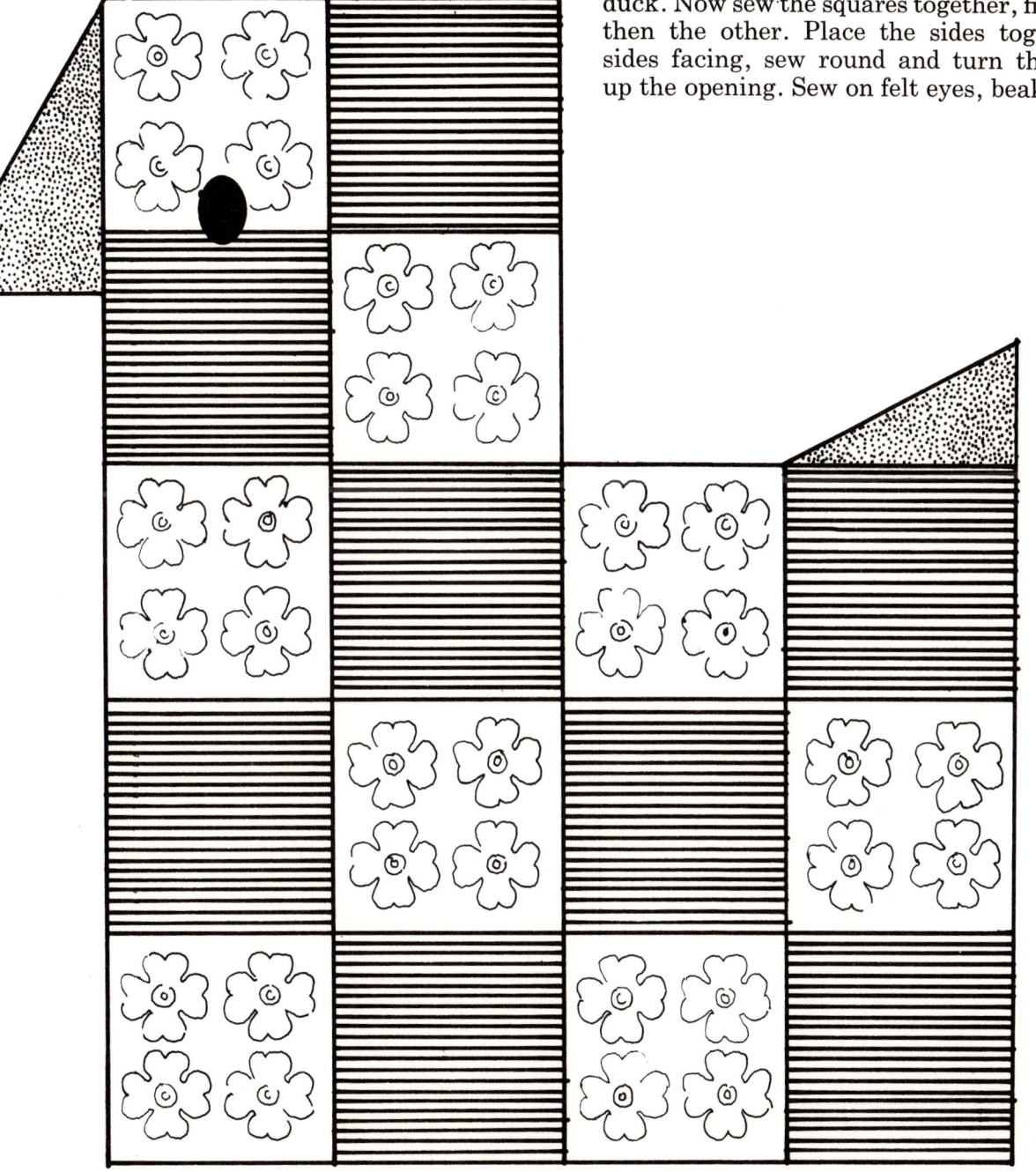

# Triangle Bird

Cut two large flower print triangles for the body of this bird. Cut four smaller triangles from navy cotton to make two wings and two small red cotton triangles for the beak. Sew two sides of the beak and turn through. Place the large triangles together, right sides facing, and insert the beak. Sew all round, leaving an opening; turn through and stuff lightly or fill with cut-out foam rubber shape. Sew the wings together in the same way as the body but do not stuff them. Sew the wings to the body and add felt circle eyes.

# Triangle Fish and Doll

The fish is made of triangles—large for the body and small ones for the tail. The body only is filled with a cut-out foam rubber or quilt wadding triangle. Sew or glue on felt circles for eyes.

The Doll is made of triangles also—one large flower print for the back and the front divided into three as shown. The face is plain and the side triangles flower print. Make as for fish.

# Square Patch Dog and Lion

These toys are made in the same way as the duck on page 11 and 2 in (5 cm) squares are a good size to use.

The lion is made up of four patches for the face, six patches for the front body and leg, four patches for the middle body, and six patches for the back body and leg. So you will need forty 2 in (5 cm) squares for front and back. Sew thick wool loops all round his face and sew black felt eyes and nose.

The dog is made up of six patches for the head, six patches for front body and leg, four patches for middle body, and eight patches for back body, leg and tail. So you will need forty-eight 2 in (5 cm) squares. The ear and eye are black felt.

These toys can be sewn flat like the duck or you can sew a ribbon or strip gusset all round as shown below.

Other animals can be made in this very simple way. A snake, worm or caterpillar can be made from a long length of single patches. A horse can be made with a wool loop mane down the side of the head. A giraffe can be made with a long neck and long legs.

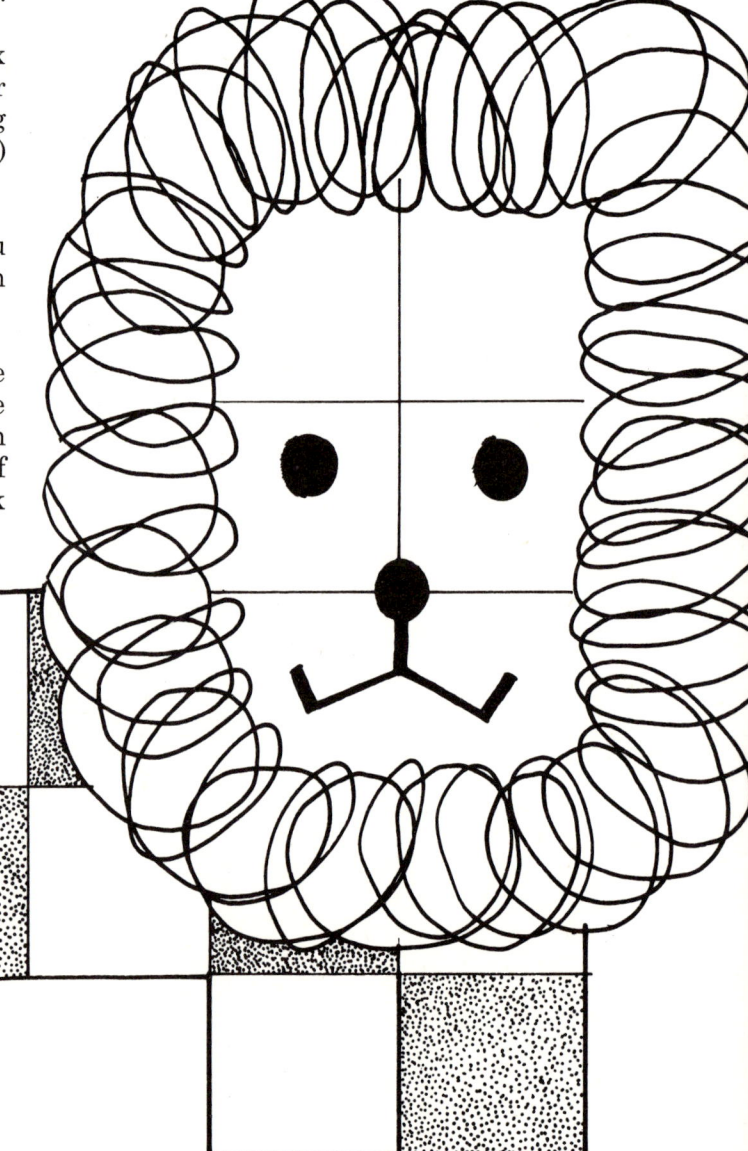

# Hexagon Spider

If you think that 'Hexagon' is a good name for a spider, then it is certainly a good name for this one. He is simply made up of two large black felt hexagon patches sewn together and firmly stuffed. His legs are pipe cleaners with strips of black felt sewn over them. The eyes are circles of white and black felt sewn to the seam so that they stand up.

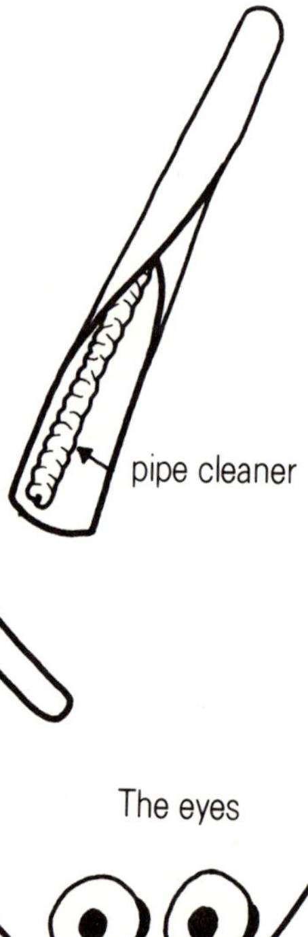

pipe cleaner

The eyes

16–3

# Hexagon Turtle

This toy is also made of hexagon felt patches. The upper body consists of six green patches for the body and one yellow for the face. The under body consists of seven yellow patches. Sew the upper patches together, then the under body patches. Now sew the under and upper bodies together, right sides facing, turn through, stuff, and close opening. The eyes are small circles of felt.

# Pentagon Dolls

By not joining all the seams of the pentagon patches you can create these dolls. The first doll requires twelve pentagon patches—six print for the back, five print and one white or pink patch for the face. Sew the patches together, then front and back, lightly stuffing the toy before sewing up the opening. Circles of felt are glued or sewn on for eyes and mouth. The second doll is made in the same way but with more patches forming a hat as well as a different body. Scraps of wool form hair.

Here are two more examples of dolls made from pentagon patches—a Chinaman and a clown. They are made just the same way as the dolls on the previous page. You might like to try making up your own dolls. Or you can use the same method to make funny little animals, like the cat and lion I have drawn here. Scraps of knitting wool form legs and tail of cat, and tail of the lion plus a piece of wool fringe for mane.

# Pentagon Ball Toys

Twelve pentagon patches sewn together and stuffed make a ball. Make pretty soft balls in felt or cotton prints—easy for small hands to grasp. Sew a smaller pentagon ball on to a larger one in felt to make the mouse. Add ears, eyes, nose, cotton-loop whiskers, and a knotted tail. Join several small green felt balls together with a larger one for the head to make a caterpillar. Give him black felt eyes (and cotton eyelashes) so that he can see where he is going, however slowly. You can make lots of other creatures in this way. A lion, made like the mouse, can have a wool loop 'mane' for example.

For the pentagon ball dolls use pink or white material for faces and hands. The hands are cut in pairs, sewn together and turned through and need no stuffing.
Fur fabric makes a cuddly doll for a baby.
Mother doll has black patches for hair. Her body is made of plain and flower print material with fringing to give a shawl effect. She holds a baby made with the two smallest patches (see Templates). The baby can be made in pink or blue and can be held to Mother with a few hidden stitches. Spotty doll, in the photograph on the next page, is made in red and white cotton material with white face and hands.

The pentagon patch dolls can easily be adapted to pentagon ball dolls, making a jolly fat clown or a Chinaman.

21–3

# Square Patch Basket

A pretty little basket is made up of nine square patches in a flower print material. Each square has a plain material lining, and these are sewn together and turned through first. Make a strip handle in print and plain in the same way. One patch is for the base, two for the front and back and three patches sewn together for one side and three for the other side. Sew each of the three side patches together first, then sew all the patches to the base. Overlap and sew the front and back patches as shown and sew on the handle. You can, if you wish, insert squares of card in each patch to make a firmer basket.

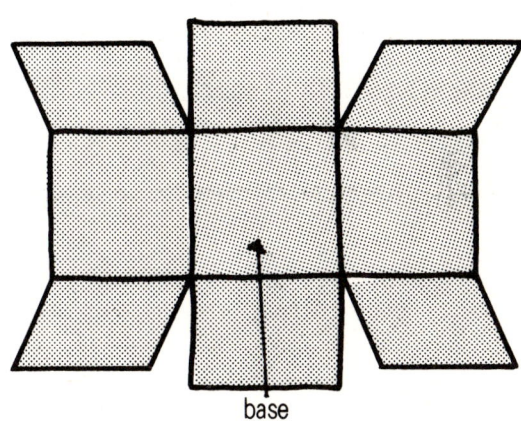

base

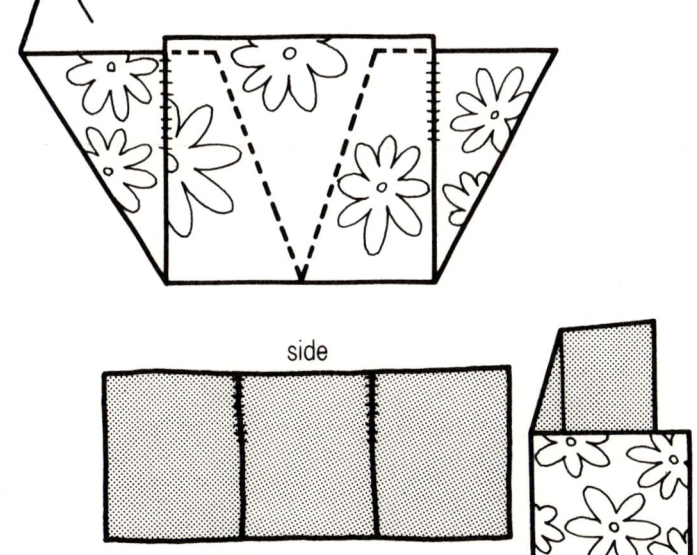

side

# Free Patchwork Doll

Here is another method of making a patchwork doll. Draw the doll shape here on a large piece of paper. Decide where the hat, face, arms, etc. should go and draw them in. Or, of course, you can draw your own doll design if you prefer. When you are satisfied with the size, shape and design of your doll, cut all the parts as shown. Allow turnings round each piece when you cut out the material parts. Cut into curves and corners and sew the patches together carefully so that all the pieces fit together again like a jig saw. The back is made the same way as the front and then the two completed parts sewn together. Leave an opening in the base seam and fill the doll with kapok, cotton wool or any soft stuffing material.

To keep the work neat in making up, press open the seams as you sew them. Keep the design simple, and avoid too many pieces, especially if your doll is small. Lines which continue from the front to the back must meet at the side seams.

Make it large and you have a pretty cushion—a small one could be filled with lavender.

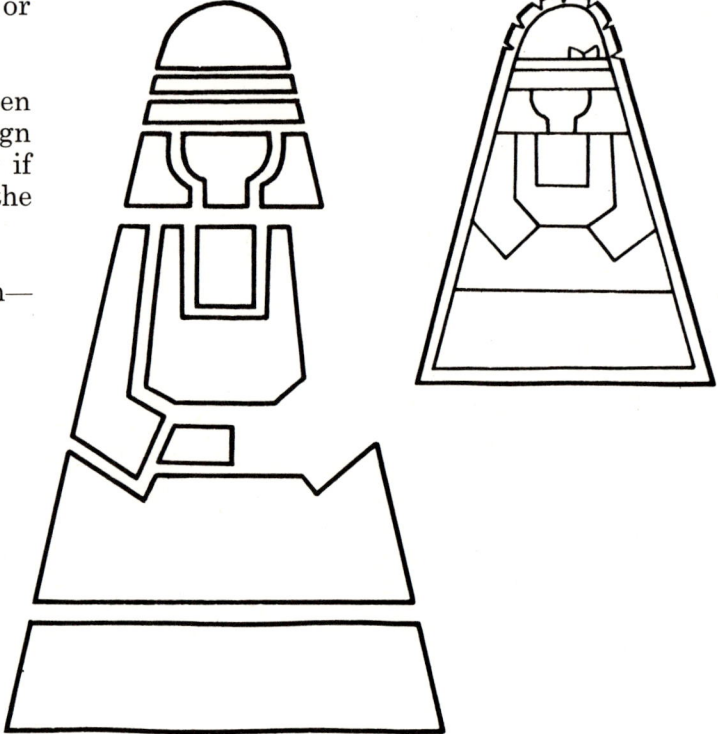

# Patchwork Pot Holders

Foam rubber or pieces of blanket are used to interline these patchwork pot holders. The actual patch designs are very simple and rely on bright materials for effect. Tape loops can be added to hang them up by. The backs can be patchwork or plain.

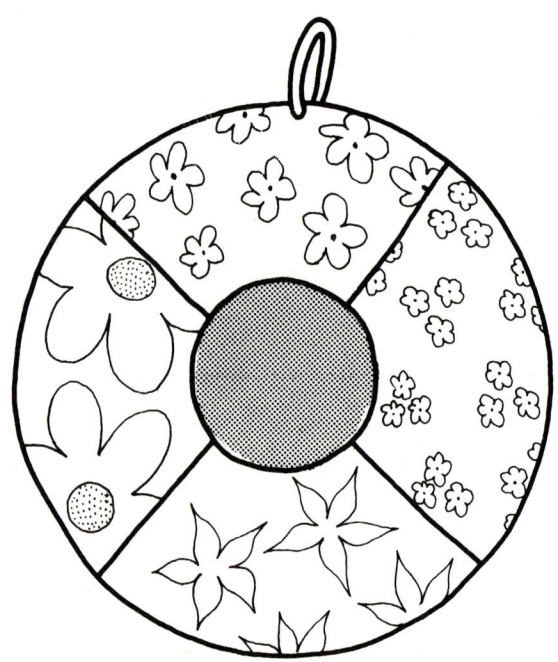

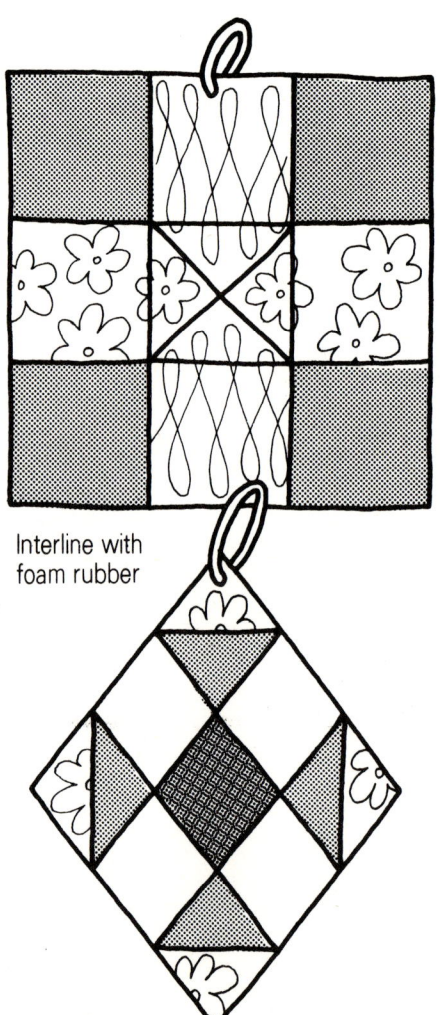

Interline with foam rubber

# Hot Water Bottle Cover

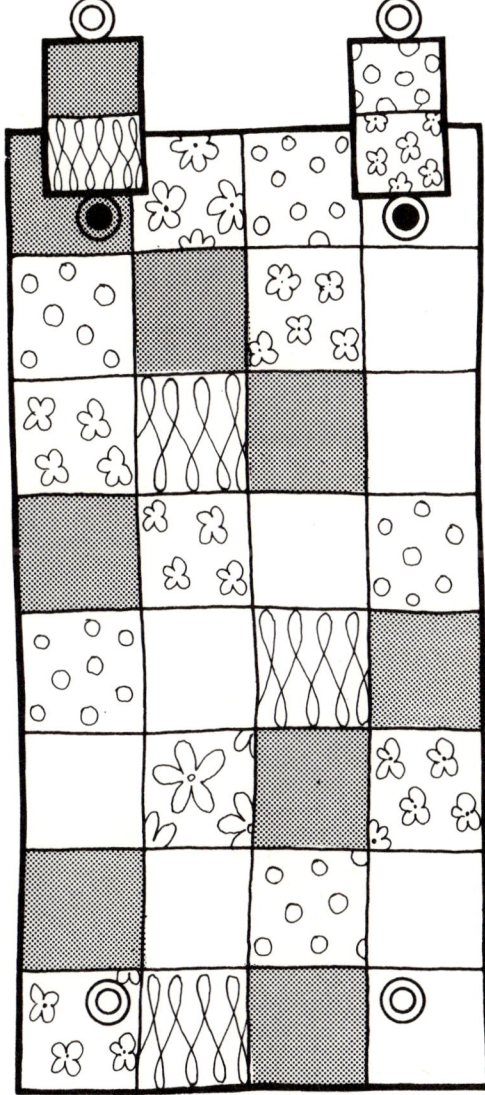

Square patches are used to make a hot water bottle cover. Sew the patches together in a long piece as shown, and sew a lining to it. Fold the piece up and neatly stitch the sides. Two squares make each tab and they also are lined. Buttons and button-hole loops fasten the tabs.

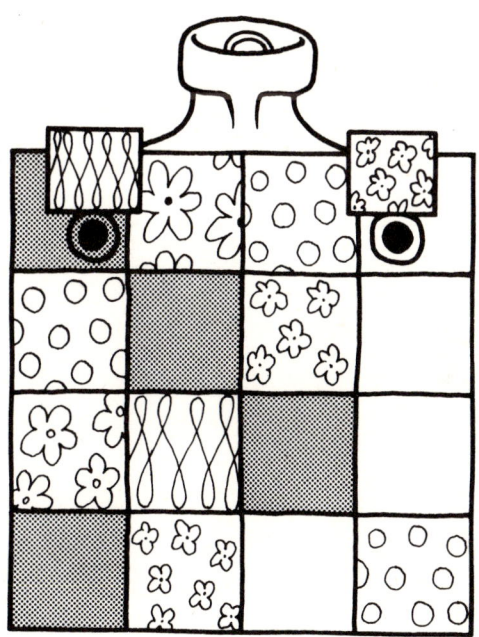

# Square Patch Bag

Five squares of card, five squares of print material and five squares of plain material make up this box-like bag. Make up the print and plain patches —the five with the seams inside, the plain ones with the seams outside. Place the card square in the base and sides between the two layers and hem all round upper edge. Sew brass rings at each corner and pass cord through them to form handles.

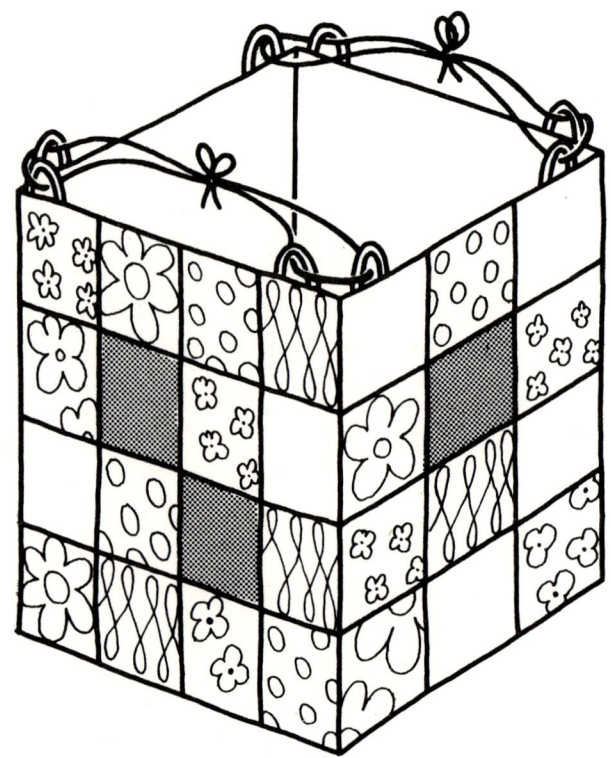

# More Patchwork Ideas

1. A pincushion made using a hexagon patch and a diamond with a point cut away. This forms a six point star which is also an attractive motif for a box for example.

2. A snake made up of diamonds has felt eyes and forked tongue.

3. A needle case with triangles using a borderprint design for effect.

4. A patchwork glove puppet has a pentagon ball head using striped material for hair. A shaped piece of striped material is sewn to the head as shown.

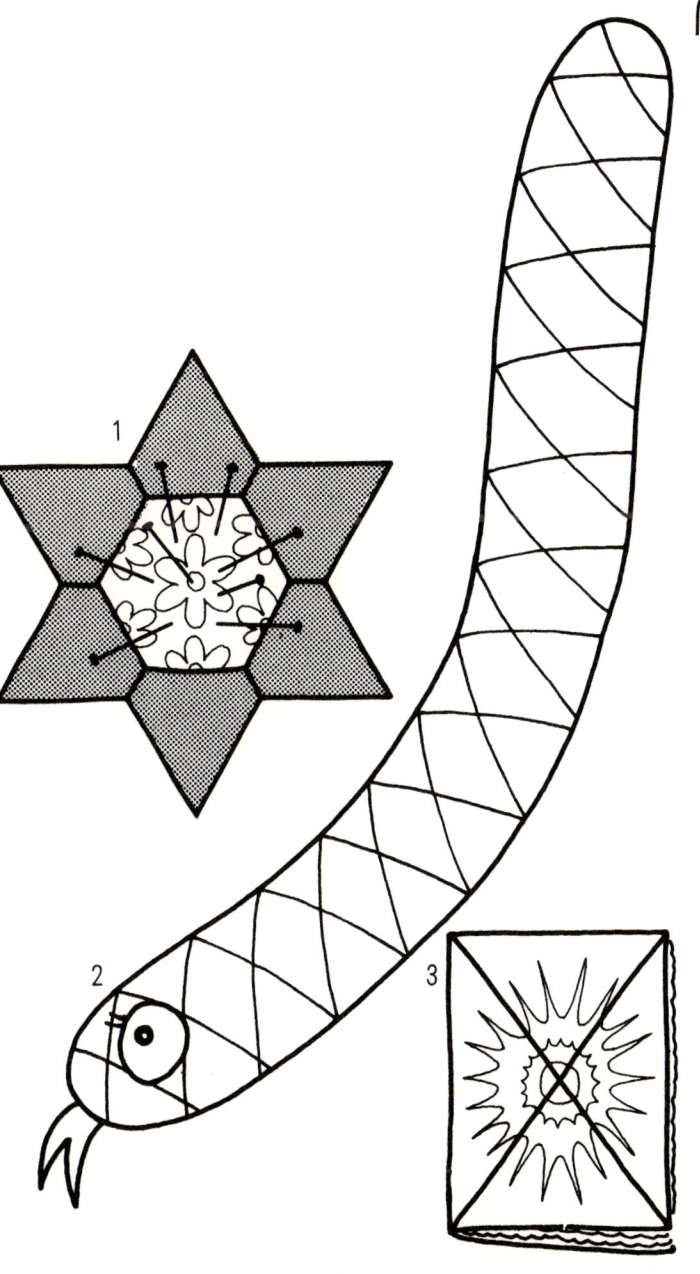

# Cushions

The backs of these cushions can be left plain.

1. Circular cushion with matching spot, stripe or check hearts.
2. Patchwork cat is appliquéd on to plain cushion and has an embroidered, appliquéd, fish (which could account for the pleased look on the cat's face!).
3. Two-tone clamshell cushion.
4. Circular plain cushion with bold patch flower appliqué.
5. Doll cushion is made in plain and print cotton. Make a wool plait to go over the head with ends left loose each side. Eyes and mouth are stitched on before making up the cushion.
6. A simple print and plain square patch cushion has decorative triangle patch edging.

For all appliquéd pieces, allow ¼ in (6 mm) turnings. Pin each piece to the background, then turn under hem and neatly sew in place. The hearts and triangles edging 1 and 6 must be cut double. Sew the shapes together, right sides facing, leaving an opening. Clip curved edge of hearts. Turn through shapes and slip-stitch opening. The hearts are sewn to the edge of the cushion after making up. The triangles are set into the seam, so be sure they are large enough. Fill the cushions with foam chips or pieces, kapok, old clean stockings or rags. Old pillows can be covered—No. 2 is ideal for these.

# Appliqué Motifs

boat
sun
fish
horse
bird
mouse

32–3

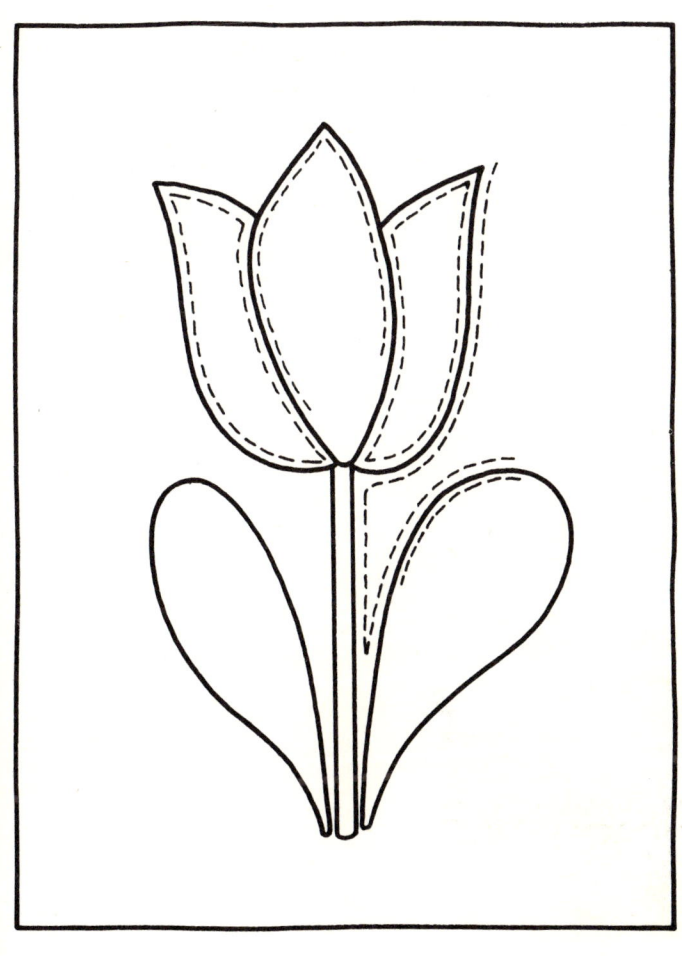

# Quilts and Bedspreads

Enthusiasm and patience are all you need to make a quilt or bedspread. Yes, you will need materials too, of course. If you feel you would like to tackle these larger items you will finish up with an heirloom, personal and beautiful, which will last you a lifetime.

Quilts or bedspreads can be made either by piecing together patchwork pieces which form the whole material, or they can be made by applying pieces of material to the background as a surface decoration—appliqué.

Below you can see two examples of motifs which can be used either singly or as an all-over design. One is a patchwork tulip motif which is appliquéd and quilted. The other is a piece of flower-print material which has been cut out, appliquéd and quilted.

A quilt has a soft interlining—decorative stitching on the quilt holds this in place. This interlining can be wadding bought by the yard, or you can use a blanket. Bedspreads are made in the same way as sheets.
If you are making a patchwork quilt or bedspread, my advice is to use large patches, squares, hexagons, diamonds or free patchwork being the most suitable.
Alternatively, you can appliqué patchwork on to a spread or quilt.

Designs 1 and 2 opposite are examples of patchwork applied to a spread and a quilt. The first is a spread with large print square patches sewn on to it in a simple design.
No. 2 is a print cotton quilt with plain strip patches sewn on to it and quilted. The plain strips (and four central squares) are so arranged as to give the whole quilt a patchwork look.

The third quilt has large bold poppies sewn on to it with squared quilting background. The lines for the quilting should be tacked or marked with an easily removable tailor's chalk, and all quilting can be stitched by hand or machine.

The fourth design here is also a quilt, with appliquéd bowl, flowers, leaves and birds. Pin, then tack all the pieces in position to achieve a good balanced arrangement. After sewing all the pieces on to the background fabric, tack the interlining to it, and quilt an outline all round them. These designs can be used for quilts or spreads as desired.

In one of the colour photographs you will see a pram or small cot quilt which has a large flower appliquéd to it. The combination of blue and white check and plain blue, and simple boldness of the design, makes a pretty quilt which is very easy to make.

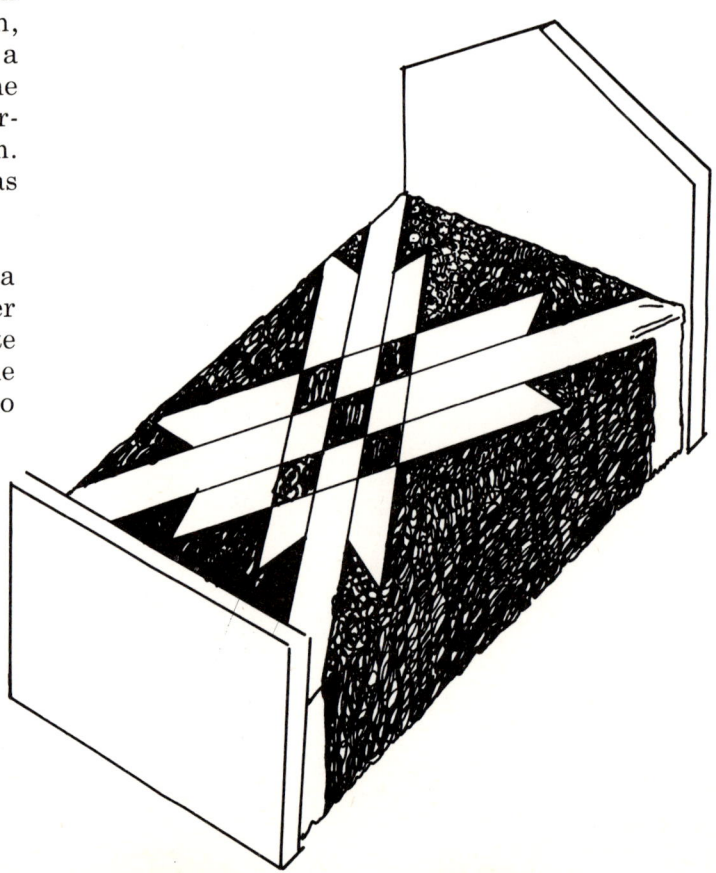

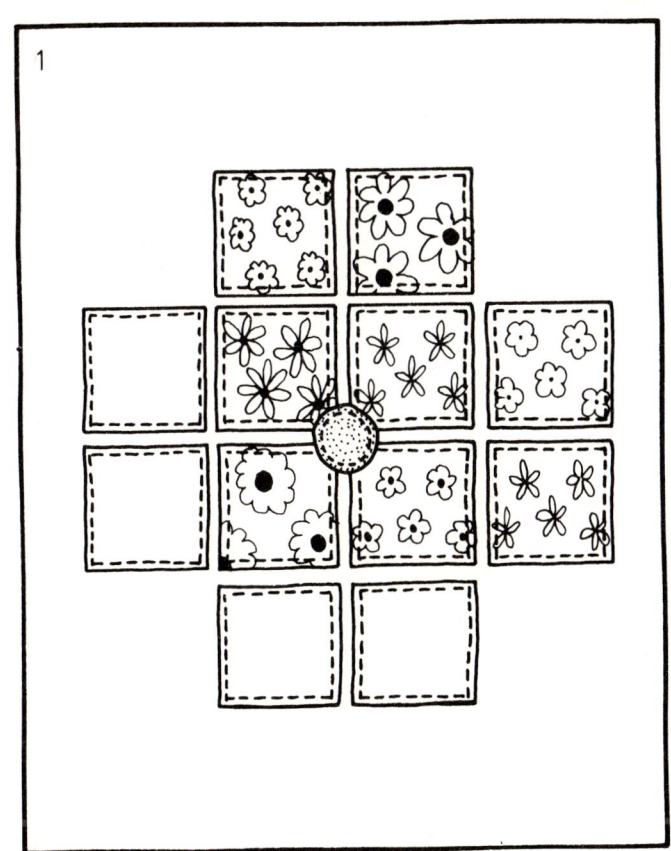

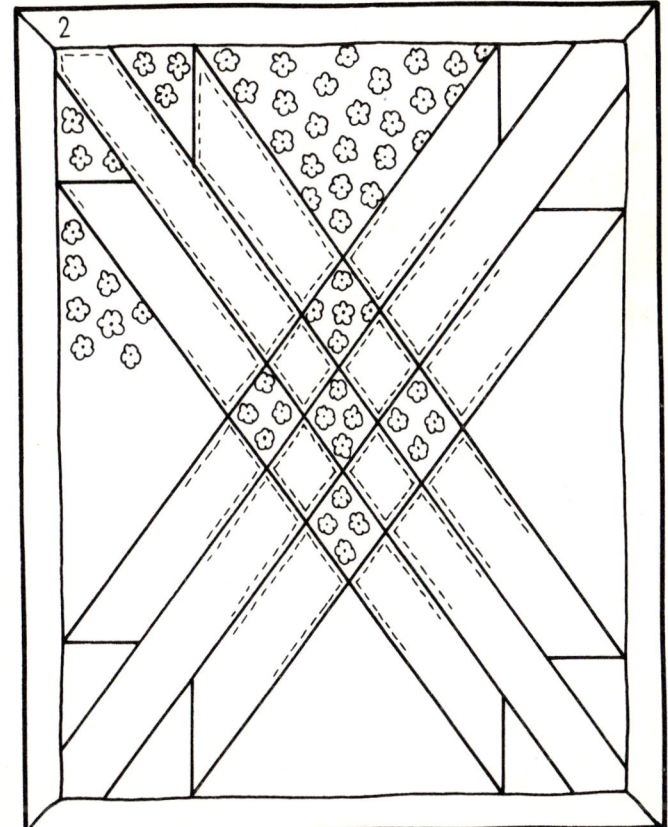

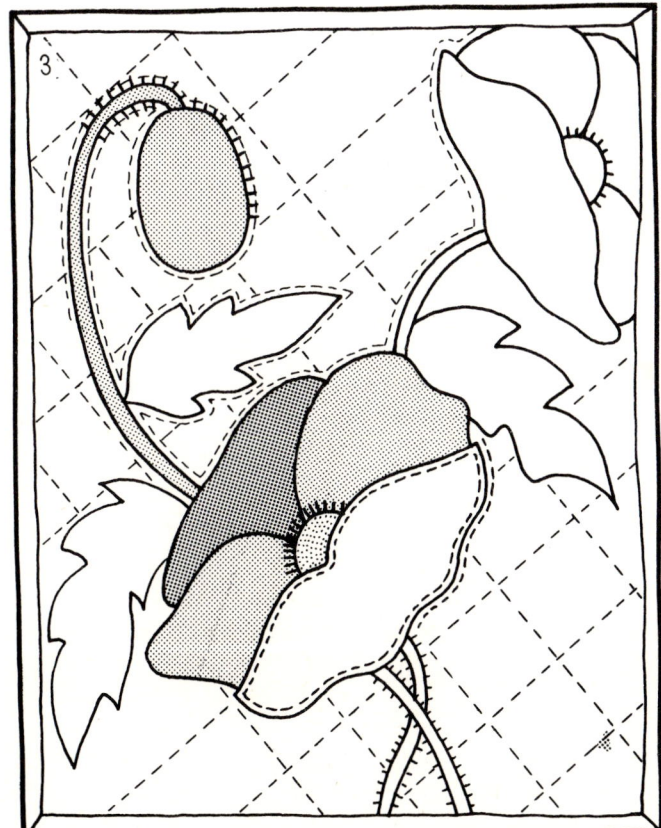

Here is a simple method of making a quilt. Large square patches have been stitched together to the required size; hearts, apples and flowers have been appliquéd to the plain squares. The interlining is 3 in larger all round and the backing is 3 in + 1 in turning larger all round than the interlining. Lay the interlining on top of the backing fabric, then the patchwork on top of the two, centring all of them carefully. Tack all layers together to hold them. Now cut away the corners of the backing fabric as shown for neat mitres. Fold down the backing fabric over interlining to edge of patchwork, turning under 1 in hem. Machine stitch all round and again at outer edge. Now machine stitch along the seams dividing the square patches.

The three designs below this quilt show how motifs found elsewhere in this book can be adapted. The spot and plain heart design is taken from a cushion on page 31. The shape of the heart is followed in the quilting.
The sunshine spread used an enlarged version of the motif shown on page 32.
Also on page 32 is a sailing boat motif which is enlarged for the third design here. The sea is indicated by quilting and a sun and fish have been added.
You may find other motifs which you would like to adapt for a quilt or bedspread. Always work out the size of quilt or bedspread you require and the type and size of design for it. This can be done on paper first.
For all the designs shown a straight stitch has been used. However, added decorative effect can be achieved by using your favourite embroidery stitches.

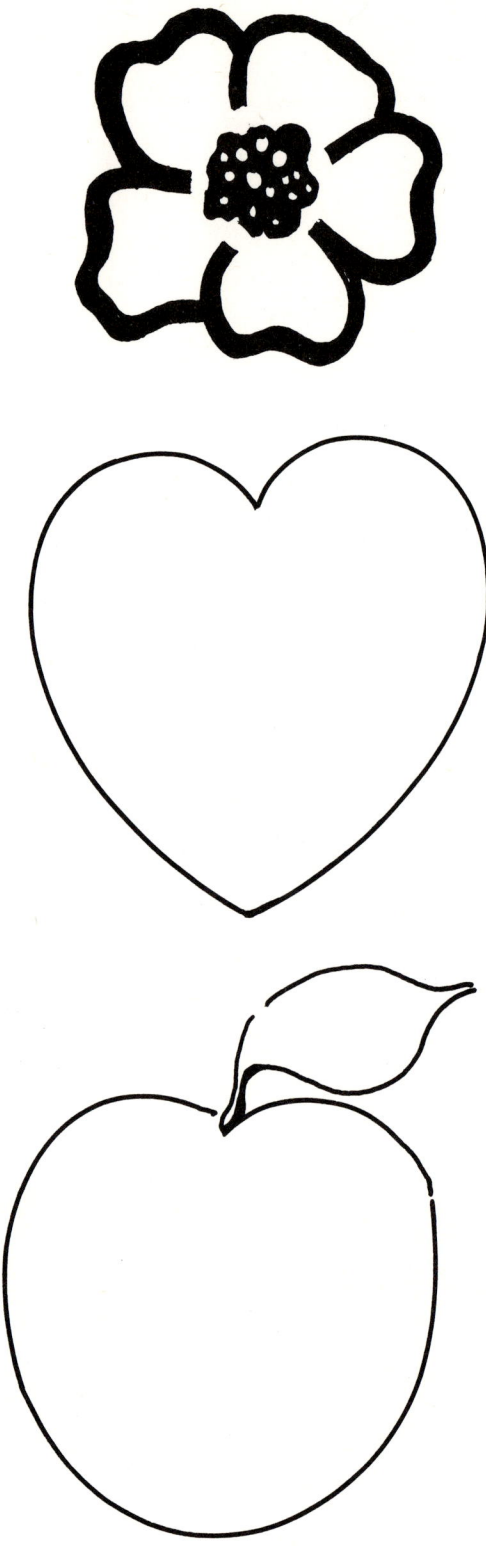

# Appliqué Gifts

1. Cat cushion in flower print and felt.
2. Gingham whale on a headscarf.
3. Gift stockings.
4. Bib with baby bull.
5. Felt Brick with appliqué and embroidery.

cushion

headscarf

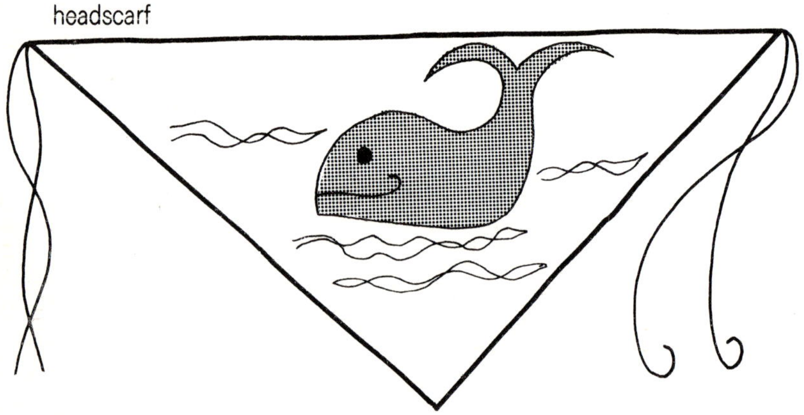

gift stockings

bib

brick

# Appliqué Box

On the next page, you will see how to make up your own box and cover it. This is a box which contained doll's house furniture. Only the lid has been covered, using blue linen, by overlapping the material and gluing it inside. The appliqué is felt and is glued on. I made a sketch of the picture and then traced off each part to use as a pattern. Cutting must be very accurate so that all the pieces fit together. Where some pieces are laid over others, glue down the underneath pieces first. This picture was inspired by a drawing in a colouring book. You can find all kinds of ideas for this type of appliqué in story books, comics, and greeting cards.

# Making and Covering a Box

Cut and score card for box in required size and cut lid $\frac{1}{8}$ in larger than the base all round. Cut material as shown and sew corners. Turn material with corner hems inside and insert the box—the sewn material will hold edges together or you can tape them. Cover lid with plain and contrast material, inserting a strip of material or tape into one long seam. Glue strip to inside of box. Make lining in contrast material in the same way as for the outer covering but turn through with corner seams outside. Place this in the box and neatly hem all round.

This covered box can have a patchwork or appliqué lid, adapting any of the designs in this book. A loop and button can be added for fastening.

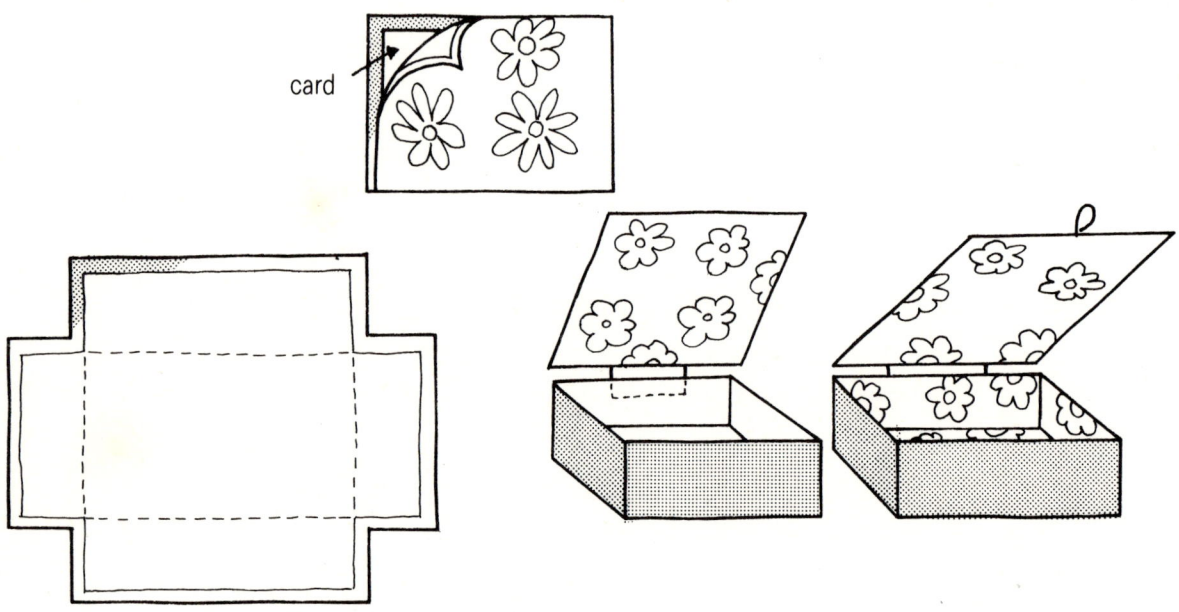

# Covering a Book

You will need a piece of material the size of your book opened out flat, with ½ in turnings all round. Cut a piece of lining material the same size and sew them together, right sides facing. Turn through and sew opening. Make pockets for the book jacket in the same way and sew to each end of the cover. If appliqué design is sewn, rather than glued, you must do this before making up.

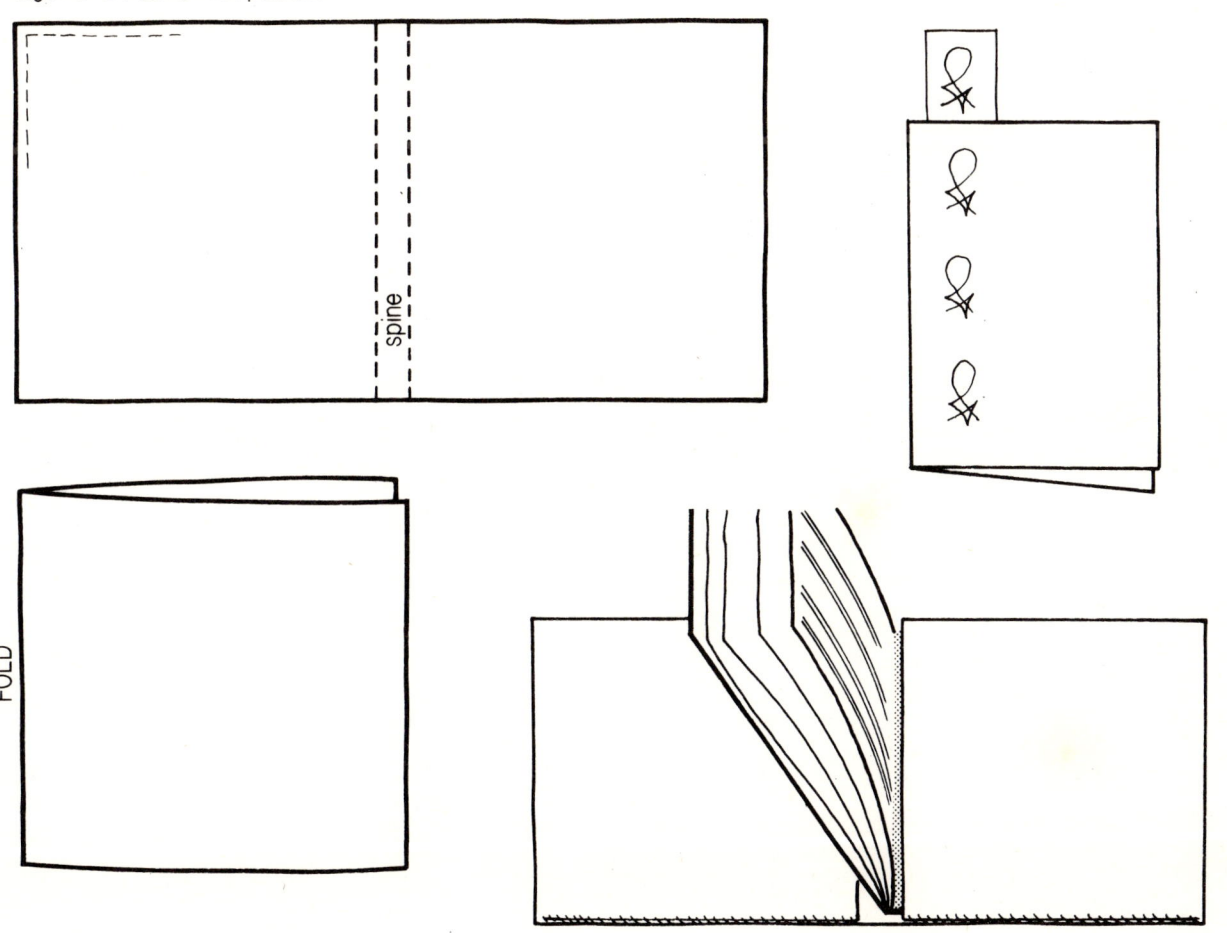

Sew fabric lining together Do same with pockets

# Little Appliqué

1. Seed bags in striped fabric have tape handles and felt appliqué.

2. Felt comb case with caterpillar and flowers in felt.

3. Simple bag-shape pencil case in fabric or felt with felt cowboy, cactus and sun.

4. A greetings card—for Easter perhaps? Gingham is glued to card, with felt appliqué—white egg shell, yellow chick, blue egg cup.

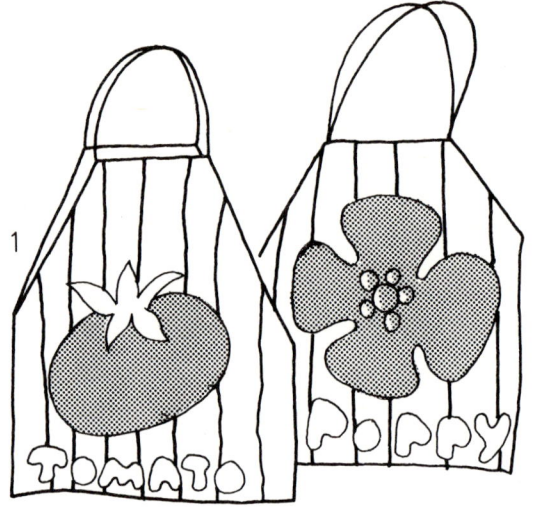
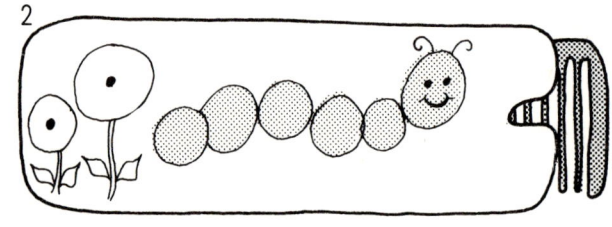

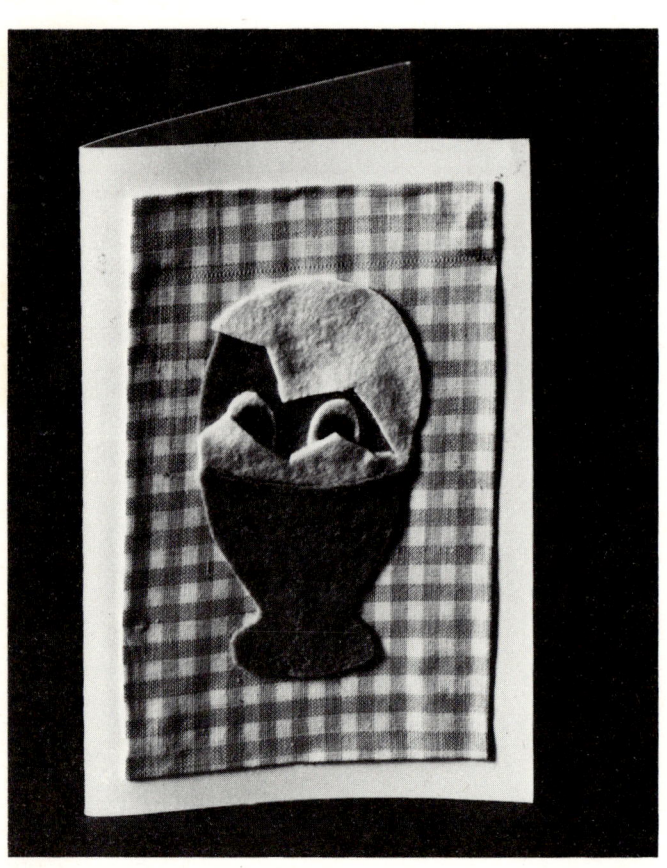

# Appliqué on Clothes

Appliqué on clothes. Always fashionable and lots of fun. Here are some ideas for you to copy.

# Appliqué Pictures

One of the most popular uses for appliqué is for pictures. As well as being able to use a greater variety of materials, it is also possible to use beads, sequins and other trimmings. Beads add much to the flower picture in the photograph on this page for example. Light padding has been used to give the petals, which have not been hemmed, a raised look. Couched wool gives a strong outline to the flowers. Also in the photograph you will see a different type of flower picture. Small panels of card have been covered with cotton material and glued to a backing. Felt flowers and leaves, with green wool stems, have been glued on to the panels. The bowler-hatted, pipe-smoking gentleman has also been made of felt. A piece of white wool gives the effect of smoke. The colour picture shows a lady with a felt profile, face and hand, wool hair and a scrap of lace for her head-dress. Each part of her dress has been cut separately and sewn to the backing to give dimension. The skirt is made as an ordinary skirt would be, and then flattened and draped and sewn to the backing. Ribbon bows and a small apron are added. See Techniques of Appliqué on page 6 for hints on appliqué methods.

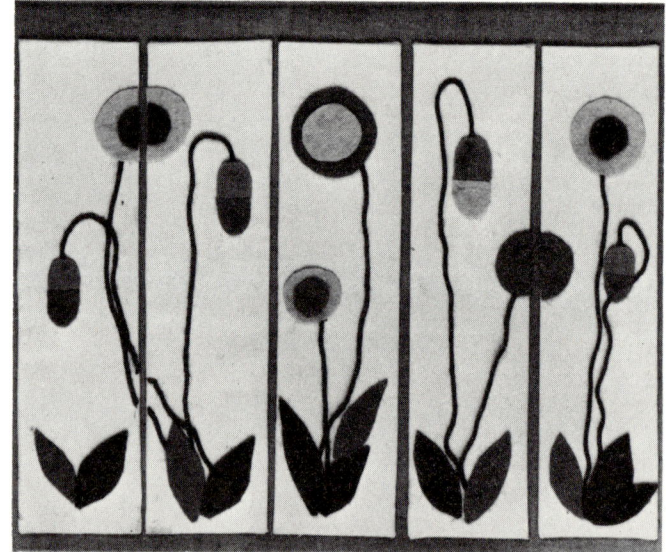

Opposite you will see more designs for appliqué pictures. The house has pockets with zips and poppers to contain favourite small items. The narrow wall hanging has an Origami-type Japanese lady sewn to it. See diagram for arranging her cotton print dress. The Father Christmas picture has gift-wrapping pockets in stripes and flower prints, complete with ribbons.

The cat all tangled up in the wool is white felt on a grey and white stripe cotton background. The 'ball of wool' is made with red and white stripe cotton with red wool strands. Birds and flowers make a pretty motif for a wall hanging with wool and bead tassels in varying lengths. The picture is made in felt.

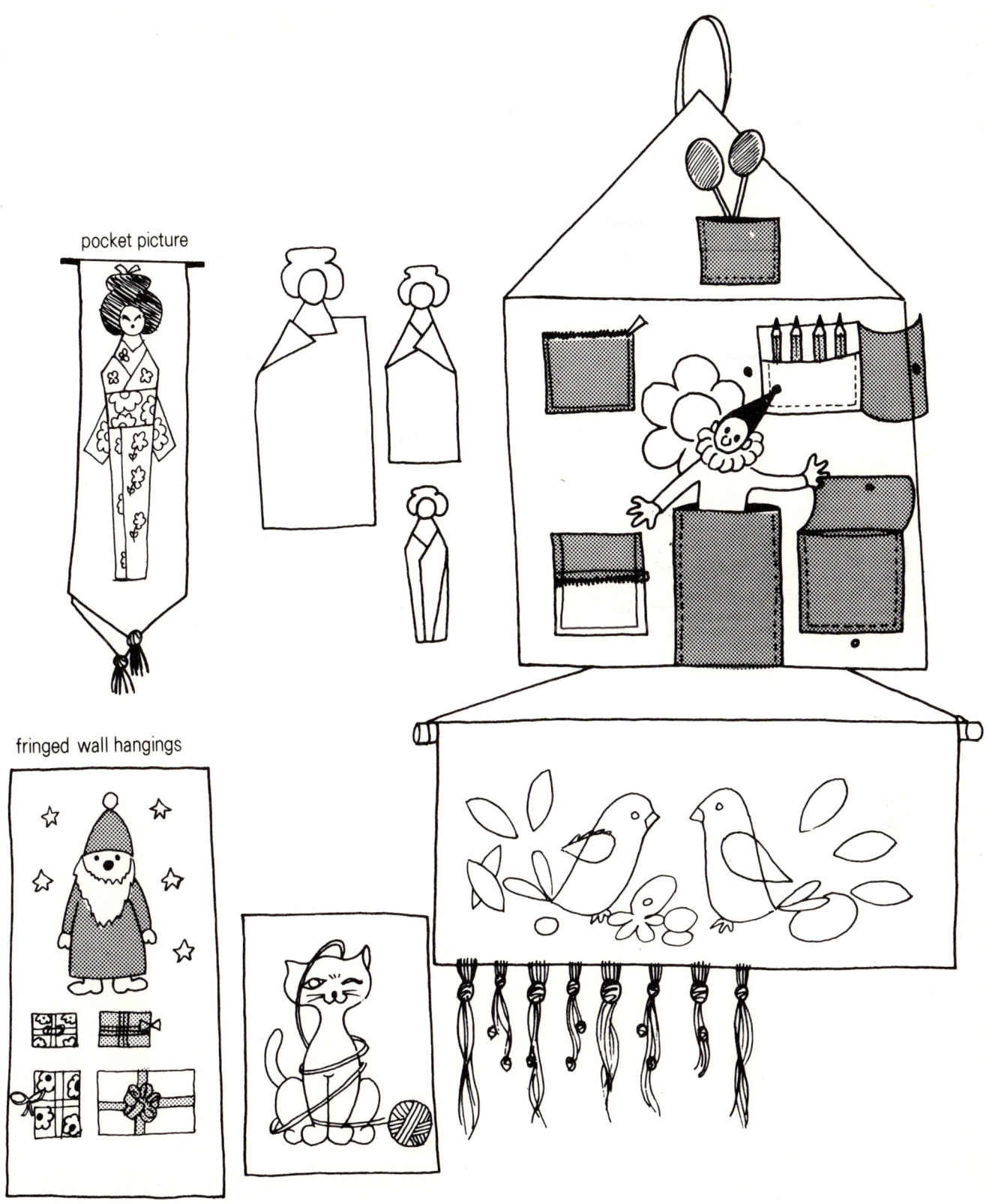

pocket picture

fringed wall hangings

45-3

# Mounting Pictures

Your photograph may be professionally framed as is the lady in the photograph, or you can mount your picture yourself. Canvas stretchers, sold by art suppliers, are strong but light and you will need a good hem all round your picture to staple to the wood. Eyelet screws in the back are used with a cord for hanging. Another method is to stitch on a backing fabric with card inserted and fabric loops for a rod to pass through. The rod is suspended by a cord.

Or you can mount your picture on thin plywood or very firm card, lacing the material at the back and then covering it with paper or fabric. A cord sewn at the back will suffice for hanging. Remember that mounting your picture well will add to its decorative effect.

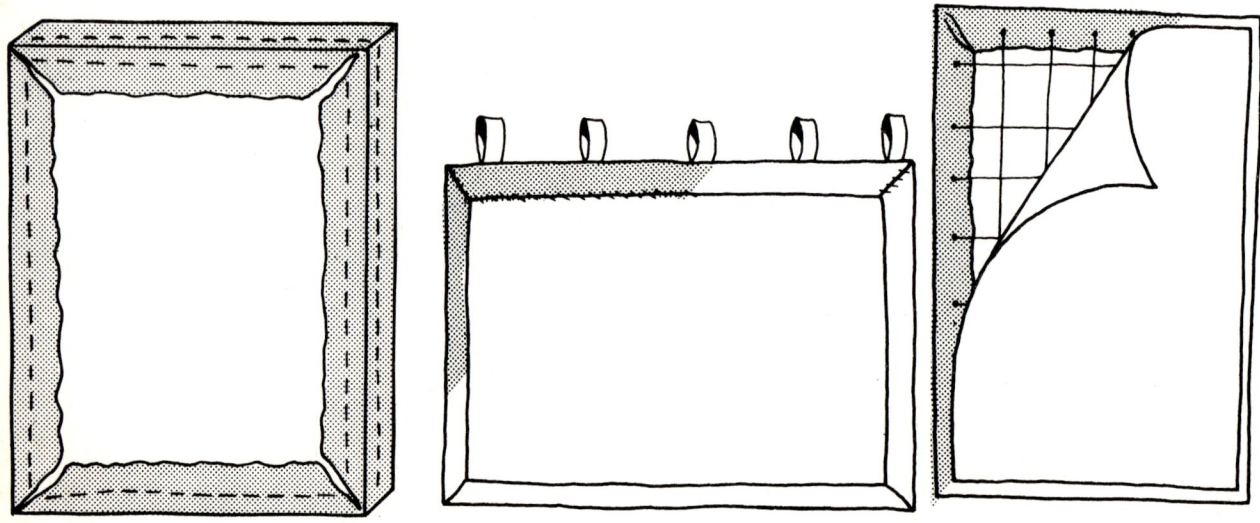

# Box Tote

This box tote is made using the same method as for covered boxes. However, here card and felt have been used with felt handles and felt appliqué motifs glued to the sides. Here you can see a house, tree and clouds (blue would make a good background colour). At the side shown here, flowers have been added. These motifs can either be repeated on the other sides or other motifs used. Since you do not need to hem felt, cut this and the card the same size.

# LEATHER & FUR CRAFTS

The luxury of fur and real leather hardly needs stressing. Leather is pliable and strong, durable and beautiful, while fur is the most spoilt-darling, deliciously soft, fabulous-looking way of keeping warm.

Today, through the ingenuity of manufacturers and modern techniques, there is a stunning variety of 'fake' furs and leathers. There is no living animal which has not been represented in one medium or the other. Indeed, some fakes are not really fakes at all, since they represent no known animal!

But whether leather and fur are real or fake, there are so many things to be made in them, apart from clothes.

Belts and bags, and purses and slippers. A fake fur hat, a green painted frog. Toys in fur and leather, a fun-fake waistcoat in fur and leather, fur mittens, even jewellery in leather and suede. Wallets and bookcovers and boxes and pencil cases and picture frames and more toys—you will surely love Fake Snake.

Leather is no longer a dull collection of shades of brown. There are paints for leather which are vivid and easy to apply. Cut thongs from brightly painted leather and try some of the attractive lacing. Or have a fling with fringing, or studs. Appliqué yourself with initials and flowers. Enjoy the added pleasure of embossing designs on things you make.

Make beautiful gifts, in fur or leather, for yourself or others, and take pleasure in the materials you make them in, and the skill you employ.

# Skins and Things

**Basic Tools**
1. Sharp shears for cutting.
2. Sharp knife for cutting and skiving.
3. Metal ruler for use with cutting knife.
4. Tracing wheel for evenly marked spaces for sewing.
5. Punch pliers—has revolving wheel with six different size punches.
6. An awl, if you prefer, to use instead of punch pliers.
7. Thonging tool—has three prongs for making slits for thongs.
8. Hammer—to use with thonging tool, awl, embossing.
9. Strong leather glue, rubber cement.
10. A wooden board—to cut on, to emboss on.
11. Glover's needles—have very sharp wedge-shaped points. Also, lacing needles with large eyes for threading laces and thongs.
12. Threads—silk threads, linen thread, button hole twist, mercerized thread. These should be drawn through beeswax. String, long shoe laces, even wool, can be used.
13. Needles. Ordinary needles can be used for fake furs which have knitted backing, but glover's needles are used for real fur.

## About Leather—Real and Fake

Real leather is the tanned skin of animals. Tanning is the process of softening and preparing the animal hide. Large skins can be shaved to obtain an even thickness, or if the skin is thick enough it may be split. The grain side of split skin is leather, while suede is the fleshside which is buffed and dyed. Some suedes have a 'nap'—that is the fibres all go in one direction. If this is so, you will have to cut all your pattern pieces also going in one direction. Calfskin is ideal for embossed work and is fine grained and flexible. Goatskin is soft and supple, as is sheepskin, though the latter is somewhat thicker. Pigskin is very popular for its distinctive look and durability. Steerhide is rather tough and stiff and is best split. Snakeskin is exactly what the name implies, and these skins are as distinctive as they are varied. The split, flesh-side of a Chamois goatskin is known as chamois. However, other soft, similarly coloured skins of small animals are also termed chamois. Is it, or isn't it? It looks like it—and yet. Well, sometimes the eye does deceive, and with the ingenuity of our age, one of the greatest deceivers is imitation leather, suede and even snakeskin. You can buy it in standard widths by the yard. Unlike most fakes it is accepted, often proudly admitted. Some imitation not only looks like leather, but feels like leather. How is it done? Most imitation leathers are created by coating a base fabric with plastic film. This surface can be shiny and stiff, or soft textured like real leather. Some fakes have a layer of foam rubber inserted between film and fabric. Another type is fabric, heated and polished and sometimes embossed with a grain. Imitation suede is made by covering a fabric surface with glue and dusting it with fibres. The backing fabric of fake leather is woven or knitted.

## Fur and Fake

A mink coat is beyond the means and dreams of most of us, but any real fur has a luxurious quality, difficult to resist. Furs can be long haired, like Fox, or short and shaggy like sheepskin or Persian Lamb. Furs like sheepskin and Persian Lamb have no nap, while long, straight haired fur has a definite direction. Fur is composed of the skin, which is leather, short hairs for warmth and long hairs for protection. The hair side is known as the face, and the way the hair lies is the grain. Fur has to be very carefully cut. To avoid cutting the hair, lay the fur face down, and using a sharp craft knife, cut the skin downwards while raising the fur from the surface. The hair will separate itself. Small pieces of fur can be sewn together from the back without seams showing. The fur pieces can be all the same type and colour, or you can achieve an attractive patchwork effect. It would be expensive to make large items in fur, but you can use fur together with leather, suede or suitable fabric.

Fake furs have a woven or knit backing which may be acrylic, polyester or cotton. The pile may be wool, rayon, nylon or various other synthetics. The pile can be fibres glued to the backing, using slightly longer fibres than for fake suede, or yarns can be woven into the backing in a similar way to tufted wool rugs. The loops can be cut or not. The pile can be sheared and polished to give a smooth glossy look like the appliqué waistcoat photographed later in the book. Fake furs can be permanently brushed to imitate the way a particular animal's fur lies. It can be dyed and printed to simulate the real thing, or it can be dyed in bright or pastel colours. Like fake leather, imitation fur can be bought by the yard, often in widths up to 60 in. Cutting long-haired fake fur is the same as for real fur. For short-haired fakes you can cut the backing with scissors, taking care not to cut the pile.

Many of the items in this book which are shown made in leather, can be made in fur and vice versa. Leather purses and bags, the fake snake and moccasins can be made in fur. The fur hat, mittens and slippers can equally be made in leather. Or combine the two, where suitable. More information for sewing leather and fur can be found on pages 42 and 43.

3–4

# Sewing and Lacing Leather

Sewing. Running stitch is quite suitable for sewing leather, but the stitches must be kept small and even. A plain back stitch can also be used. The neatest and most widely used is saddle stitch. For this you will need two threaded needles—glover's needles for real (or thick fake) leather. Stitch first needle from front to back and then second needle from back to front. Pull threads taut and repeat as before. Continue in this way until seam is finished. Lacing. Use a thonging tool to make slits or make holes with a punch. Cut a point on end of thong. Thongs can be bought, or cut as described below.

(a) Simple oversewn lacing.
(b) Oversewn with two colours.
(c) Cross lacing. Oversewn one way. Second thong oversewn in opposite direction through same slits.
(d) Couched lacing. Oversewn thong over contrast strip.
(e) Slanted lacing.
(f) Straight lacing.

Thongs can be cut from circles of leather 5 in or more in diameter. Begin cutting from the outside edge and spiral in, keeping the thong an even width.

Always round off corners to be laced. Glue ends of thongs inside work.

Eyelets and Grommets (the larger version) are also used for decorative lacing and come with a fixing tool. You can use them not only for closing, but for a decoration—on a pocket for example, or on the front of a plain dress or skirt. Side seams can also be made attractive with lacing over them.

Studs are another form of decoration and useful for strengthening corners of pockets. The prongs are pushed through to the back of the material and then bent over.

Hammer-on Snaps. These are ideal fastenings for leather and are applied with a special tool. For details of sewing fur see pages 42 and 43.

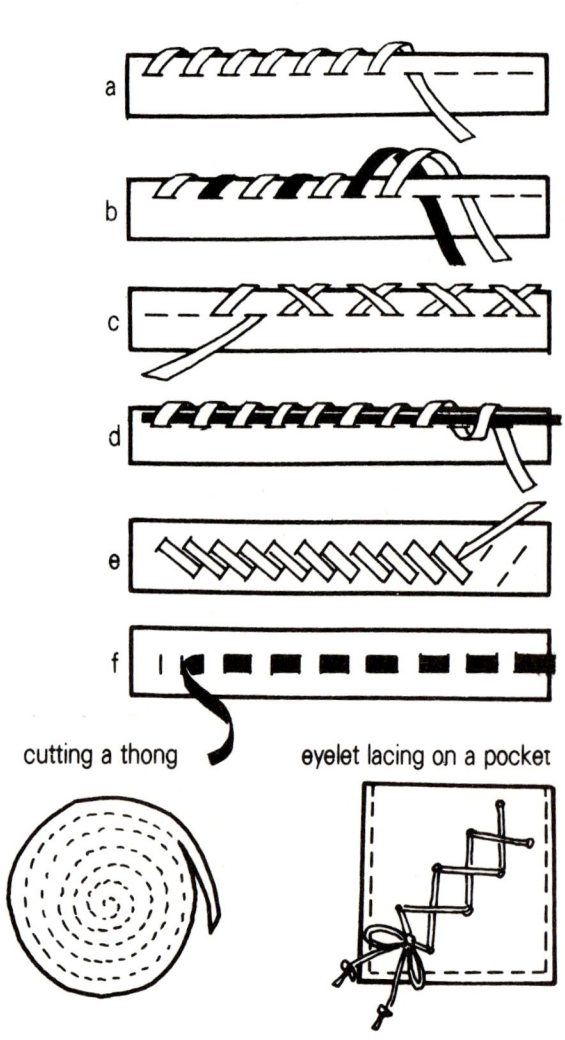

cutting a thong

eyelet lacing on a pocket

# Skiving and Decorating

Skiving. To make a neat flat overlap, both ends of the leather should be skived. This is done by holding the leather face down on a hard surface and, using a sharp knife, shaving or paring away thin layers of the leather at the edge. The edge may also be gently hammered, laying a piece of card over the leather to prevent marking.

Embossing. This is purely decorative, and is easy and satisfying to do. Large headed nails can be filed into different shapes, and you can use small blocks of very hard wood, like pinewood. The leather must be damped (not soaked) all over, to prevent water marks. You will need a small hammer and a board to place the leather on. When using wooden stamps, soak briefly in water and then dry them. Hold the stamp vertically on the leather and strike it sharply with the hammer. A linking tool and ruler can be used to make straight line designs.

Appliqué. Another form of decoration and effective for leather and suede as it does not have edges which will fray. There are many examples of it in this book for you to copy. The cut-out shapes should be positioned with fabric glue or rubber cement and can then be hand sewn.

Painting leather. The painted leather items in this book were done with shoe paints which come in a great variety of colours. The applicator gives a smooth even colour and finish, and you should paint and allow it to dry before cutting out. Acrylic paints can be used with fine brushes for painting detail if you wish; and felt tip pens are also effective. You cannot emboss or paint fur or fake fur, but you can certainly decorate it. There are textile crayons on the market—you draw with them on paper then transfer the design to fabric by ironing like a transfer. I have found that this worked very well on a short-piled fake fur-fabric. A little furry jacket with flowers on it would look very pretty. The colour does not penetrate the depth of the pile, just the tips being coloured. This gives a pretty soft effect.

Fur and fakes look good trimmed with leather or suede as you can see in the Clothes section.

5–4

# Some Small Items – Leather and Suede

1. Comb case. Comb size. Made and thonged in suede.
2. Purse. Cut out shape in suede and felt. Cut slit in suede only. Lay felt on suede, fold up and thong sides and around flap.
3. Visiting Card Case. Made and thonged in suede.
4. Notecase. Straight piece of suede $8\frac{3}{4}$ in x $3\frac{3}{4}$ in (20·5 cm x 8 cm). Fold $1\frac{1}{2}$ in (3·7 cm) each end and thong sides with suede.
5a. Bookmark. Suede strip with cut fringe and contrast suede heart glued to it.
5b. Bookmark. Corner-of-envelope type. Suede with contrast suede heart glued to it, and suede thonging.
6. Small notebook. Length of notebook opened out plus 2 in (5 cm) turn up ($\frac{1}{4}$ in (7 mm) glued at sides) x width plus $\frac{1}{2}$ in (13 mm). Made in leather with felt lining. Punch out holes, then glue to felt. Punch holes in contrast (or painted leather) and glue small spots into holes.
7. Pochette. Leather. 10 in x $7\frac{1}{2}$ in (25 cm x 18 cm) piece of leather with $3\frac{1}{2}$ in (7·7 cm) folded up. Stitch up sides of pocket and around flap. Fasten with press-studs. Suede initials are stitched on flap.
8. Needle Case. Leather with thin felt lining. Main part 12 in x $3\frac{1}{2}$ in (30·4 cm x 7·7 cm). Pocket $2\frac{1}{4}$ in x $3\frac{1}{2}$ in (5·7 cm x 7·7 cm). Two pieces felt for needles 7 in x 3 in (18 cm x 7·5 cm). Fold leather and mark position for press stud. Fix press stud. Stitch centre channel of pocket, and felt for needles (folded) to felt lining. Glue lining to leather and thong with leather all round.

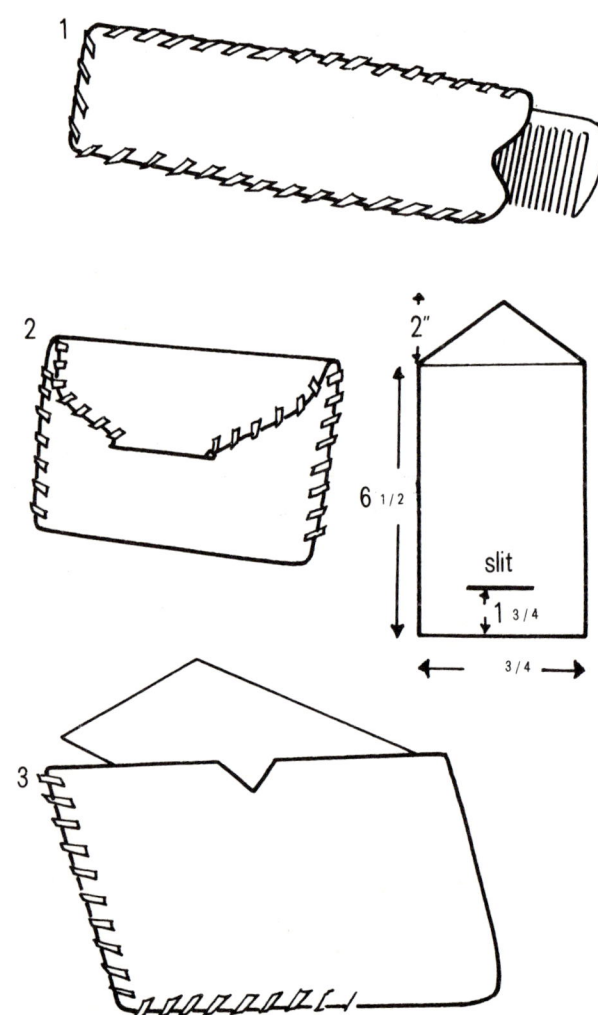

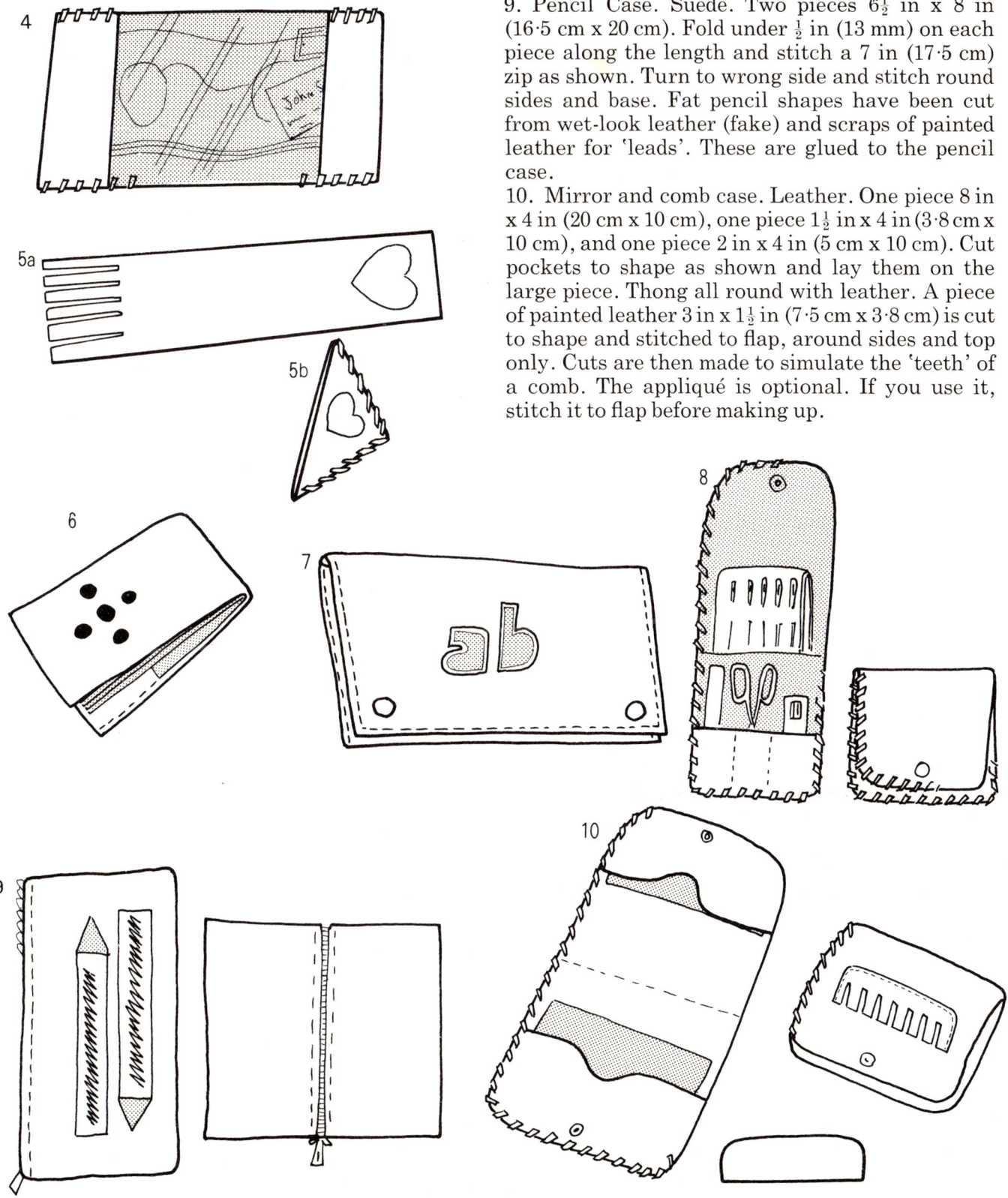

9. **Pencil Case.** Suede. Two pieces 6½ in x 8 in (16·5 cm x 20 cm). Fold under ½ in (13 mm) on each piece along the length and stitch a 7 in (17·5 cm) zip as shown. Turn to wrong side and stitch round sides and base. Fat pencil shapes have been cut from wet-look leather (fake) and scraps of painted leather for 'leads'. These are glued to the pencil case.

10. **Mirror and comb case.** Leather. One piece 8 in x 4 in (20 cm x 10 cm), one piece 1½ in x 4 in (3·8 cm x 10 cm), and one piece 2 in x 4 in (5 cm x 10 cm). Cut pockets to shape as shown and lay them on the large piece. Thong all round with leather. A piece of painted leather 3 in x 1½ in (7·5 cm x 3·8 cm) is cut to shape and stitched to flap, around sides and top only. Cuts are then made to simulate the 'teeth' of a comb. The appliqué is optional. If you use it, stitch it to flap before making up.

# Jewellery in Leather and Suede

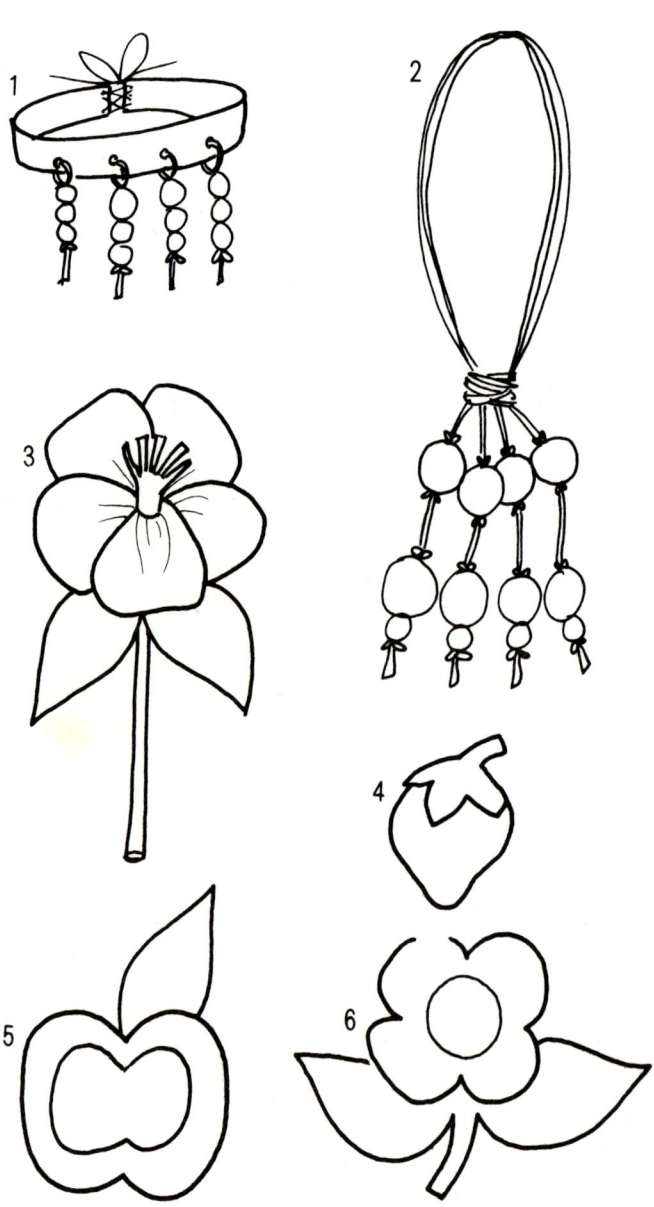

1. Suede neckband with laced edges. Four holes are punched at the front, and suede thongs are looped through them, with beads knotted onto them.
2. Leather thong and bead necklace. Two strands about 20 in (51 cm) long knotted at front with large beads knotted on to the strands.
3. Suede flower brooch. The stem is a piece of suede 1¼ in x 4 in (3 cm x 10 cm). Roll and give up to 1 in from top. Cut slits into top and fan out. Cut petal shapes from suede and wrap and glue round stem. Cut two leaf shapes and glue to back of flower. Sew pin to back.

    Brightly painted scraps of leather are used to make these brooches.
4. A bright red strawberry with green leaf and stem glued to it. Small felt shapes with pins sewn to them are glued to the back of these brooches for fastening.
5. A red apple with yellow centre shape glued to it. A green leaf is glued to back edge.
6. A blue flower with white centre glued to it. Green leaves and stem are cut in one piece and glued to the back.
7. Shiny wet-look leather (fake) heart-shaped locket is cut double, slightly stuffed and stitched round. A loop is inserted into seam and a thong threaded through loop for necklace.
8. A silver leather fish, cut double and glued together with narrow loop inserted between. Can be hung on thong, cord or chain.
9. A suede thong necklace has suede 'beads' made by cutting small strips of suede and wrapping and glueing them around the thong.
10. A pretty necklace made up of tan leather, bright orange wool and orange, pale pink and white beads. Cut the pendant shape twice and

glue them together back to back. Punch four holes at top and three at bottom of pendant. Take four long strands of wool. Pass two ends through the first hole marked 1 and knot at back. Pass two ends through hole 2 and knot at back. Knot four strands a little way up, then thread 5 beads on two strands and 5 on the other two strands. Make a knot. Bring ends of wool round and repeat on holes 3 and 4. With a macramé knot fix one strand of wool to 1st hole at base. Thread 5 beads on each strand and knot together leaving ends loose. Repeat for other two, only on the centre hole use 2 strands. You will need 50 beads.

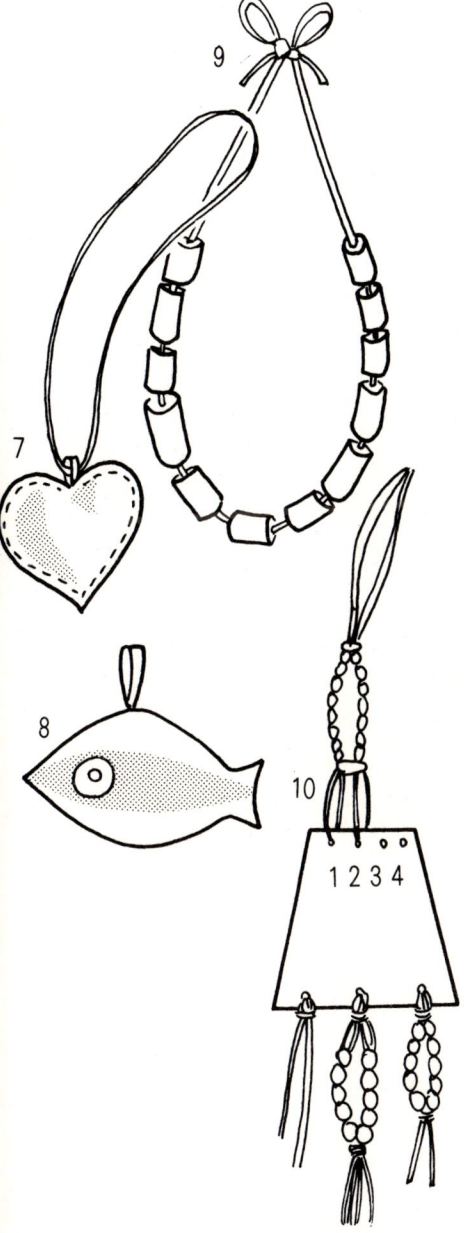

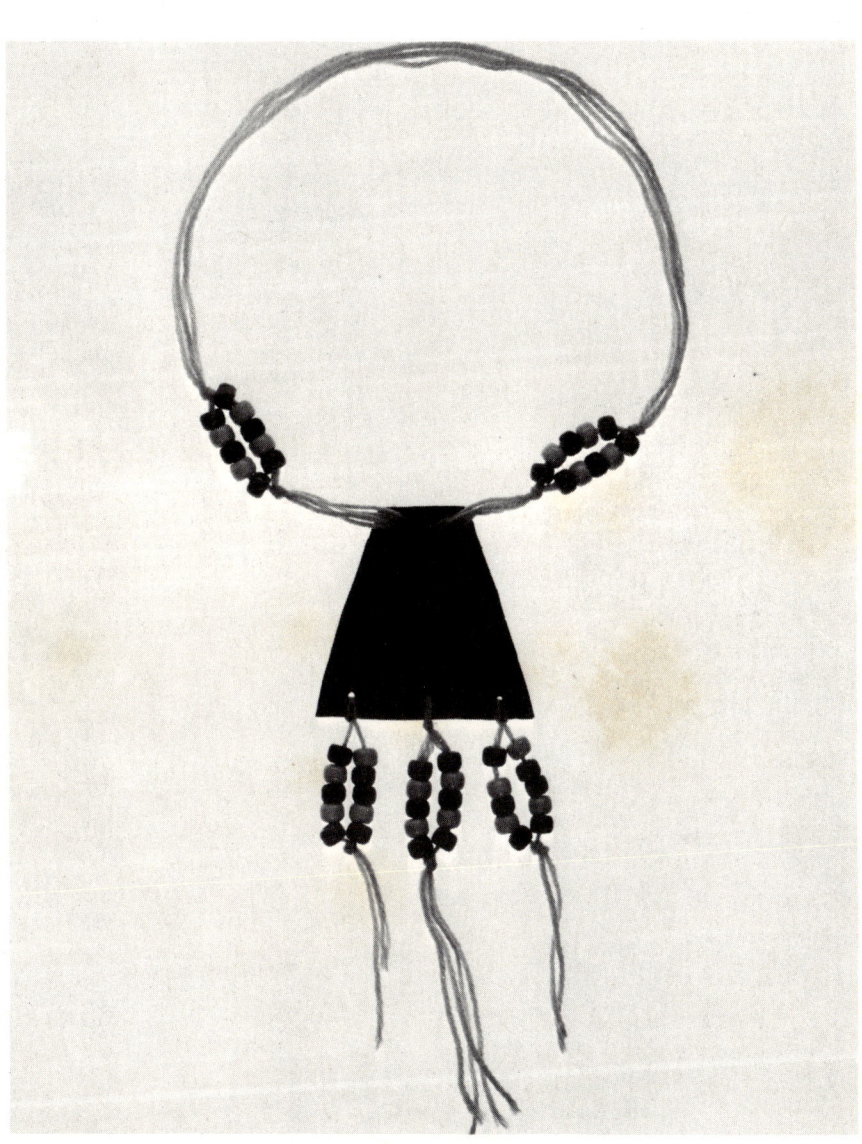

# Chamois Sewing Doll

The prettiness of this useful little doll is enhanced by the use of soft chamois leather. You can make it any size you like. Her body is a card tube wrapped in chamois which is glued. Tuck in at top and bottom and glue in place. Her head is a table-tennis ball or a larger wooden ball, depending on the size of doll, which is painted and glued to the body. Gather a skirt on to a waistband and sew this round the body. The arms are cut in a long strip, rounded for hands. Cut this piece double and glue together for firmness. The hat is a circular piece of chamois, gathered and stuffed, then glued to the head, making a neat little pin cushion. Tie a narrow strip round the neck in a bow at front. The thimble holder is a small roll of card covered with chamois. A straight piece is joined and then sewn to a small circle. Insert card and glue top edges of chamois inside. A second roll of card covered with chamois is glued to the back of the doll to contain crochet hook, knitting needles, scissors etc.

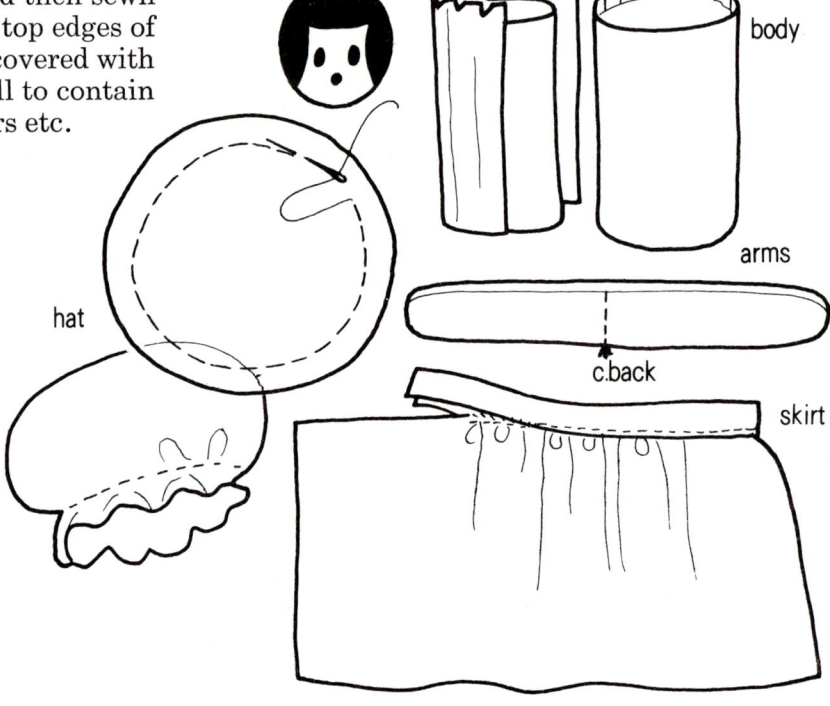

# Doll in Leather and Fur

This doll can be made in real leather and fur or look just as good made from 'fakes'. The head is a table tennis ball with painted eyes and mouth. The hair is fur cut to the shape shown to fit with pieces cut out to make darts. When glueing the fur to the head, you will need to shape it to fit. Bring the darts edge to edge and glue. The body is a half circle of card with a piece added (shaded area) for overlapping and glueing. A piece of leather is cut to this shape up to the broken line, and glued to the card cone edge to edge. A strip of fur is glued round the hem. The arms are made as for the chamois doll, but in leather, with small strips of fur glued round for cuffs. A red painted leather heart is glued to the body with the hands glued over it.

# Fur Bird

Fur Bird is simply a piece of rabbit fur wrapped around a roll of card—the card tube of a toilet roll has been used here. Hold the fur back loosely as you cover the roll and leave enough to tuck in and glue at the top and the base. As the hair of this fur is long it will give a continuous all-over furry look. A leather beak is cut as shown, folded and glued and then glued into the fur. Black beads are glued into the fur for eyes. The eyes and beak will swing about a bit since they are glued to loose fur, but the effect is quite amusing.

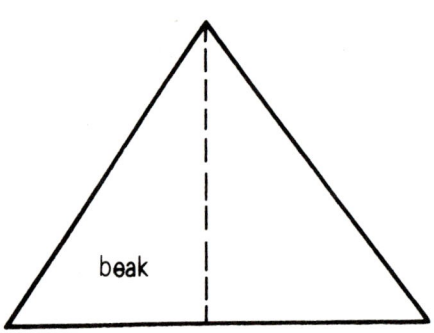

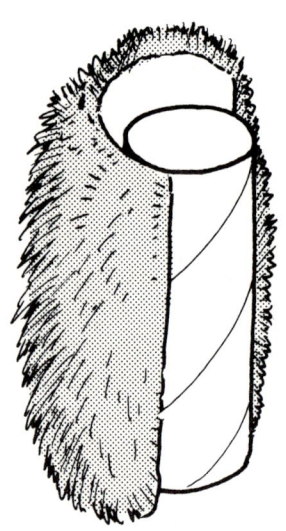

# Fur Mouse

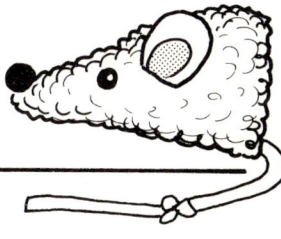

Is it, or isn't it? No, it can't be a real mouse as he is made of fake fur! A lovely, soft, creamy coloured, imitation. Using thin tracing paper, trace off the body pattern. Only half is given here so use the paper folded then cut out the shape and open it out. Trace off the base. Mark round the patterns on the underside of the fur and cut out carefully, holding back the fur at the edges so that the seams will not show when you sew it. Fold the body part in half, with the fur inside, and sew the upper body seam. Sew the base to the opening just half way round. Turn through, and with a pin pick out any fur that may be caught in the seams. Stuff the body firmly and sew up the opening. Cut out two white felt ears, and two smaller pink ones, and glue them together. Glue them into the fur. Cut a narrow strip of white felt, tie a knot in it—just for fun—and glue edge to base. Pink beads are sewn on for eyes and a black bead for nose.

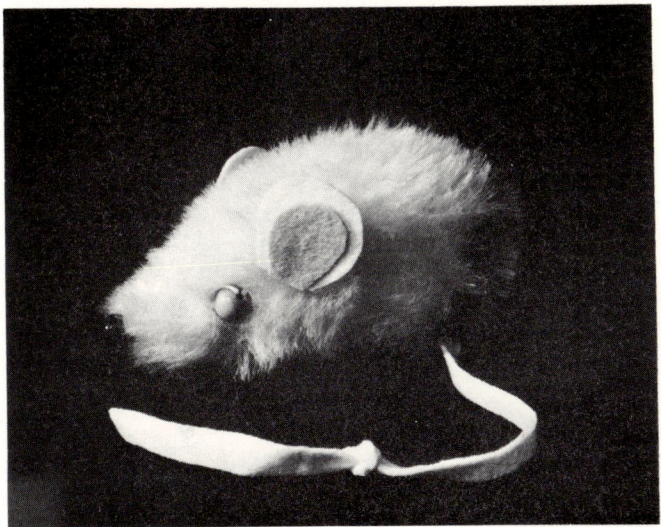

13–4

# Fake Snake

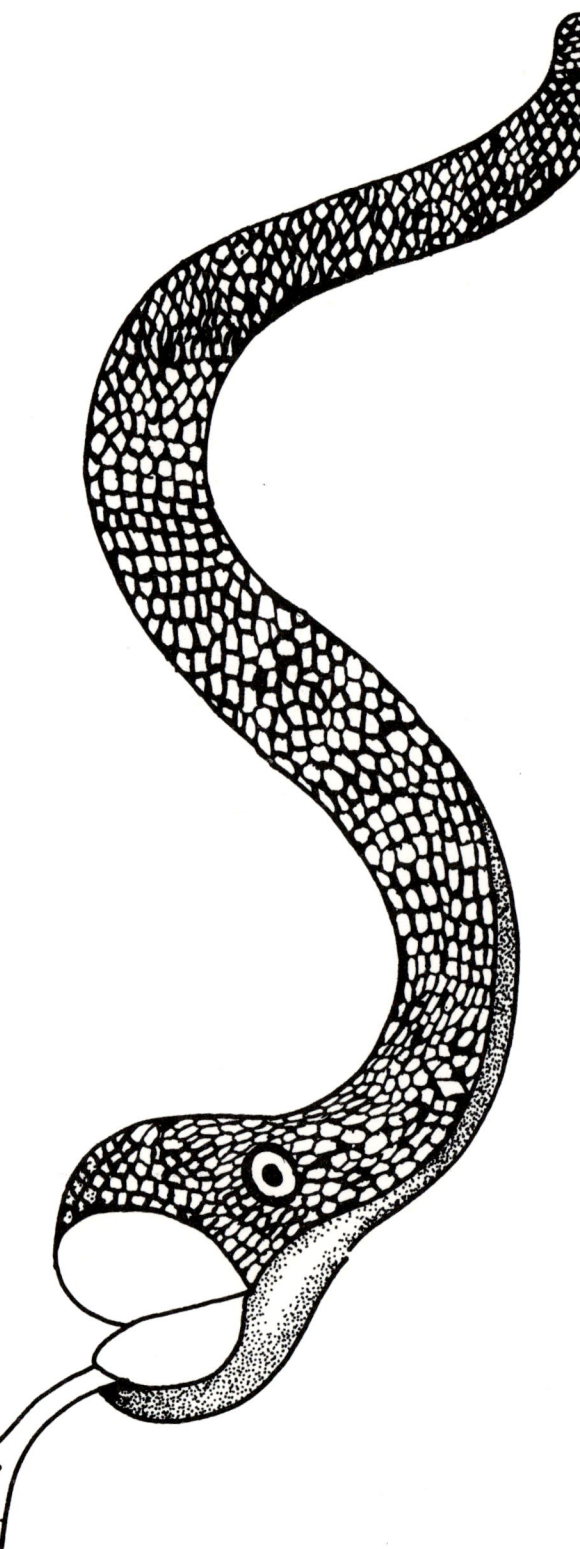

What a big mouth—still, fake snakes don't bite! It is impossible to get all of this reptile on to the page, but it is quite simple to make the pattern. The snake is 20 in (51 cm) long so you will need a piece of tracing paper at least that length. Trace off the body up to the broken line. Measure a 5 in (12·7 cm) space then trace off the half head pattern. Draw the upper line to meet the neckline. Turn the paper over, and trace the other side of the head—it should show through but if not you can pencil over it on the right side. Now draw the lower line to meet the neckline, so that you have one continuous snake shape. Be sure to make the space you have filled the same width as the rest. Across the head pattern you will see a broken line. Trace this on to your pattern. Now fold a piece of tracing paper and lay the fold against the broken line. Trace across this line and round the front head.

This is the mouth pattern.
Cut the upper body out of imitation snake-skin and the lower body out of chamois—you may have to join pieces of chamois to obtain the length. Open the mouth pattern flat and cut one shape in card and fold it; and one, plus turning, in pink felt. Overlap and glue the felt to the card. Place the body parts together, right sides facing, and sew all round leaving the front head—marked x—unstitched. Stuff the body very firmly up to this point. Insert the pink mouthpiece and sew neatly around lower edge. Stuff this area. Now sew half way round upper mouth to upper head and stuff this part. Hold the stuffing in as you sew up opening. Cut out a long red tongue like the one shown and sew it to the fold in the mouth. Cut out white felt circles and smaller green ones. Glue the green circles on to the white ones and glue the eyes to the head.

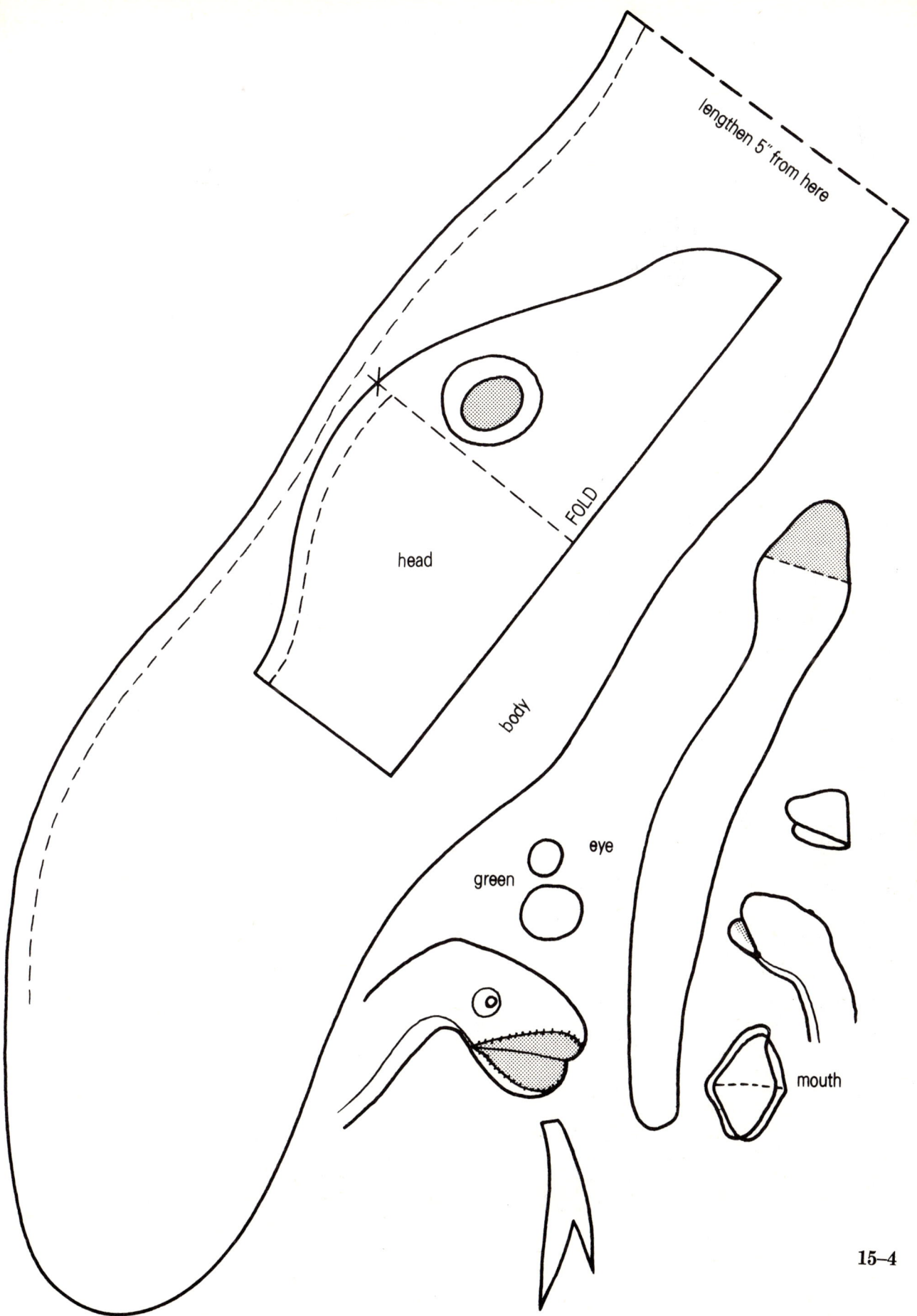

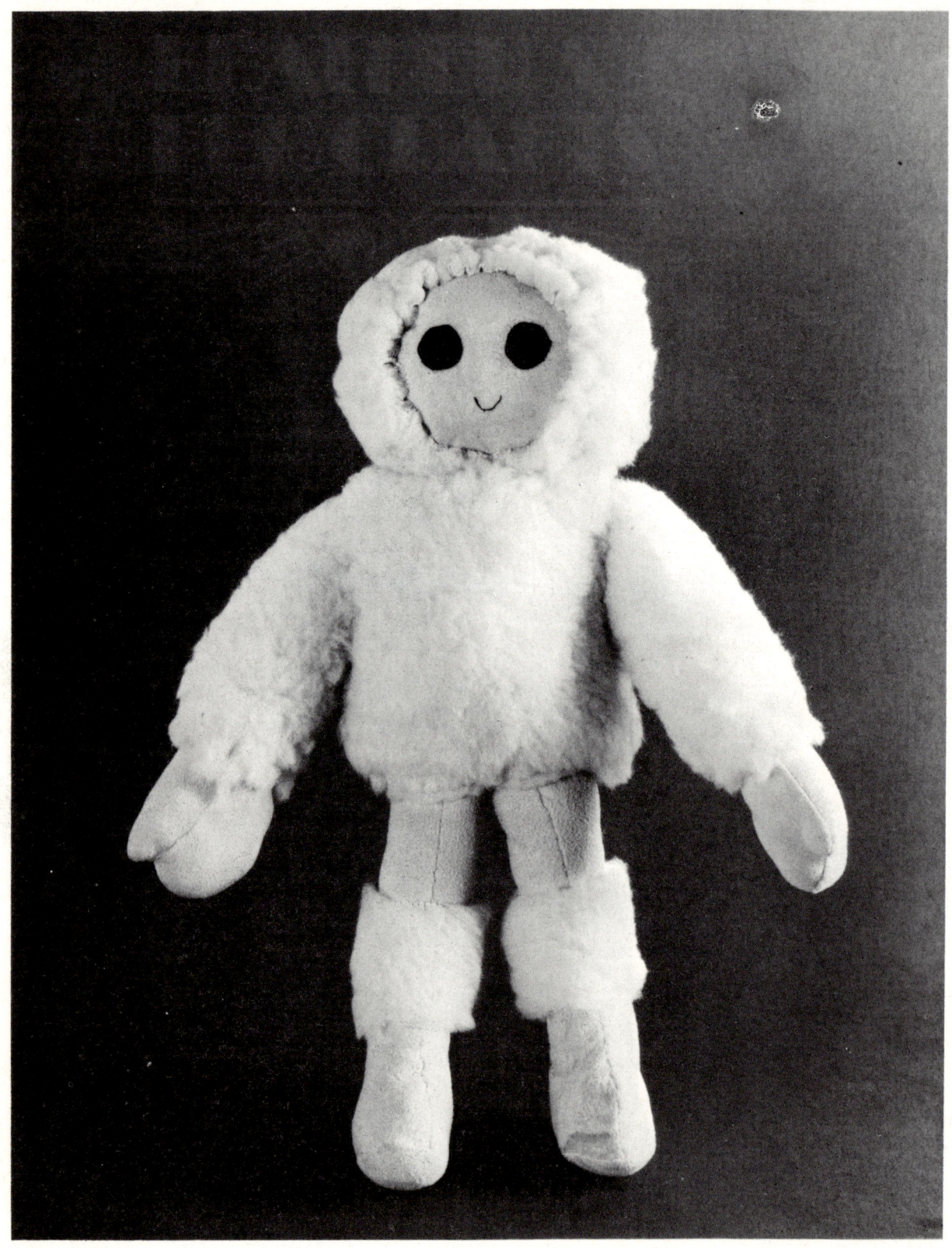

16–4

# Doll in Chamois and Fur

Chamois is ideal for dolls because it has such a soft 'skin' feel and look. This little Eskimo doll is particularly soft, being made in chamois and fur. The fur used here is fake but if you have some of the real thing (it doesn't need much), so much the better.
On the next page you will find the patterns and diagrams for making the doll. Each piece is clearly marked, and you make it up as you would a fabric doll.

The head. The back head, cut in fur is slightly larger than the face which is cut from chamois. Run a thread round the edge of the fur and gather it in to fit round the face. Stitch the two, fur inside, leaving an opening. Turn through and stuff, firmly, and sew on the opening. The felt circle eyes are glued on and the mouth is sewn. The body. The pattern for the body is on the fold. So fold a piece of tracing paper and trace the body. Cut out the pattern and open it out. This is cut twice from fur. The arm pattern is made and cut in the same way, twice, from fur. The hands and legs and soles are cut from chamois. Sew the body across both shoulders on wrong side. Open out flat. Lay the arms, fur facing fur, on the body, fold of arms at shoulder seam, and stitch down. Fold body and arms and stitch under arms and sides. Turn through and stitch head into neckline. Sew the hands in pairs and sew round them to arm edge. Stuff body and arms firmly and sew opening. Sew the legs together in pairs and sew the soles in. Turn legs through and stuff firmly. Flatten legs to have seams at back and front and sew top openings. Stitch legs to lower edge of body, holding back the fur as you go.
Finally, sew strips around both legs to indicate boot tops.

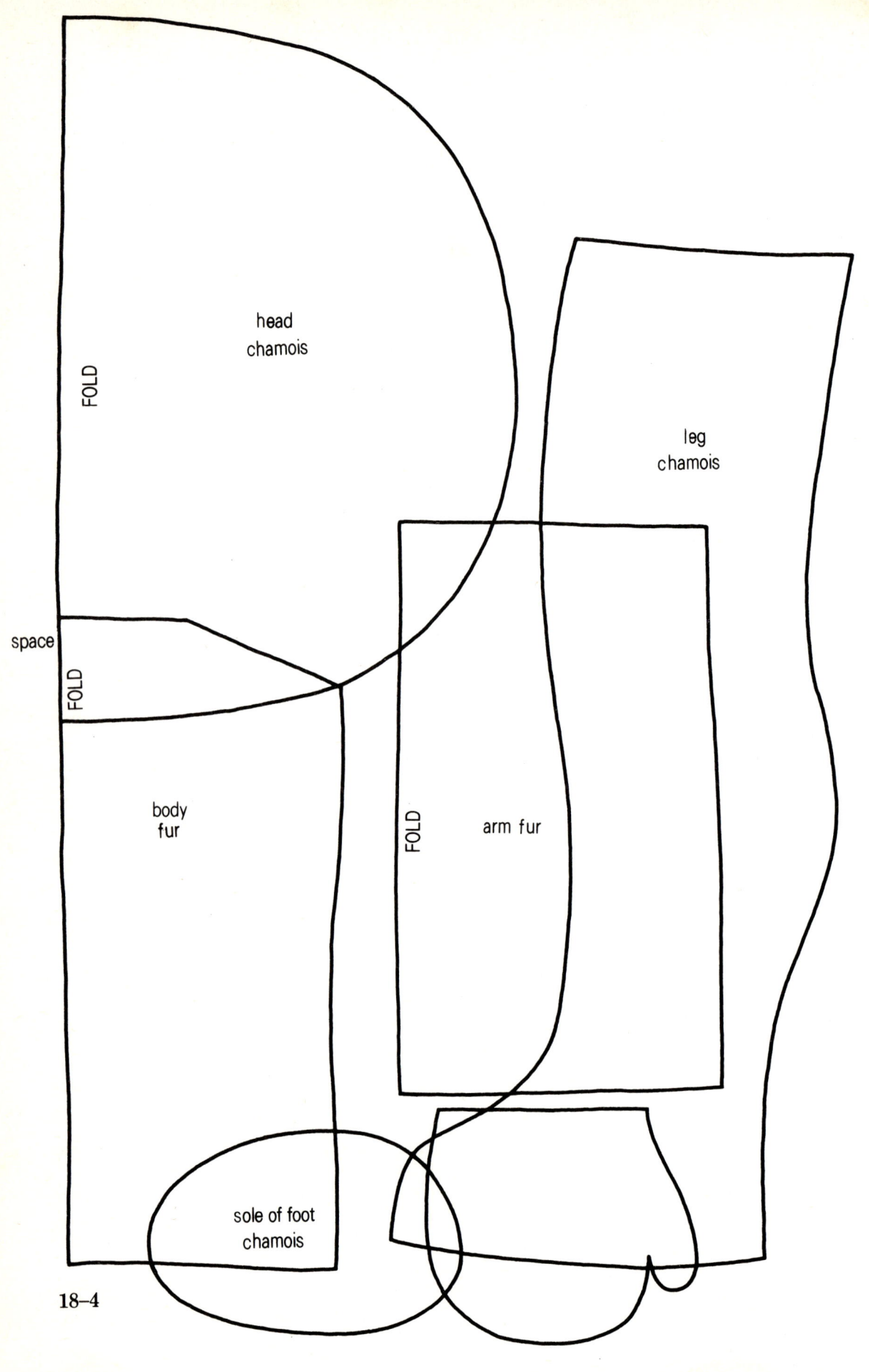
18-4

19-4

# Painted Leather Frog

This vivid green frog, which is a bean bag, is made out of imitation leather. It is the type produced by heating and polishing fabric to resemble leather and has an ideal, smooth, surface for painting. Bright green shoe leather paint has been used to paint a piece 11 x 10½ in (28 x 27 cm) for the upper body. The underbody is cut from a piece of chamois the same size.

Trace off the body pattern in the usual way. Cut one in fake leather (when the paint is thoroughly dry of course!) and one in chamois. The two parts are joined together, all round, working blanket stitch in green wool. You will not need to punch holes for this and can use an ordinary sewing needle. Leave an opening between the back legs and, through this, fill the frog with beans. Continue blanket stitch to close the opening. The eyes are two large black beads sewn to the wool chain stitch at the front edge of the head. You can see the vivid impact of the toy in the colour photograph.

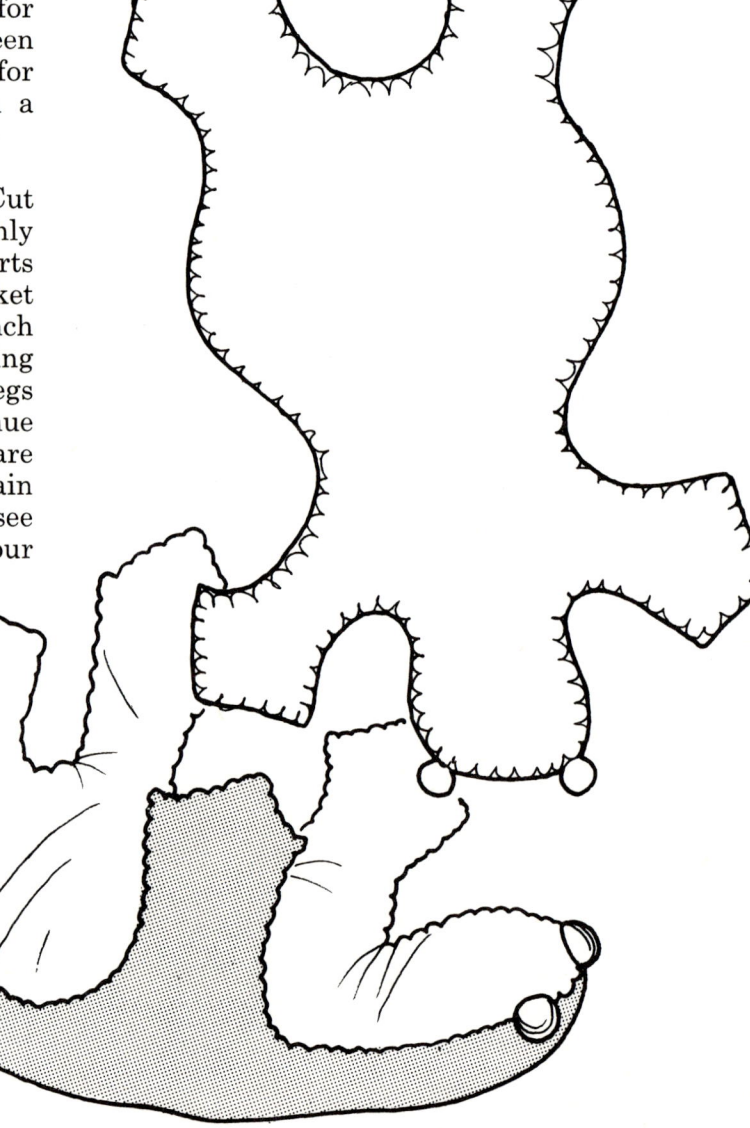

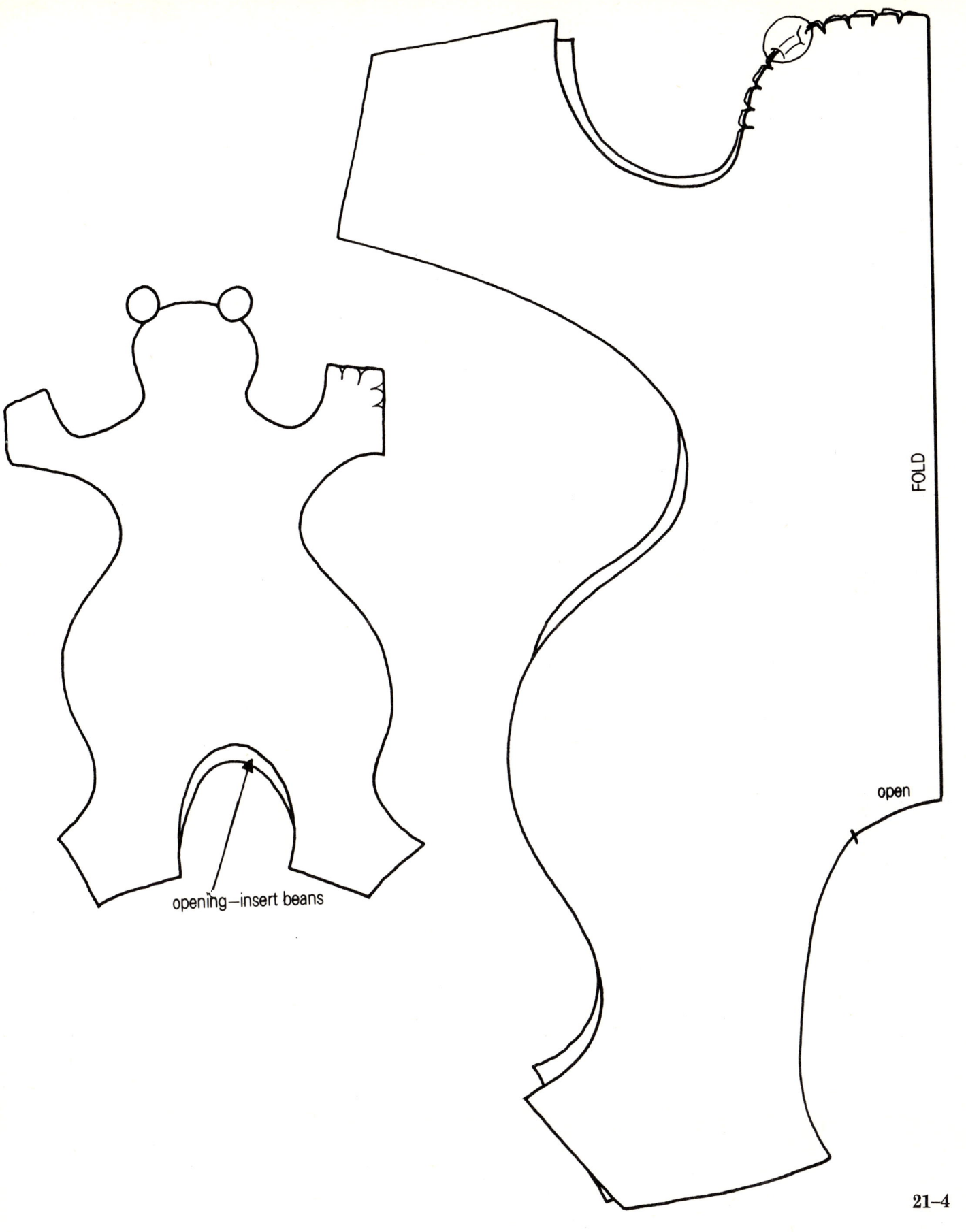

21–4

# Purses

1. Neat little zip-up purses, made in suede or leather. For each purse cut two 5 in (12·7 cm) squares. Fold under ½ in (13 mm) to wrong side on each piece along one edge. Stitch a 4 in (10 cm) zip between them as shown. Fold purse to wrong side and sew both edges. Open zip and turn through. You can do this with thin leather or suede. If your leather or suede is rather heavy, top stitch outer edge seams on outside. The appliqués are sewn on before making up purses.

2. Fringed leather or suede purse is cut in two pieces. The back piece is 11 x 4 in (28 x 10 cm), and the second piece is 8 x 4 in (20 x 10 cm) (shaded area in diagram). Cut the pieces to shape as shown. Sew a button on the front pocket and a buttonhole loop to top flap point. Lay pocket front on back piece and stitch round pocket only. Make cuts for fringe to just below stitch line.

3. Steam open the 'seams' of an unused envelope. Use this as a pattern for the third purse. You can make it in suede or leather, real or fake—in fact, it would look very effective in a brightly painted fake leather. The stitching is a little tricky as you will have to hold it with your hand inside to hold the pieces together. Fold the two side flaps first—use your envelope as a guide if you like. Glue a strip under the upper flap at the point, and make a small slit at fold of lower flap, through which you insert and glue another strip. These are the ties. Put your hand inside, palm against the flaps and hold together with thumb on top. Sew across these seams as shown. Sew up sides, for neat edges, and around flap. Keeping your hand in this position, fold up lower flap and sew round it through the lower flaps.

4. The fourth purse is very easy to make and is cut in one piece 13 x 6 in (33 x 15 cm). The strap

22–4

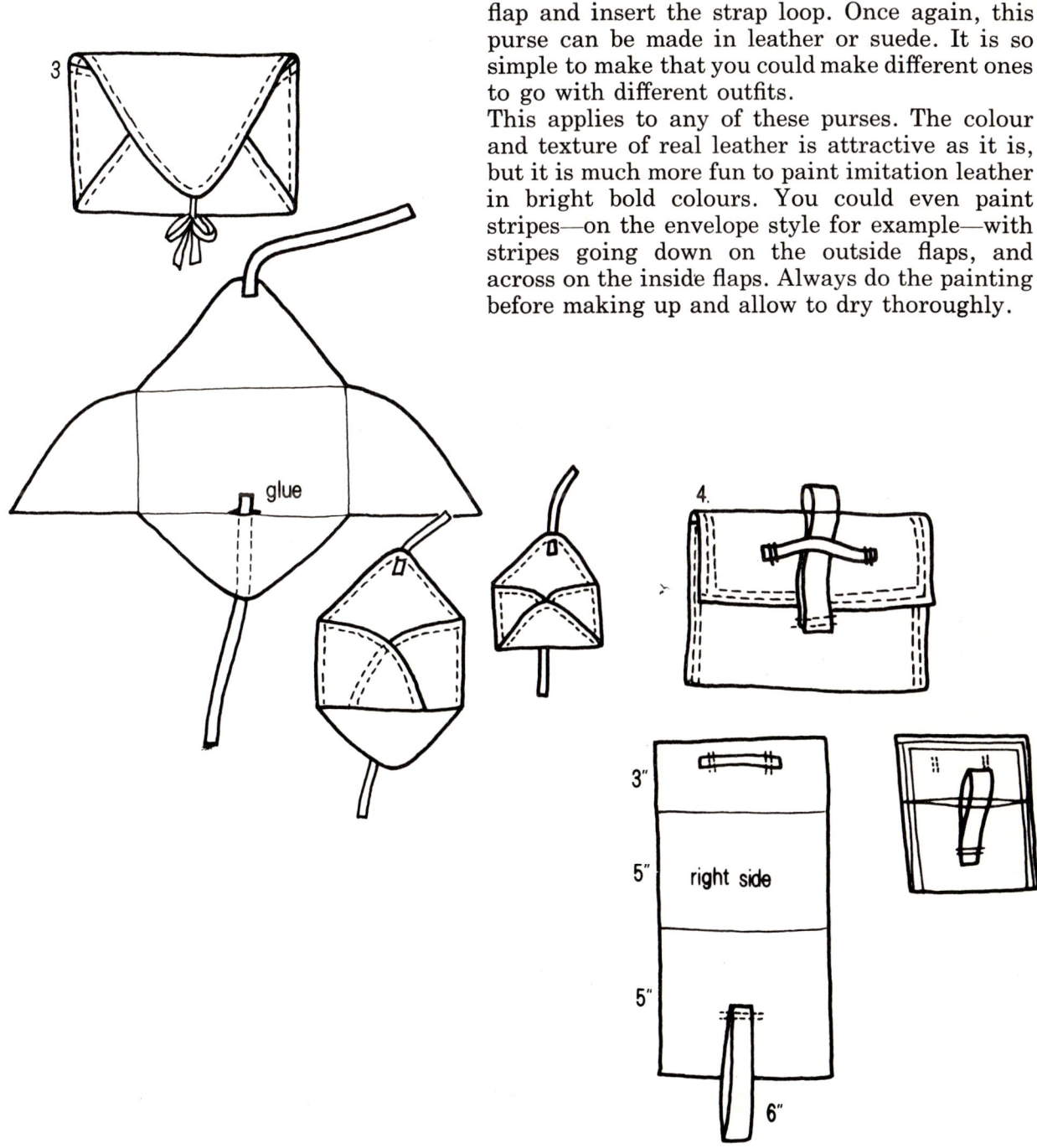

loop is a piece 8 x 1½ in (20 x 3·7 cm) and you will need a strip piece 2½ x ¾ in (6·3 cm x 19 mm). On the right side of the main piece place and stitch the strap loop and the narrow strip. Use the diagram as a guide for placement. Turn over and fold up 4 in (10 cm) pocket and make two rows of stitching up sides and round flap. Fold down the flap and insert the strap loop. Once again, this purse can be made in leather or suede. It is so simple to make that you could make different ones to go with different outfits.

This applies to any of these purses. The colour and texture of real leather is attractive as it is, but it is much more fun to paint imitation leather in bright bold colours. You could even paint stripes—on the envelope style for example—with stripes going down on the outside flaps, and across on the inside flaps. Always do the painting before making up and allow to dry thoroughly.

# Bag and Purse

Bag. This attractive bag is made in suede with string, yes string! for fringing and sewing. You will need two pieces of suede 9 x 7 in (23 x 18 cm) plus one piece for flap, 9 x 5 in (23 x 12·5 cm). Cut the flap to the uneven shape shown and round off the lower corners of the two bag pieces. Punch holes, evenly spaced and matching exactly, round sides and base of bag, and along top of bag and flap. Using a large-eyed needle and thin smooth string, sew bag together with blanket stitch. Sew flap to bag with blanket stitch. Knot long lengths of string to edge of flap, using macramé knots.

Purse. The purse is made in chamois or suede. The back is 7 x 3½ in (18 x 9 cm) and the flap is 3½ x 2½ in (9 x 6 cm). Punch evenly spaced holes along the folded-up sides of purse and along top of purse and flap. Punch two holes in one side of flap, and three at centre of lower fold of purse. Sew purse together with string in blanket stitch, as above. Knot one piece of string through one hole on flap and thread two beads on to it, knotting end. Repeat for second hole on flap. Knot strings into lower three holes and thread 3 beads on each string, knotting at ends.

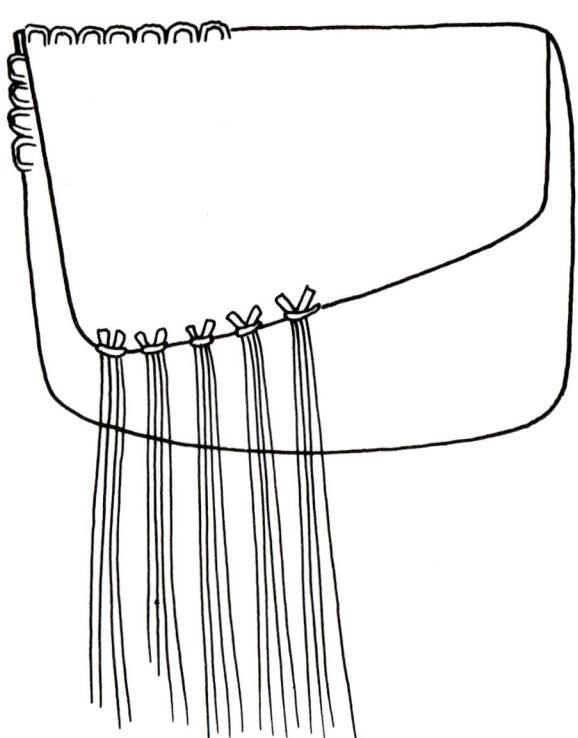

The appeal of this simple bag and purse is in the attractive look and texture of the fake snakeskin, which is light grey and white. Bright green felt is used as a strong contrast to line the bag and purse. They are both made in one piece. For the bag, cut a piece 13½ x 7 in (34 x 18 cm) in leather and one in felt. Glue the felt to the wrong side of the leather, fold up 5 in (12·5 cm) and stitch round pocket only. The purse is made in exactly the same way from a piece 8 x 3¾ in (20 x 9 cm). Glue the same size felt to it as before and fold up 3 in (7·5 cm) and stitch. Fasten with hammer-on snaps.

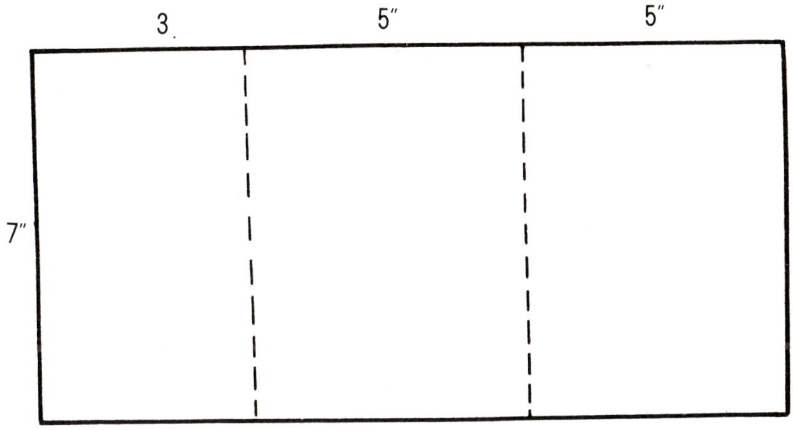

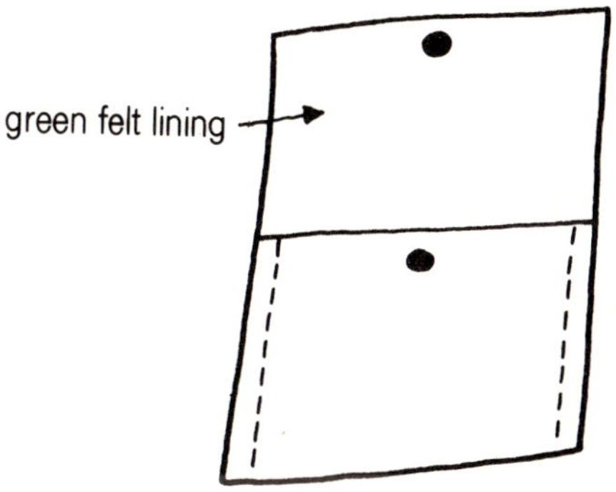

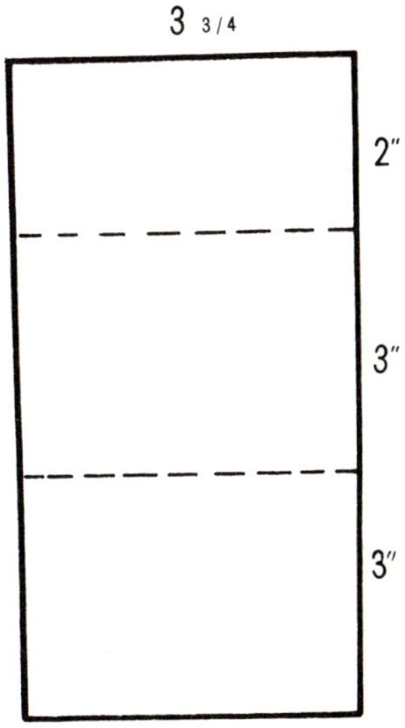

# Drawstring Bag and Beaded Bag

**Drawstring Bag.** This lively bag has an amusing appliqué cut from scraps of painted imitation leather glued to it. The apple is bright green, the head of the ladybird black and the two body sections red. The bag is very simply made to any size you like in leather or suede. Cut a folded bag shape plus 2 in (5 cm) hem at both ends. Fold up and stitch bag on inside and turn through. Glue in or sew the 2 in (5 cm) hem and insert thong, knotting ends together.

**Beaded Bag.** The decoration for this suede bag is made from wooden beads sewn to the front in a design. The bag can be any size you like, and has two squares (front and back) and a welt stitched all round to the squares. The beads are sewn on first. Allow $1\frac{1}{2}$ in (4 cm) at each end of welt to fold in and stitch with brass rings in the loops. A strap is then folded over the rings at each end and stitched.

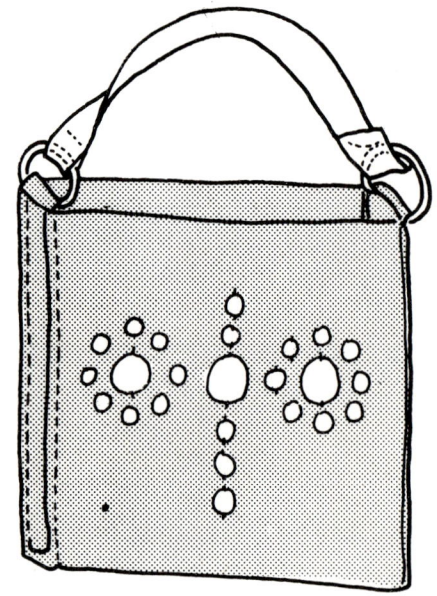

# Knitting Bag

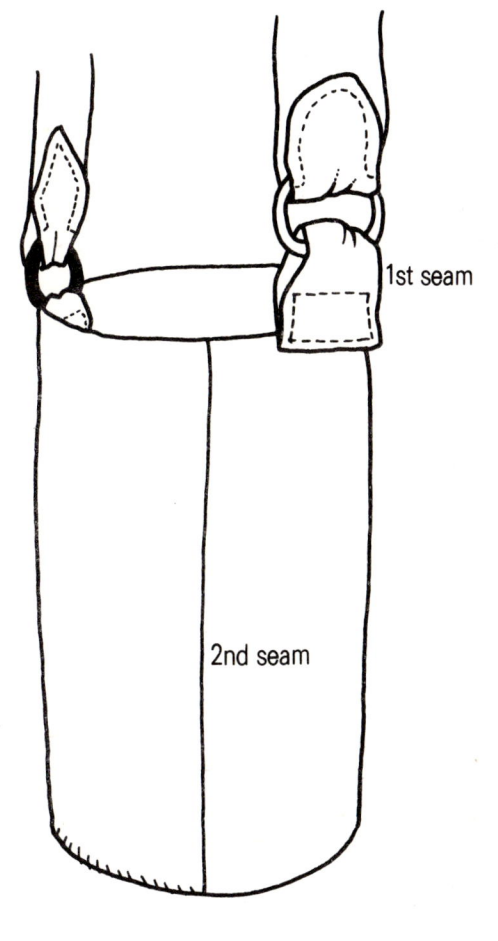

This sturdy, useful bag, might be used for other things as well as knitting. It is made in leather with a felt lining. To make the pattern, cut a circle from a 6½ in (15·5 cm) square of card. Cut a circle of leather allow ½ in (13 mm) turning and a circle of felt the size of the card. Cut a straight piece of leather 20½ in (51 cm) (½ in (13 mm) turnings have been allowed) and of felt the same size. Wrap and glue the leather circle over the card, make small cuts to draw together. Glue felt circle over this side. Lay leather and felt lengthways together and sew first seam. Open out and stitch down second seam. Fold the felt into leather and glue round at base to hold in place. Neatly sew circle to base. Cut a strap 14 x 2 in (35·5 x 5 cm) and two strap loops 6½ x 2 in (16·5 x 5 cm). Fold the loops with large rings in them and stitch to bag. Insert ends of strap through rings and stitch ends to strap.

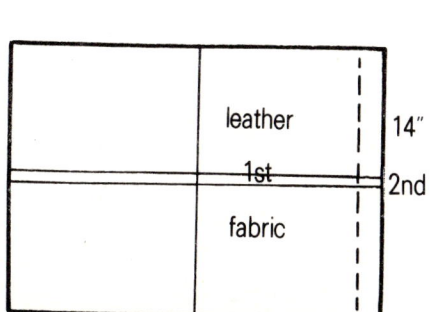

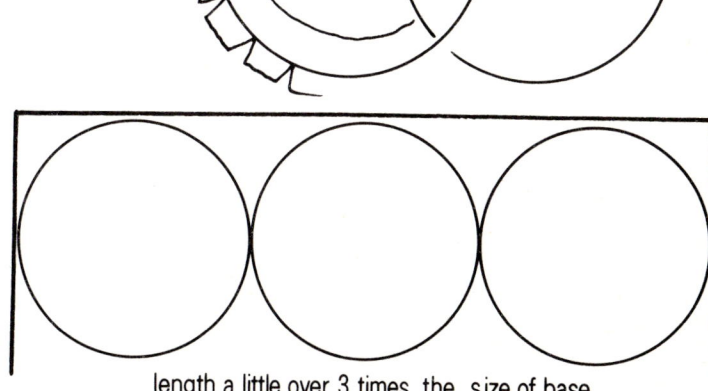

length a little over 3 times the size of base

# Fur Mittens

You can make these mittens with the fur inside or outside, as you prefer. The photograph shows them with the fur outside. Knit-back fake fur has been used. Trace off the mitten and thumb pattern, the last in one opened-out piece. Cut four mitten shapes and two thumbs. Stitch the thumbs into the holes on one piece of each mitten on the wrong side, then sew round mitten edge. Fold the wrist edge under and glue. If you reverse the making up to have the fur inside, fold the fur wrist edge to the outside and glue. I have used a brown short pile fake fur, but if you use a longer haired real fur they will be even more luxurious. You can make them with the fur inside, if the skin side is good-looking suede, or an attractive fake design. I made my daughter a pair in imitation leopard skin which showed the pattern on the knit side. They were made with the fur inside, and the cuffs folded to the outside to give a good contrast. They were too well-worn to photograph so you can tell how popular they were!

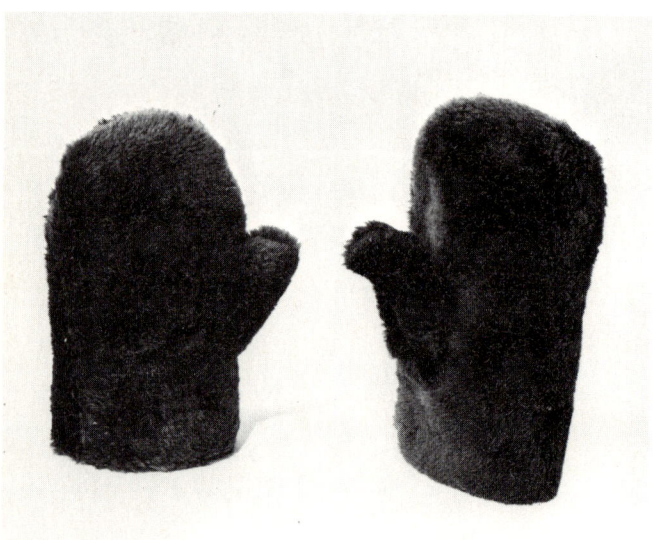

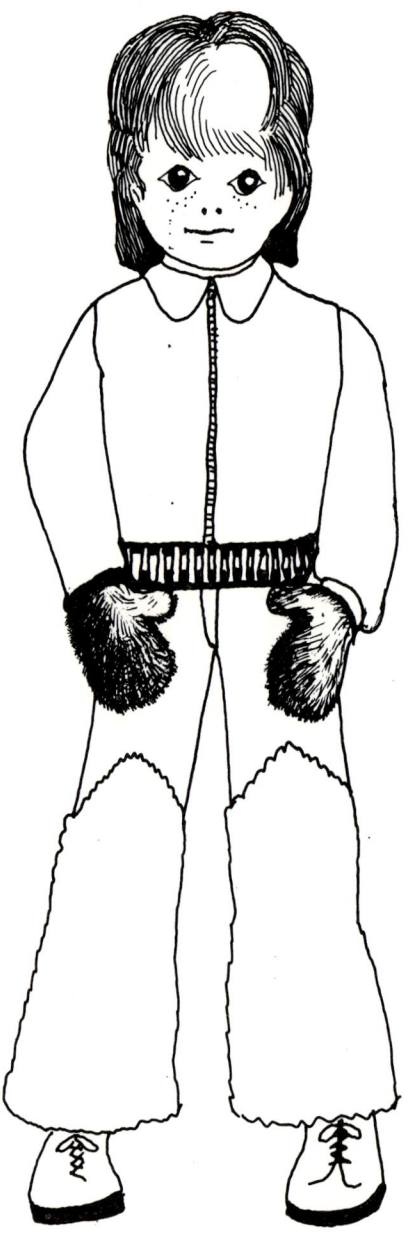

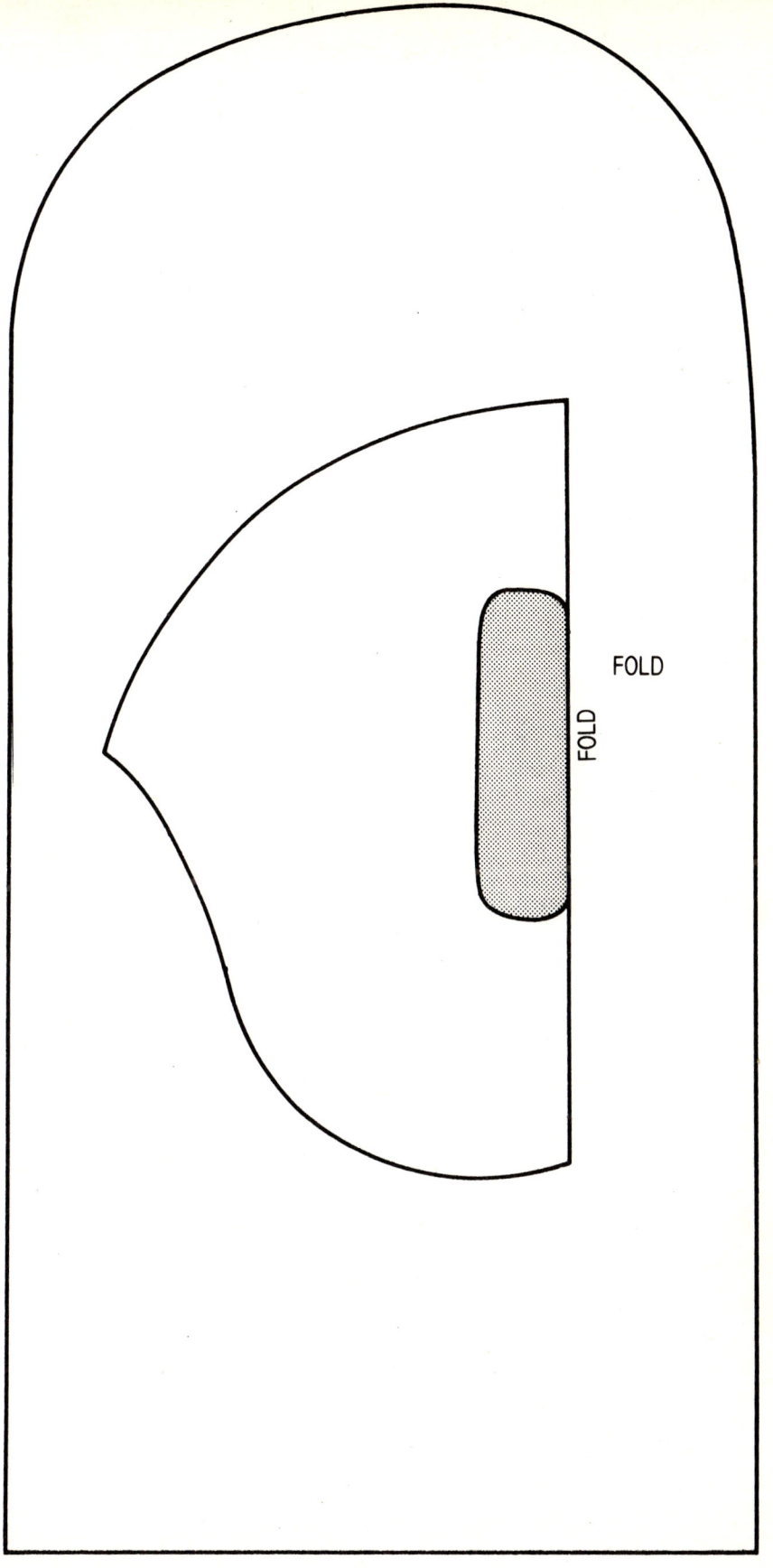

# Slippers

These cosy mule slippers could not be easier to make—in fake fur with leather soles. Place your foot on a piece of paper and draw round it for the sole pattern. Now measure across your foot, from one side, up over to the other, and allow ½ in (13 mm) turnings. Cut a piece of fur this length x 7 in (18 cm). Cut 2 soles, two leather soles, and two bought inner soles cut down to your size if necessary. Glue the leather and inner soles together to make a pair. Fold the upper across and sew taking ½ in seam. Repeat for other upper. Turn through and flatten to place the seams underneath. Glue one securely to each inner sole at both sides. Glue the fur soles to the inner soles underneath the uppers.

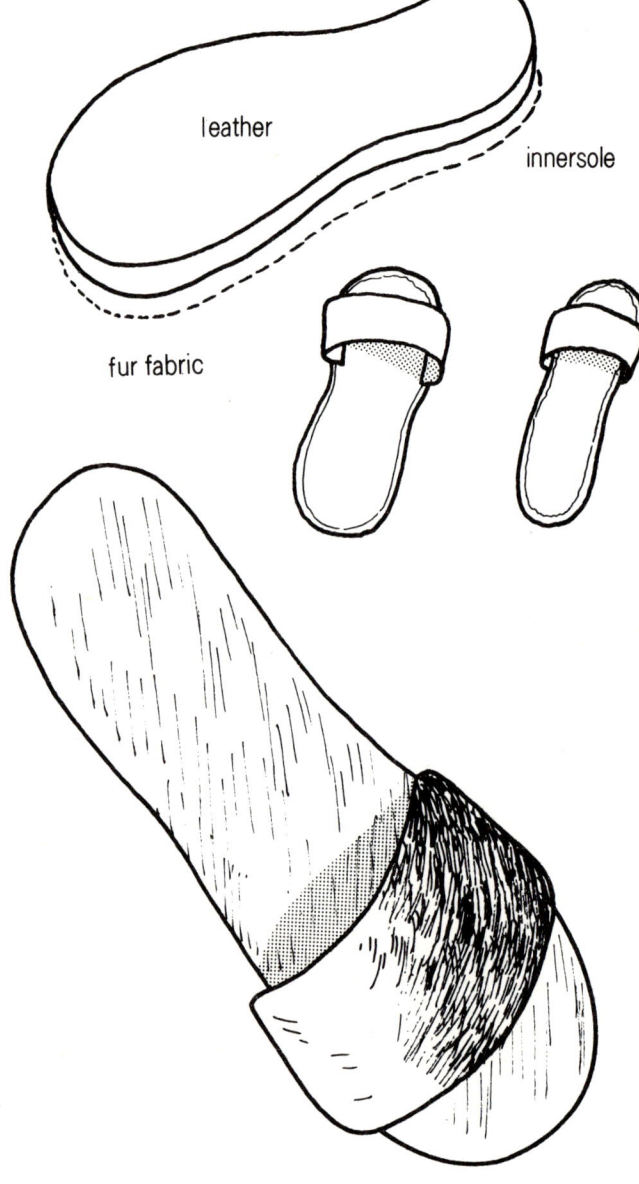

# Slippers Slipper

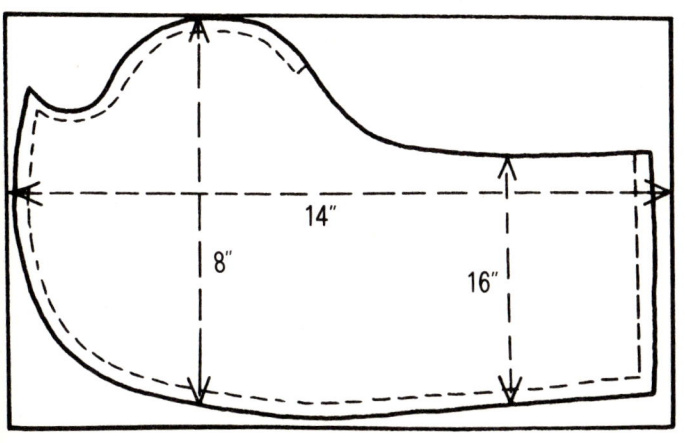

Make one big doggy slipper to contain your pair of slippers and sit by your bed. Cut the pattern from a piece of paper of at least the length of 15 in (38 cm) including ½ in (13 mm) turnings x 9 in (23 cm) also including turnings. Copy the diagram to draw the shape. Cut the ear 10 in x 3 in (25 x 7·5 cm). Make the slipper dog in fake fur or leather. Cut the body shapes, one ear, a nose, and eyes. If the slipper is in fur, stitch on inside. If it is leather, stitch outside. Stitch round slipper, leaving back part open (for inserting slippers). Sew ear at centre to top head seam. Glue nose over point bringing ends together. Glue eyes in place.

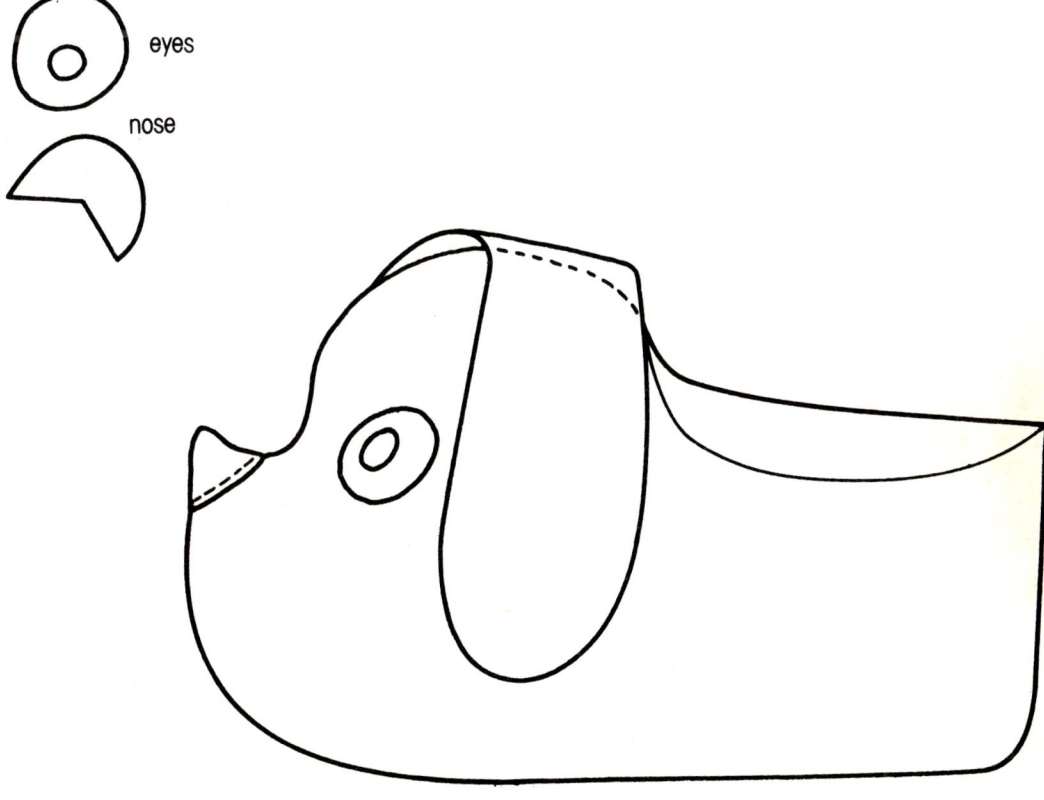

31–4

# Moccasin Slippers

This type of slipper can be made in fur, leather or suede, but whichever you use, it should be soft enough for gathering the front edge. Make the pattern in an odd piece of cloth before cutting out precious fur or leather. Draw round your foot in the centre of the cloth. The measurement A is the depth from your big toe (which usually is the longest!) up and over to form uppers. The measurement B is the depth at the side and C is the depth at heel. Draw the shape and cut out. Pin the heel to get a snug fit and gather front to check for fit. If it is right, cut out two in fur or leather, gather front and stitch heel. Cut two round tongue shapes and stitch to front edge. The slippers can be edged in fur, or you could stitch beads to the tongue, or use an appliqué decoration.

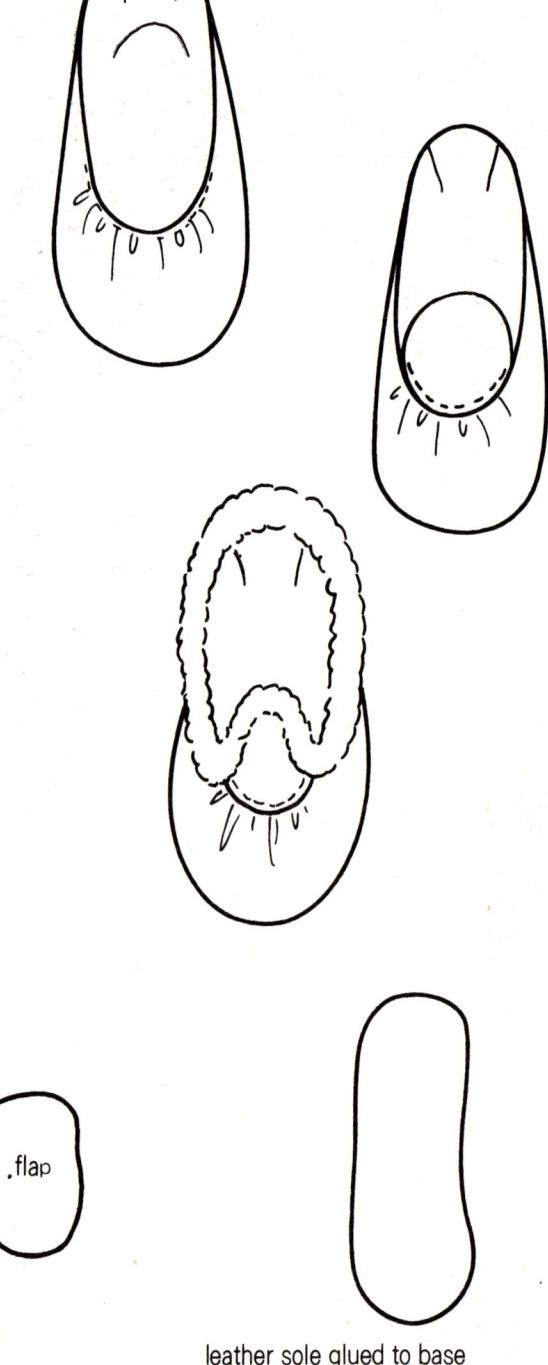

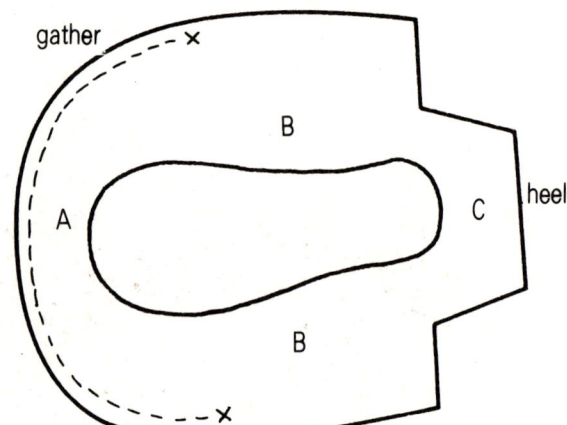

leather sole glued to base

32–4

# Leather Gloves

Patterns for leather gloves can be bought, or you can make your own pattern by cutting up an old glove which fits you well. Cut up the side seam, carefully remove the thumb and cut along seam, and cut the narrow pieces that are sewn between the fingers—these are called fourchettes, and there are six of these. The gloves can be made in suede, leather, or a medium chamois. It is possible to buy suitable chamois for gloves which is somewhat firmer than the type for household use. The latter is the type recommended for the toys described earlier. Keep one glove by you to follow when sewing. Cut out all the pattern pieces in the leather of your choice. Sew the fourchettes together in pairs. Sew the thumb into the glove. Sew the fourchettes between the fingers, and sew the side seam. Use linen thread drawn across beeswax, and a gloving needle for sewing. If you are using thick leather use a hole punch for sewing. The wrist can be shaped and stitched as shown.

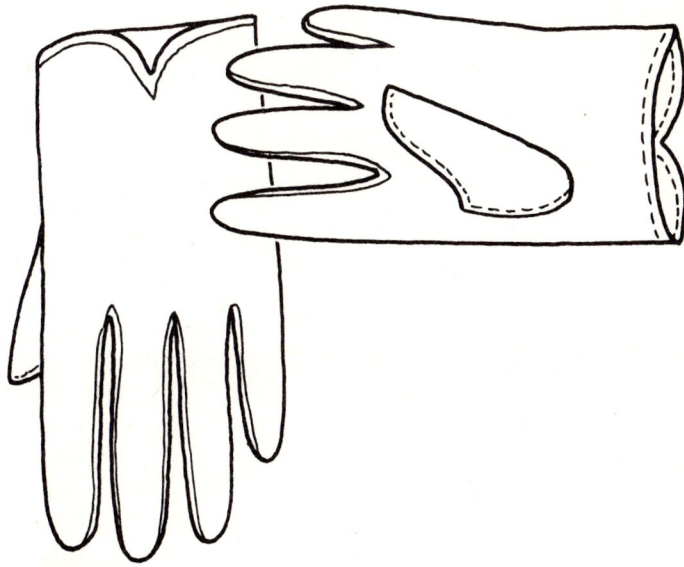

# Some Bright Ideas

1. A leather appliqué picture, wrapped and glued over card, with cord.
2. A simple flap bag with painted leather appliqué.
3. Stitch leather soles to bright socks for around the house.
4. A long bag with zip and painted leather appliqué. Holds brush and comb. Based on pencil case in 'Small Items'.
5. Funny little chamois pets with painted leather cheese and carrot. Appliqué all parts before making up toys. Cut double, stitch round, turn through and stuff in usual way.
6. A little suede mole, cut double, sewn and stuffed, has fur wrapped round and sewn to him.
7. A neat notebook, covered in leather. Take out the 'drawer' of a matchbox and wrap and glue leather round box. Glue appliqué to it, replace 'drawer' and glue to notepad. Keep small rubber and pencil sharpener in it.
8. Wrap and glue leather strip over a circle of card after decorating with crossed lacing and sewn-on beads. Can be used as a bracelet, or make a set for table napkin rings.
9. A monkey purse with zip grin. Cut a circle of brown leather or suede for the back. Draw this on to a piece of paper, then draw face. Cut one piece like shaded area 1 in brown leather and one mouth part like area 2 in light suede or yellow painted leather with line drawn across. Cut along line and allow ½ in (13 mm) seams on both straight edges. Fold under edges and sew a zip between. Sew mouth to face and face to back, inserting ears. Cut larger ears in brown and smaller ears in light suede or yellow painted leather. Glue black felt eyes and nose to face.
10. A useful needle and wool container that rolls and ties; could also be converted for pencils with narrower spaces in strip. Cut a long straight piece in suede or leather and cut one also in felt. Cut a longer narrow strip and sew to felt leaving spaces between. Stitch all round, inserting ties at one end. Roll and tie.

35–4

# For the Real Thing — Leather

1. Folding photograph frame. One main piece 12½ x 6 in (32 x 15 cm) three frames 4 x 6 in (10 x 15 cm). Cut out windows and back with clear plastic. Leave ¼ in (7 mm) spaces between frames. Stitch all round. Front decorated with two contrast strips glued down with decorative lacing over them.
2. Leather Book Cover. Continuous piece to fit book with pockets folded back, laced edging. Has embossed design on front, done before sewing. (See Embossing.)
3. Laced Wallet in leather. Finished size is 5½ x 8 in (14 x 20 cm)—opened out 11 x 8 in (28 x 20 cm). Sew stamp and card pocket to larger pocket, sew strap and loop of purse side, before making up. Make pockets and purse to fit, leaving good space between for folding. Emboss diamond shape on front before making up.
4. Hanging Photograph frame, made in required size. Two pieces same size in leather stitched into pockets at sides, base and between. Before making up, stitch two leather loops on back part. Cut out windows and back with clear plastic. Emboss design above middle window.
5. Pencil case, made in leather. Cut main piece 9½ x 7 in (24 x 18 cm) and shape flap as shown in diagram. Fix press studs in correct position. Cut two pieces of card 7 x 2 in (18 x 5 cm) and wrap and glue leather pieces over them having first stitched a strap, sewn into four loops, on to the leather. Glue the cards into positions indicated in diagram. An appliqué initial can be sewn to flap.
6. Pencil Pot. Cut a piece of leather long enough and deep enough to cover a tin can plus overlap for top and bottom, and a small overlap at side. Decorate with lacing and beads all round. Glue the leather to the tin, and glue seam overlap and

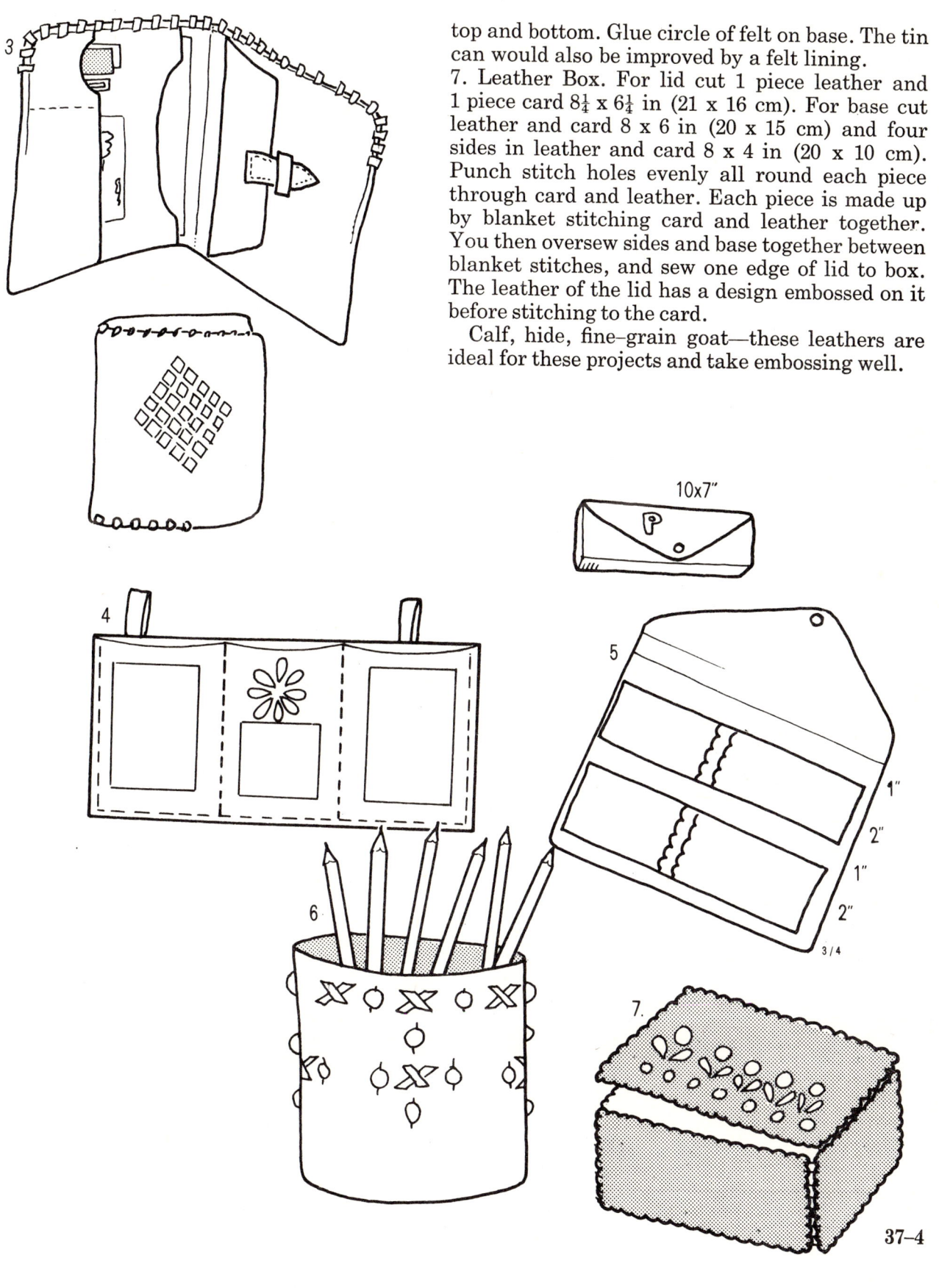

top and bottom. Glue circle of felt on base. The tin can would also be improved by a felt lining.

7. Leather Box. For lid cut 1 piece leather and 1 piece card $8\frac{1}{4} \times 6\frac{1}{4}$ in (21 x 16 cm). For base cut leather and card 8 x 6 in (20 x 15 cm) and four sides in leather and card 8 x 4 in (20 x 10 cm). Punch stitch holes evenly all round each piece through card and leather. Each piece is made up by blanket stitching card and leather together. You then oversew sides and base together between blanket stitches, and sew one edge of lid to box. The leather of the lid has a design embossed on it before stitching to the card.

Calf, hide, fine-grain goat—these leathers are ideal for these projects and take embossing well.

# Ten Belts

1. Deep belt in suede, has painted leather appliqués of trees sewn on to it. The ends are folded under and stitched, and a thong threaded for tying.
2. Make this belt from a blue painted leather strip, sewing on white beads in a wavy line and white leather fish. Make eyelet holes for lacing.
3. This belt is worn laced at the back, the shaped wider part at the front. Paint it blue and glue or sew a white cloud and a red sun.
4. Cut out flowers from painted scraps of leather and glue them to this narrow leather belt. A press-stud is fixed behind the larger flower.
5. Narrow suede belt fastens as for number 1. Punch holes, evenly spaced, on both sides of the front. Thread narrow thongs through holes and make a knot. Thread beads on to thongs and knot ends.
6. Plain leather belt with buckle, slightly curved. Punch hole for prong of buckle, attach the belt, fold end back and stitch. Make eyelet holes other end, and stitch all round edge for neat finish.
7. Made as for 6 but with wider shape at back. Butterflies are cut out of painted leather and stitched on.
8. Deep belt made of shiny black fake leather has large holes cut out with a knife (draw round a small eggcup) and spotted scarf knotted through.
9. Cut three wide suede thongs and stitch them to a piece of suede as shown. Plait the thongs and finish end in the same way as beginning. Use hook and eye type belt fastening, wrap suede strips over ends of buckle parts and stitch edges to plaits.
10. Another shiny black fake leather belt. This one has a lining of bright flower print material. Cut the material ½ in (13 mm) larger all round than shaped belt. Turn under edges and stitch through all round. Cut flowers and hearts from painted leather to match colours in lining and stitch to belt. Punch eyelet holes and lace with narrow thong.

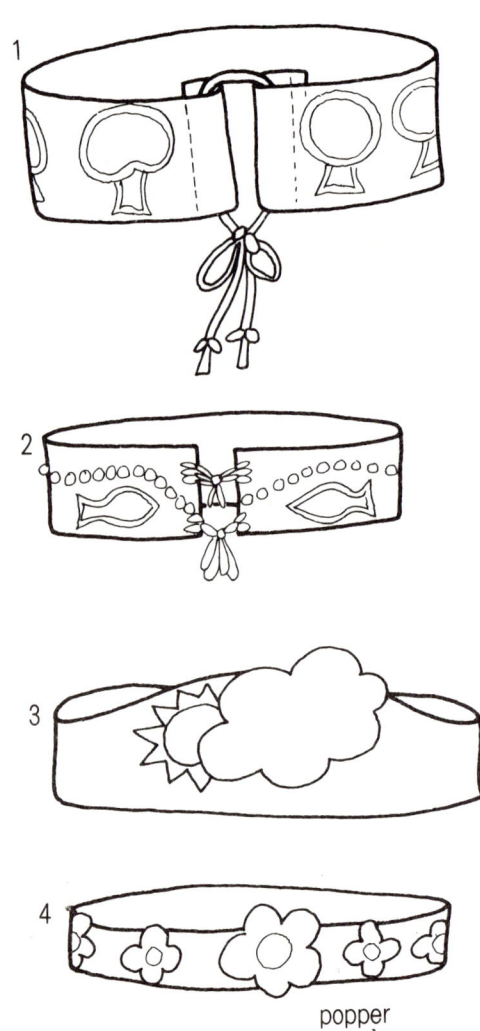

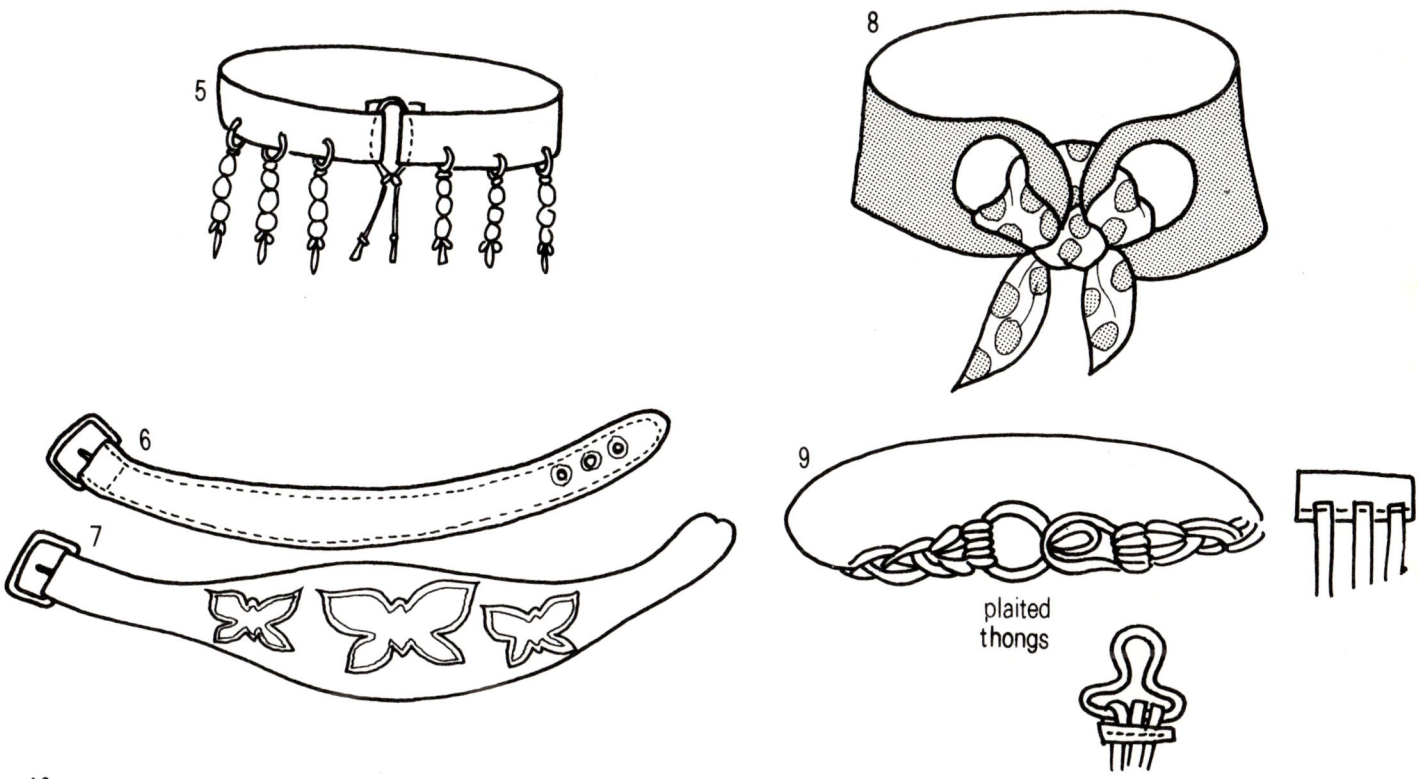

39–4

# Fur Hat

This pretty, soft hat is made in a short pile fake fur. The crown is cut in four parts, the brim in two. As there is not enough space for the whole brim pattern, only a quarter of it is shown here. To make the whole pattern which you will need for cutting out, fold a piece of paper and lay a tracing of this ¼ pattern on it, broken line against the fold. Draw round, cut out, and open out new ½ pattern. Repeat this once more to make the full brim pattern. Cut out all parts and sew the four crown pieces together as described on p.42 and 43. Sew the two brim pieces together (fur inside) up to each end. Open each end out flat, lay edge to edge and sew straight across. Turn brim through. On the right side lay crown inside brim and sew edge to edge. Sew a band of grosgrain, or similar ribbon, to this edge, turn it to the inside and catch it down with neat stitches. A row of stitching round the outer edge of the brim gives a firm edge. This hat would also look good in leather. You can see a drawing of it on page 45 with a big floppy leather flower trimming it. Make it in a shiny fake leather to use as a rain hat. Make it in leather and paint flowers over it using shoe leather paints. Make it in suede and fur, suede at the front and fur at the back. Make it in suede with leather diamonds stitched to it.

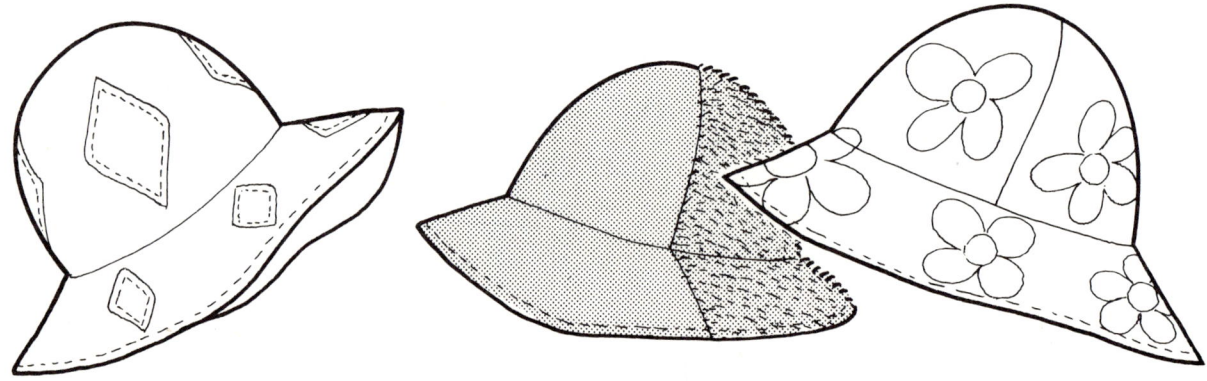

41-4

# Sewing Leather and Fur for Clothes

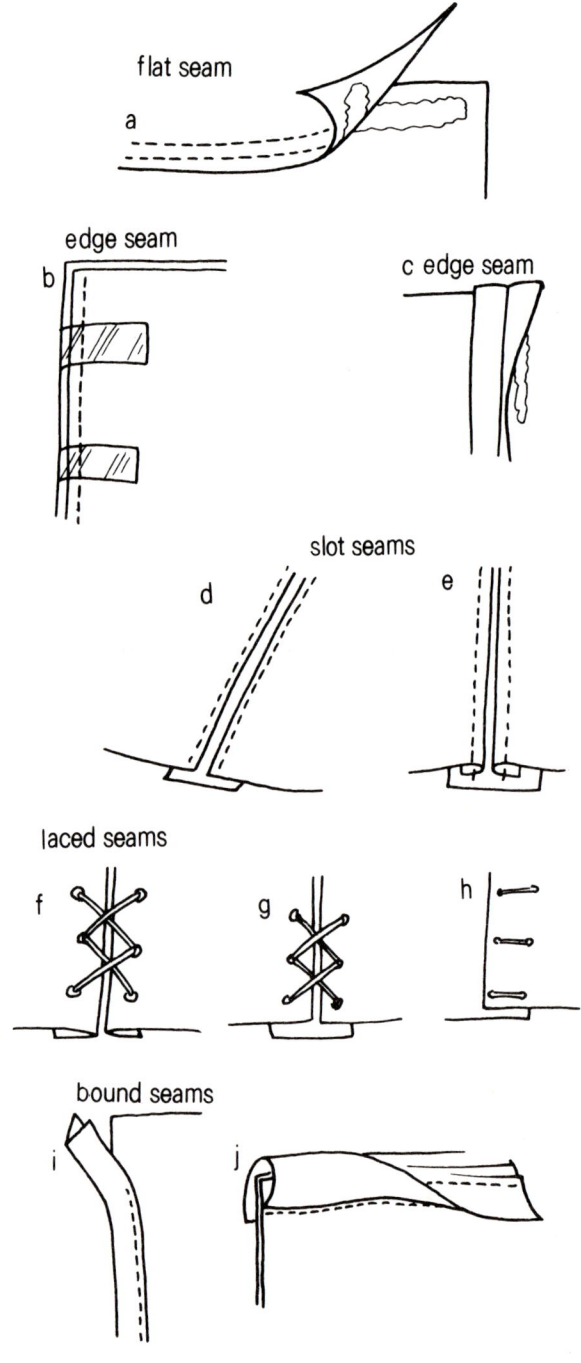

Leather. The *flat seam* (a) is overlapped, glued, then stitched. *Edge seam* (b). Hold edges with Sellotape and stitch. (c) Fold back turnings and glue with rubber cement. *Slot seams*. Edges are placed edge to edge on a strip of leather and both edges stitched, (d) and (e). *Laced seams* (f) and (g) are made in the same way, while (h) is an overlapped laced seam. *Bound seam* (i) is a strip of thin leather, or tape, wrapped over edge and stitched right through; (j) has a strip stitched to one side, then rolled over and stitched right through. *Buttonholes* are cut and sewn as shown in (k), (l) and (m). The first *fringe* is cut in one with the piece—a wider seam is allowed for this (n). The second has a piece set between two layers flat and stitched (o).

Fur. 1. Cutting the skin side with sharp craft knife.
2. To avoid bulk cut away fur on seam edges after stitching. These turnings can be glued back.
3. After stitching seam, cut away some of turning allowance and oversew, or buttonhole stitch narrow edge.
4. Shows gluing of seam edge after cutting fur away.
5. Another, very neat, way of seaming. (a) Oversew edges with tape on both sides. (b) Lay work flat, then bring each tape across to meet and oversew edges. The buttonhole shown is made in the following way. Securely glue tapes (except for long edges arrowed) round buttonhole which is cut between tapes with a knife (a). On the fur side, sew two strips of leather or grosgrain to edges of

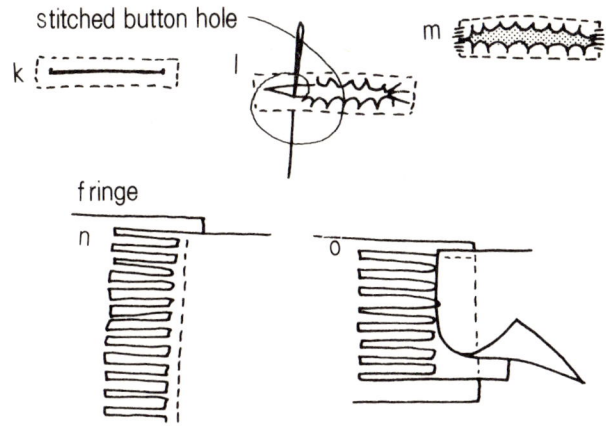

buttonhole with blanket stitch (b). Turn leather or grosgrain through to back and catch edges to edges of tapes (c). Finished buttonhole (d).

*Buttons.* Shank buttons are best for fur and can be sewn with button or carpet thread allowing a good length thread shank. Or you can use very narrow strong tape, threaded through the button shank, and passed through a small hole made in the skin. The tape ends are then sewn back.

Large hooks and eyes, and large snaps can be bought for fastenings.

cutting fur

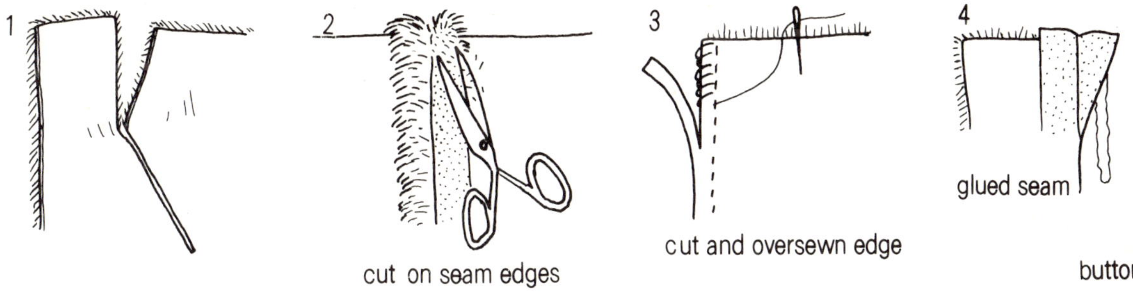

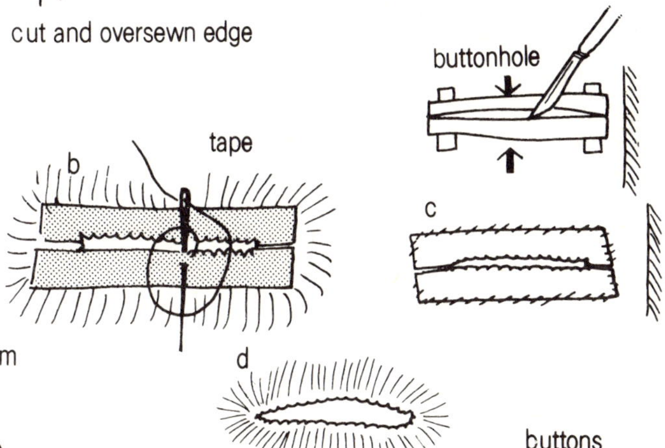

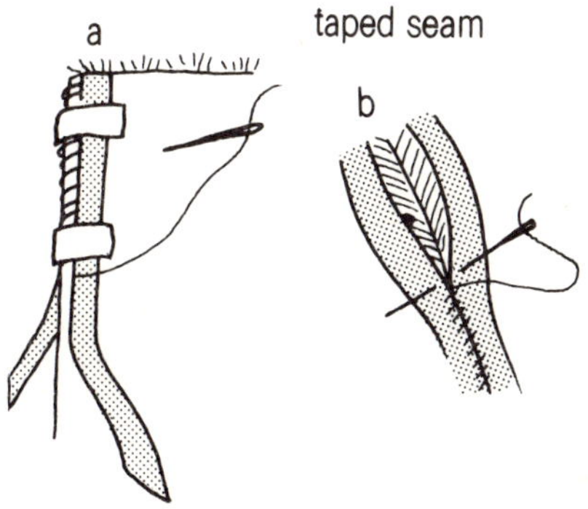

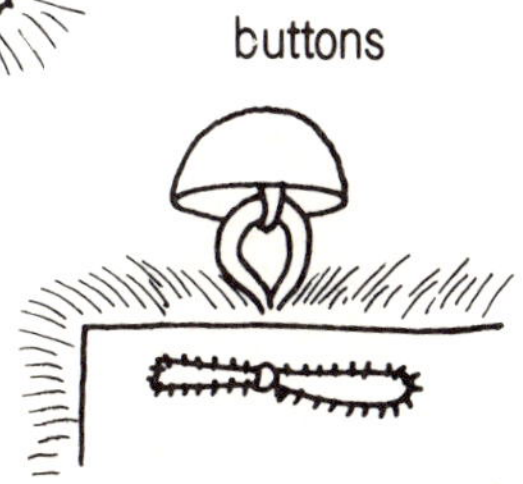

# Clothes in Fur and Leather

Just to show the kind of fun you can have making clothes in fur and leather, here are a few ideas. All are cut from conventional patterns. The waistcoat in the photograph shows the back view. It is made in a smooth shiny fake fur, and the appliqué is cut out of black and white shiny fake leather. The tongue is painted red.

On the next page—all are fake leathers, suedes and furs.
1. Short laced top and trousers have overlap fringing.
2. Suede top and trousers contrast with fake sheepskin for a tough look.
3. Knitted cloche has apple appliqué (see leather jewellery). Trouser suit has suede initial appliqué on sleeve, flowers and leaves in suede on trousers.
4. Leather version of fur hat. It has a flower and leafy stem cut from painted scraps of leather.
5. A plain zip-up jacket is made smart by use of fur and suede. The suede edging is best for inserting zips.
6. Jerkin is fur with suede band, has large hook-and-eye fastening.
7. A plain coat pattern, midi length, has a look of luxury in fake suede and fur.
8. A simple hood with attached scarf—made in fake fur. Could be worn with the coat for the warmest winter ever!
Tough Guy Looks.
9. Edge a sleeveless cardigan with suede, including the pockets.
10. Leather belt has simple gun holster stitched to it. It consists of the back piece, the actual holster, which is one piece wrapped over and sewn, and a narrow strap fixed to the back to slot the holster

into. Attach the holster to the back with a stud and the back to the belt with three studs. Studs also decorate the belt.

11. Leather sleeve cuffs have press-stud fastenings and leather gun appliqués glued to them.

Look through pattern books with fur and leather in mind and you will be surprised by the number of suitable styles. The plainest styles are the best ones to choose and, made more important by fur, leather and suede, they have that special 'boutique' look that lifts them out of the everyday rut.

9 leather or suede edging to cardigan

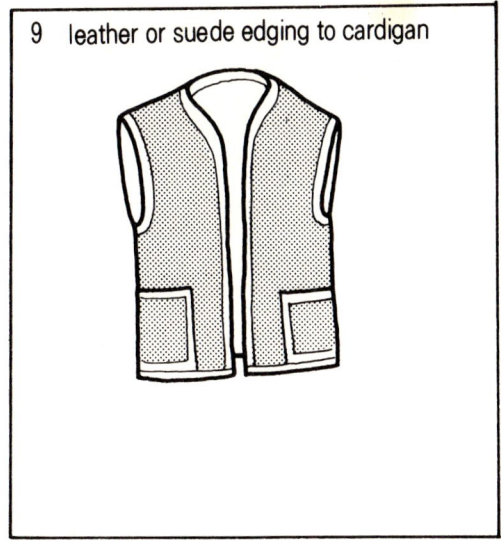

10 leather gun holster

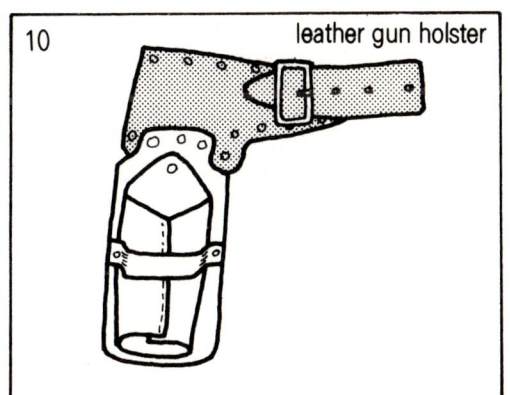

11 leather sleeve cuffs

appliqué with gun

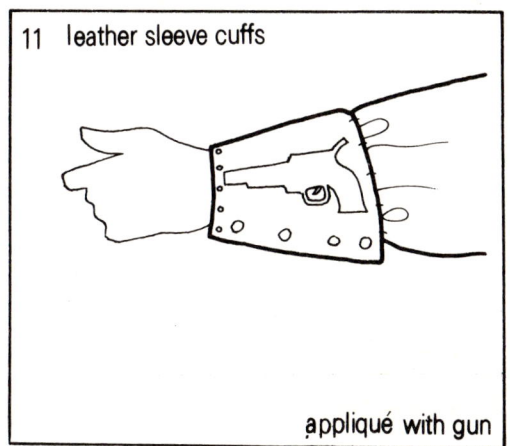

tough guy

# Cleaning Up

Real leather should be kept away from excessive heat or cold. If it gets wet, wipe away excess water with a soft cloth and leave it to dry in an open cool place. Dirty spots can sometimes be removed with soap and warm water, but don't make it too wet. It can be cleaned with saddle soap, which also softens the leather, or it can be cleaned by rubbing the surface over with well-beaten egg white and polishing with a soft cloth until dry. Leather clothes should be sent to leather cleaners annually. If suede gets wet, allow it to dry, then brush up the nap with a soft brush. There are suede cleaners available on the market.

Fake leather. Excessive heat will make it self-adhesive and too much cold can make it crack. You can give it the same at-home cleaning treatment as real leather. Happily, some fake leathers can be dry cleaned, but you should check first.

Real fur can be brushed, using a natural bristle brush, first against the nap, then with the nap. A mixture of water and white vinegar 50-50 can be used to damp the brush. Allow the fur to dry, then brush again. Hang in open air until the smell goes. *Never* store real fur in plastic, or use cleaning fluids or moth balls. A fabric bag is best, and a padded hanger. Faded patches in fur can be touched-up with hair or fabric dye, applied with a vegetable brush and rinsed in cold water. Test first, on a spare scrap or a part that will not show. Fake fur can also be brushed. Some can be hand or machine washed, and even machine dried, while others must be dry cleaned. It is very important when buying it to look for cleaning instructions or to ask the salesman the best way to treat it.